D1069022

Matthew's Gospel and Formative Judaism

J. ANDREW OVERMAN

Matthew's Gospel and Formative Judaism

The Social World of the Matthean Community

Fortress Press • Minneapolis

For Janet

MATTHEW'S GOSPEL AND FORMATIVE JUDAISM
The Social World of the Matthean Community

Scripture quotations, unless otherwise noted, are translated from the original languages by the author. Some translations are from the Revised Standard Version of the Bible, copyright © 1946, 1952, and 1971 by the Division of Christian Education of the National Council of Churches.

Cover design: Pollock Design Group

Cover art: Matthew 9:32–36 from a twelfth-century parchment manuscript in the library of the Greek Patriarchate in Jerusalem

Internal design and typesetting: The HK Scriptorium

Library of Congress Cataloging-in-Publication Data

Overman, J. Andrew, 1955–
   Matthew's gospel and formative Judaism : the social world of the Matthean community / by J. Andrew Overman.
     p.   cm.
   Includes bibliographical references and index.
   ISBN 0-8006-2451-3
   1. Bible, N.T. Matthew—Criticism, interpretation, etc.
2. Sociology, Biblical. 3. Jews—History—168 B.C.–135 A.D.
4. Judaism—History—Talmudic period, 10–425. 5. Christianity and other religions—Judaism. 6. Judaism—Relations—Christianity.
7. Palestine—Religion. 8. Palestine—Social life and customs.
I. Title.
BS2575.6.O83   1990   90-43386
226.2′06--dc20   CIP

Manufactured in the U.S.A.   AF 1-2451

94   93   92   91   90   1   2   3   4   5   6   7   8   9   10

Contents

Acknowledgments

It is a delight to have the opportunity to thank the many people who over the years have helped with this work. Pride of place must go to Howard Kee, who served as my thesis advisor at Boston University. He gave unselfishly of his time and insights. He offered thoughtful direction and was both challenging and gracious from start to finish. Peter Berger, also of Boston University, helped provide much of the initial impetus for this, read the entire manuscript, and provided helpful direction and encouragement. The framework and methodology of the book reflect the influence his work has had on my reading of Matthew. The comments and suggestions of Anthony Saldarini of Boston College were invaluable. He read each chapter thoroughly and offered many important insights. Richard Horsley of the University of Massachusetts—Boston and Hugh Anderson of the University of Edinburgh have helped more than they realize with their comments and criticism over the years. I would also like to thank the staff of the Wellesley College Library for their cooperation.

Above all I wish to express my deepest gratitude and admiration to my family: Janet, Amy, Matthew, and now Alison, who endured the hardships and inconveniences such an undertaking imposes on a family. Without their love and support this book could not have been written. This book is dedicated to my companion throughout life, my wife, Janet.

Abbreviations

AnBib	Analecta Biblica
ANRW	*Aufstieg und Niedergang der römischen Welt*
ARNA	*Abot Rabbi Nathan* version A
ARNB	*Abot Rabbi Nathan* version B
ATR	*Anglican Theological Review*
BASOR	*Bulletin of the American Schools of Oriental Research*
BEvT	Beiträge zur evangelischen Theologie
CBQ	*Catholic Biblical Quarterly*
CD	The Cairo (Genizah text of the) *Damascus Document*
EKKNT	Evangelisch-Katholischer Kommentar zum Neuen Testament
ETL	*Ephemerides theologicae lovanienses*
EvT	*Evangelische Theologie*
HSM	Harvard Semitic Monographs
HTR	*Harvard Theological Review*
HUCA	*Hebrew Union College Annual*
IEJ	*Israel Exploration Journal*
JAAR	*Journal of the American Academy of Religion*
JBL	*Journal of Biblical Literature*
JBR	*Journal of Bible and Religion*
JES	*Journal of Ecumenical Studies*
JJS	*Journal of Jewish Studies*
JQR	*Jewish Quarterly Review*
JR	*Journal of Religion*
JSJ	*Journal for the Study of Judaism*
JSNT	*Journal for the Study of the New Testament*
JSNTMS	Journal for the Study of the New Testament Monograph Series
JTS	*Journal of Theological Studies*

NT	*Novum Testamentum*
NTS	*New Testament Studies*
OTP	*The Old Testament Pseudepigrapha (edited in 2 vols. by James H. Charlesworth)*
PAAJR	*Proceedings of the American Academy of Jewish Research*
4QFlor	*Florilegium* from Qumran Cave 4
1QH	*Thanksgiving Hymns* from Qumran Cave 1
1QM	*War Scroll* from Qumran Cave 1
1QpHab	*Pesher on Habakkuk* from Qumran Cave 1
1QS	*Manual of Discipline* from Qumran Cave 1
SBLDS	Society of Biblical Literature Dissertation Series
SBS	Stuttgarter Bibelstudien
SJT	*Scottish Journal of Theology*
SNTSMS	Society for New Testament Studies Monograph Series
TDNT	*Theological Dictionary of the New Testament*
ZNW	*Zeitschrift für die neutestamentliche Wissenschaft*
ZTK	*Zeitschrift für Theologie und Kirche*

Introduction

THIS IS A STUDY of the life and world of the community represented by the Gospel of Matthew. As Max Weber recognized, every community must order its life, and develop means by which it can preserve and protect itself.[1] It is clear that the Matthean community was in no way exempt from this sociological necessity. Matthew's community, like any other, was confronted with the task of explaining the experiences and convictions of the community to ensuing members as well as developing structures and procedures that would help protect it from alien forces and beliefs. This study focuses on those developments.

The nature and shape of a community owe much to the social forces and dynamics which surround that community. It is the problems and issues of day-to-day life in any given community that more than anything else provoke and shape its social development and transformation.[2] The roles, patterns of behavior, and the institutions emerging within a community will to a large degree be in response to the questions and struggles the community must regularly face. Such is the case with Matthew's community. Much of the life and reality reflected in Matthew's Gospel was socially constructed.[3] That is to say, the developments and issues evident in Matthew's Gospel

---

[1] See M. Weber, *Essays in Sociology*, ed. H. Gerth and C. Mills (Oxford: Oxford University Press, 1946) 262; idem, *Economy and Society*, ed. G. Roth and C. Wittich (Berkeley: University of California Press, 1978) 246ff. See also P. L. Berger, "The Sociological Study of Sectarianism," *Social Research* 21 (1954) 470.

[2] B. Holmberg, *Paul and Power: The Structure of Authority in the Primitive Church as Reflected in the Pauline Epistles* (Philadelphia: Fortress Press, 1978) 165. Max Weber's term for routinization (*Veralltäglichung:* literally, "everydayization") specifically draws attention to the issues and questions of everyday life as the driving force behind a community's development and institutionalization.

[3] See, for example, some of the more well-known literature on the subject of the sociology of knowledge and the social construction of reality: A. Schutz and T. Luckmann, *The Structures of the Life-World*, trans. R. Zaner and H. Engelhardt, Jr. (Evanston: Northwestern University Press, 1973); P. L. Berger and T. Luckmann, *The Social Construction of Reality* (Garden City, N.Y.: Doubleday, 1967); P. L. Berger, *The Sacred Canopy: Elements of a Sociological Theory of Religion* (Garden City, N.Y.: Doubleday, 1969).

are responses to the social setting, situation, and world of that community. No text is autonomous, isolated from the events transpiring
around it.[4] What one reads in a text such as Matthew's Gospel is
inevitably a product of the world in which it participated and from
which it came. Throughout this study close attention will be paid to
the world or larger context and horizon within which the developments in Matthew's community can best be understood and
explicated.

The factor within the locale and setting of Matthew's community
which most profoundly influenced its development was the competition and conflict with so-called formative Judaism—a group which,
like the Matthean community, was involved in a process of social
construction and definition. Like Matthean Judaism, formative
Judaism was in the process of *becoming*. The years following the
destruction of the Jerusalem temple and the first Jewish revolt were
significant for both Matthean and formative Judaism. It was during
this period that these two groups most actively ordered and defined
their life and beliefs. At the time of the writing of Matthew's Gospel
these two groups, formative Judaism and Matthean Judaism, were
obviously in competition and, it would appear, formative Judaism
was gaining the upper hand.[5] This has a significant impact on the
shape and substance of Matthew's Gospel. Many of the developments within the life of the Matthean community were in response
to the impact that an organizing and consolidating formative Judaism
was having on the people within the Matthean community and their
world.

In certain ways formative Judaism, as J. Neusner has shown, was
a precursor of the eventually dominant authorities within Judaism in
late antiquity, rabbinic Judaism. In no way, however, should formative Judaism be understood as synonymous with rabbinic Judaism,
which began to emerge about one hundred years after the writing of

---

[4] Contrary, it would appear, to J. D. Kingsbury, *Matthew as Story* (Philadelphia:
Fortress Press, 1986) 2—though I am not completely sure what Prof. Kingsbury
means by "autonomous," and the extent to which he is willing to allow for inter-
action between the world of the text and the social world. The vast majority of
Kingsbury's works would seem to suggest that he does not advocate a radical
distinction between the world of the text and the social world within which it must
be placed and interpreted.

[5] Against Sjef Van Tilborg (*The Jewish Leaders in Matthew* [Leiden: E. J. Brill, 1972]
171) and D. Hare (*The Theme of Jewish Persecution of Christians in the Gospel According
to St. Matthew* [Cambridge: Cambridge University Press, 1967] 127), who suggest
that Judaism is no longer serious competition for Matthew's community.

Matthew's Gospel.[6] While there is some relation between the two groups, they should not be confused. The evolution from formative to rabbinic Judaism was a protracted and complicated historical process that was played out over a several-hundred-year period. In the conflict between formative and Matthean Judaism we are exposed to one rather small slice of the overall process of Jewish self-definition and consolidation in the post-70 period.

Formative Judaism during the period in which we find it contesting with the Matthean community was one of several movements struggling to gain more influence and control in the post-70 period. At this stage formative Judaism should not be envisioned as a broad movement that represents or speaks for Judaism. Apocalyptic movements were alive in many communities during this period as *2 Baruch*, *4 Ezra*, and the *Apocalypse of Abraham* attest. Also, the revolutionary option retained considerable appeal and resiliency, as the Bar Kochba revolt of 133 shows. Matthean and formative Judaism, then, in the period between the two Jewish revolts, are two emerging movements, among several, involved in the process of self-definition and consolidation in a society that was fragmented and divided following the upheavals associated with the Roman period in Palestine—not least of which, of course, was the destruction of the temple in Jerusalem.[7] It is this process of self-definition and the struggle for influence that loom so large in the Gospel of Matthew.

Both formative and Matthean Judaism share the same fluid matrix and indeed have much in common. This accounts for the number of ways in which the Matthean community and formative Judaism overlap and appear to be similar. This is because formative and Matthean

---

[6] See, for example, the following works by J. Neusner: *From Politics to Piety: The Emergence of Pharisaic Judaism* (Englewood Cliffs, N.J.: Prentice-Hall, 1973); *Rabbinic Traditions about the Pharisees before 70* (3 vols.; Leiden: E. J. Brill, 1973); "The Idea of Purity in Ancient Judaism," *JAAR* 43 (1975) 15–26; "Judaism after Moore: A Programmatic Statement," *JJS* 31 (1980) 141–56; "The Formation of Rabbinic Judaism: Yavneh from A.D. 70–100," in *ANRW* II.19.2, 3–42; "Two Pictures of the Pharisees: Philosophical Circle and Eating Club," *ATR* 64 (1982) 525–38; "Religious Authority in Judaism: Modern and Classical Modes," *Interpretation* 39 (1985) 373–87.

[7] For a history of this period, see S. Freyne, *Galilee from Alexander the Great to Hadrian* (Wilmington, Del.: Michael Glazier, 1980); M. Hengel, *Judaism and Hellenism* (Philadelphia: Fortress Press, 1974); D. S. Russell, *The Jews from Alexander to Hadrian* (Oxford: Oxford University Press, 1967). See now also the interesting and suggestive work of R. Horsley and J. Hanson, *Bandits, Prophets and Messiahs: Popular Movements in the Time of Jesus* (Minneapolis: Winston, 1985); and A. J. Saldarini, *Pharisees, Scribes and Sadducees in Palestinian Society: A Sociological Approach* (Wilmington, Del.: Michael Glazier, 1988).

Judaism share the same social setting and context. These two groups share a similar background, the same cultural context, and, in short, inhabit the same world. Before attempting to study the nature and development of the Matthean community and its relationship and conflict with formative Judaism, one must attempt to understand the background and setting that helped to shape both formative and Matthean Judaism. This larger background and horizon constitute the world which set the stage for the emergence and development of formative Judaism and the Matthean community. This world must be discussed and outlined before attempting to understand and analyze the specific groups represented by Matthew's Gospel and formative Judaism.

It has been suggested that Christianity and Judaism are "fraternal twins."[8] These movements share the same historical matrix and often defined themselves in light of and over against one another.[9] If that is true of Christianity and Judaism generally, it is all the more true where Matthew's Gospel and formative Judaism are concerned. I believe what the reader encounters in Matthew's Gospel is a Jewish community, which claims to follow Jesus the Messiah, discovering that they are now different from what is emerging as the dominant form of Judaism in their setting. Where do we as a community now stand in relation to the Jewish authorities in our setting? How do we understand and interpret the law? How do our beliefs in Jesus of Nazareth relate to all this? Now that Matthean Judaism is emerging as different or deviant from the evolving norms, how do we order our life and articulate our position? In what way are we different? Such are the questions that provoked the writing of Matthew's Gospel. The defensive posture of the Gospel and strident attacks on the Jewish authorities, represented in Matthew by "the scribes and Pharisees," comprise all the emotion and tension of a family falling apart. Matthean Judaism and its struggle with formative Judaism are perhaps the first chapter in the long and difficult separation of these fraternal twins Judaism and Christianity.

In time the descendants of the Matthean community and the tradition to which they belonged came to be called "Christians" and saw

---

[8] This is one of the major thrusts of A. Segal's recent work, *Rebecca's Children: Judaism and Christianity in the Roman World* (Cambridge, Mass.: Harvard University Press, 1986); see especially p. 179.

[9] As the title reveals, this is the point of R. Hummel's monograph, *Die Auseinandersetzung zwischen Kirche und Judentum im Matthäusevangelium* (Munich: Kaiser, 1963).

themselves as distinct and at best only vaguely related to Judaism. At the time of the writing of the Gospel of Matthew, of course, no such self-understanding existed. The people of Matthew's community did not understand themselves as "Christians." On the contrary they were Jews. Like many of their contemporaries and competitors, however, they understood themselves as the "true Israel" and set themselves over against those they believed to be the false covenant people and false leaders who would lead the people astray.[10] The Gospel of Matthew is full of such exclusive claims and the tension and conflict these claims inevitably provoke.

The Gospel of Matthew cannot be accurately understood apart from the competition and conflict with formative Judaism. That conflict played an essential role in the development and in the world of the Matthean community. For a time formative and Matthean Judaism developed and grew up alongside each other. At a certain point, about the time the Gospel was written, these two groups began to diverge. The Gospel of Matthew not only then records a critical moment in the history of these two early movements; it also constitutes an invaluable chapter in the larger history of Jewish–Christian definition, conflict, and relations. A close study of the Gospel of Matthew then may not only shed light on the history of this one community, the origins of formative Judaism and Christianity, and their subsequent separation but also, one would hope, help to bring about greater mutual understanding and appreciation between these two fraternal religions.[11]

---

[10] This point has been made forcefully by W. Trilling in *Das Wahre Israel: Studien zur Theologie des Matthäus-Evangeliums* (Munich: Kösel, 1964).

[11] See the review of A. Segal's *Rebecca's Children* by J. A. Overman in *Theology Today* 45 (1989) 512–13, where this point is developed.

The Background and Horizon
of Matthean and Formative Judaism

Issues and Antecedents
in Judaism 165 B.C.E.–100 C.E.

A NY GENUINE SOCIAL HISTORY of a community and its development must begin by attempting to understand the background and broader setting in which a community is placed. The shape and nature of a community and many of the specific constructions within it are in response to the issues and questions that are part of the broader world and setting of that community. The sociology of knowledge has described this broader setting as the *life-world*.[1] The life-world, or what we will refer to as the social world, stands for the reservoir of assumptions and experiences shared by a society or community, which inform the social development of that community. What deserves note in this definition of the life-world is the emphasis placed on the assumptions shared by a community. The social world of a community includes not only explicit ideas and experiences but also implicit assumptions and meanings.

This combination of the explicit issues and developments within a society and the implicit assumptions constitutes "all that passes for knowledge" in a society. The common experiences and background and the force that shared reality has brought to bear on the members of a community provide for a host of implicit meanings and things which are "taken for granted."[2] "Every word . . . , every gesture . . . ,

[1] See A. Schutz, *Collected Papers* (The Hague: Nijhoff, 1962) 1:149; and P. L. Berger and T. Luckmann, *The Social Construction of Reality* (Garden City, N.Y.: Doubleday, 1967) 16.

[2] A. Schutz and T. Luckmann, *The Structures of the Life-World*, trans. R. Zaner and H. Engelhardt, Jr. (Evanston: Northwestern University Press, 1973) 7, 241; Berger and Luckmann, *Social Construction*, 3, 18ff.; Schutz, *Collected Papers*, 1:121ff.

every work of art and every historical deed is intelligible because the people who express themselves through them and those who understand them have something in common; the individual always thinks and acts in a common sphere, and only there does that person understand."[3] Engaging and interpreting this wider context or social world are essential for accurately understanding the development and nature of any given community and the text it has produced. Throughout this study careful attention will be paid to the wider setting and social world of both formative and Matthean Judaism in order to interpret more accurately and fairly what these communities are saying and how they developed.

E. D. Hirsch has expressed the necessity for understanding the wider setting and social world for accurately interpreting a text with his application of the notion of the *horizon*. The horizon, like the life-world, represents a spectrum of typical expectations and assumptions for the text and the person or people who stand behind it.[4] The horizon frames reality. As the frame of a picture may not constitute part of the picture per se, the frame does define the picture "and helps to constitute its wholeness."[5] In this chapter we will discuss certain aspects of the background and horizon for Matthean and formative Judaism which appear to have figured significantly in the development, claims, and eventual competition and conflict between these two communities. These aspects help "frame the reality" of these two communities and provide the proper context for our understanding and study.

The period 165 B.C.E.–100 C.E. in Palestine was fluid and diverse. A review of some of the salient issues that emerged during this period cannot claim to be exhaustive and will by nature be somewhat selective. However, within this diversity certain themes do emerge as both widespread and central for many of the communities that flourished during this period of Judaism in late antiquity. The five aspects of the horizon of Matthean and formative Judaism offered

---

[3] Wilhelm Dilthey, as cited by H. C. Kee, *Christian Origins in Sociological Perspective* (Philadelphia: Westminster, 1980) 21.

[4] E. D. Hirsch, Jr., *Validity in Interpretation* (New Haven: Yale University Press, 1967) 221. This notion of the horizon had a significant influence on Alfred Schutz, one of the leading figures of the sociology of knowledge. See Schutz's essay "Phenomenology and the Social Sciences," in *Philosophical Essays in Memory of Edmund Husserl*, ed. M. Farber (Cambridge, Mass.: Harvard University Press, 1940) 164–86.

[5] H. Kuhn, "The Phenomenological Concept of the Horizon," in *Philosophical Essays in Memory of Edmund Husserl*, ed. M. Farber, 107.

here are important not only because a number of other communities struggled with the same questions but also because these five aspects obviously emerged as crucial for Matthean and formative Judaism. These aspects of life in Palestine from 165 B.C.E. to 100 C.E. must be taken into account when interpreting Matthew's Gospel and trying to understand the nature and development of his community.

Fragmentation and Factionalism: The Sectarian Nature of Judaism

This period in Judaism has been characterized by a number of scholars as sectarian in nature.[6] While avoiding a comprehensive definition of the term *sect*,[7] we follow J. Blenkinsopp in taking the term *sectarian* to mean a group which is, or perceives itself to be, a minority in relation to the group it understands to be the "parent body." The sect is a minority in that it is subject to, and usually persecuted by, the group in power. The dissenting group is in opposition to the parent body and tends to claim more or less to be what the dominant body claims to be.[8]

The sociologist Bryan Wilson also has sought to avoid a lengthy definition of the term *sect* and focuses instead on what he calls the group's "response to the world."[9] This aspect of Wilson's work draws attention to what Blenkinsopp emphasized—the group's view of its relationship to those setting the social and cultural norms, who thereby wield the power in that context, that is, the so-called parent group. These sectarian groups feel alienated from those in authority and often openly denounce or oppose them. They, in contrast to the

---

[6] The sectarian nature of this period has been discussed by J. Blenkinsopp, "Interpretation and Sectarian Tendencies: An Aspect of Second Temple History," in *Jewish and Christian Self-Definition*, ed. E. P. Sanders (Philadelphia: Fortress Press, 1981) 2:1–26; M. Simon, *Jewish Sects at the Time of Jesus* (Philadelphia: Fortress Press, 1967); T. L. Donaldson, "Moses Typology and the Sectarian Nature of Early Christian Anti-Judaism: A Study in Acts 7," *JSNT* 12 (1981) 27–52; R. Scroggs, "The Earliest Christian Communities as Sectarian Movements," in *Christianity, Judaism and Other Greco-Roman Cults* (Leiden: E. J. Brill, 1975) 2:1–23; L. Schiffman, "Jewish Sectarianism in Second Temple Times," in *Great Schisms in Jewish History*, ed. R. Jospe and S. Wagner (New York: KTAV, 1981) 1–46.

[7] See particularly the discussion on sectarianism in P. L. Berger, "The Sociological Study of Sectarianism," *Social Research* 21 (1954) 467–85.

[8] Blenkinsopp, "Interpretation and Sectarian Tendencies," 1.

[9] B. Wilson, *Magic and the Millennium: A Sociological Study of Religious Movements of Protest among Tribal and Third World Peoples* (London: Heinemann, 1973) 16–26.

leaders or "parent group," understand the truth, possess it, and will one day be vindicated by God.

Social unrest and division are certainly evident in the documents we possess from the immediate postexilic period.[10] However, it would seem that through a variety of influences and historical circumstances, the period from around 165 B.C.E. to 100 C.E. showed an increasing tendency toward factionalism and sectarianism. The harsh treatment of many Israelites by their Seleucid rulers, the encroaching Hellenism and its appeal to some Israelites and abhorrence to others, and the abuses of later Hasmonean rulers all led to division. Among the elements that provoked fragmentation in the first century C.E. were the Roman occupation, the competing Jewish schools, and the destruction of the Jerusalem temple.

Throughout the period 165 B.C.E.–100 C.E., the leadership, or parent body, changed. This was by no means a fixed group. Both those who were in power and those who felt oppressed and alienated changed often during this period. Throughout this period these sects were competing for control of and influence within Jewish society. Awareness of the factionalism characteristic of this volatile period in Israel's history is crucial for properly understanding formative and Matthean Judaism.

Numerous communities were outspoken in their criticism and denunciation of those who comprised the parent body in this period. The Dead Sea community at Qumran is a clear example of this kind of response to those in power. In terms of Wilson's notion of a community's response to the world, it is worth recalling that this group physically removed itself from the world which it so obviously rejected. In a self-imposed exile, the community through its writings castigated the Jerusalem leadership and anticipated its vindication by God through a holy war. The community's faithfulness would be rewarded, and the apostasy of the majority of Israel, the priests and religious leadership in particular, would be punished.[11]

The *Damascus Document* begins by stating that God has "hid his face from unfaithful Israel, and from the sanctuary and delivered them up to the sword." Remembering his covenant with the forefathers, God left a remnant and did not deliver it up to be destroyed. That remnant, to be sure, was the Qumran community, who alone remained

---

[10] For a recent discussion of this period, see Paul Hanson, *The People Called* (San Francisco: Harper & Row, 1986) 291–311.

[11] G. Vermes, *The Dead Sea Scrolls in English* (New York: Penguin, 1975) 96 (hereafter cited as Vermes, *DSS*).

faithful.[12] The very structure and order of the community were grounded in its being the holy people of God. The rank or organization (*serek*) of the community was based on the level of holiness the member had achieved and was a reminder that the community replicated a holy place, the temple.[13] God has given to the chosen ones an everlasting possession. They are the holy people and the foundation of the building of holiness for all ages to come.[14] God has hid the teaching of the law from the men of falsehood and revealed it only to the men of his chosen way.[15] The Qumran sectaries understood themselves to be the remnant, the only ones who kept the covenant which God had made with their ancestors.[16]

Another document which dates from approximately the same period as the Qumran writings, *1 Enoch,* holds a similar view of those who are in power. They are corrupt and faithless and soon will be judged. The author describes them above all as "sinners" (96:2; 98:4; 100:7). These sinners commit idolatry (99:7; 104:9), blaspheme (94:9; 96:7) and curse (95:4). They oppress the righteous and just (94:6; 96:7; 97:6). They bear false witness in order to persecute the righteous (95:6; 99:1). They coerce the righteous with their power (96:8) and pervert the law for their own means (99:2).[17]

Like the members of the Dead Sea sect, the author of *1 Enoch* viewed his community as the righteous. The author highlights the imminent judgment of the wealthy sinners and the vindication of the oppressed righteous through a series of woes (94:6-11; 95:3-6; 96:5-8; 97:1ff.; 99:1-2, 11-16; 100:7-9) in which the sinners and their corrupt attitudes and actions are described. The sinners are vilified and assured of judgment, and the righteous are promised their reward and vindication.

The first century B.C.E. *Psalms of Solomon* appear also to have their provenance in sectarian Judaism in this period.[18] This is seen in the sentiments expressed in this document concerning the faithlessness

---

[12] CD 1; Vermes, *DSS*, 97.

[13] L. Schiffman, *The Halakah at Qumran* (Leiden: E. J. Brill, 1975) 60ff.

[14] 1QS 11; see Vermes, *DSS*, 93.

[15] 1QS 9; see Vermes, *DSS*, 88.

[16] 1QM 14; see Vermes, *DSS*, 142.

[17] G. W. E. Nickelsburg, Jr., *Resurrection, Immortality, and Eternal Life in Inter-testamental Judaism* (Cambridge, Mass.: Harvard University Press, 1972) 30. See also *The Old Testament Pseudepigrapha*, ed. J. Charlesworth (2 vols.; Garden City, N.Y.: Doubleday, 1983, 1985) 1:7 (hereafter cited as *OTP*).

[18] P. N. Franklin, "The Cultic and Pious Climax of Eschatology in the Psalms of Solomon," *JSJ* 18 (1987) 15.

of Israel and its leaders or parent body in particular. Despite the widespread corruption within Israel and the devastating critique of the Jewish leadership, the *Psalms of Solomon* do reflect the belief that God will save a remnant. These are the righteous who follow God's commandments (14:1-2). These righteous, who are faithful and do not corrupt God's statutes, are a tree firmly planted which will not be uprooted (14:4), and they shall live forever (14:3). In the view of the author, God will gather a "holy people" and lead them to righteousness (17:27, 30).

Here again we see a community alienated from and hostile toward the dominant body of leaders and their supporters. In *Psalms of Solomon* the majority of these authorities and their followers are viewed as the unfaithful who have not followed God's commands. The leaders are lawless (1:8, 12); they have defiled the sanctuary and profaned the offerings (1:3). For this the leaders will finally be rejected. Again it is said that these lawless people are those in power. They have the authority to pass judgments on sinners, and they "sit in the council of the devout." They are excessive in appearance, excessive in words, and live in hypocrisy (4:1ff.).

The people of this dissenting community understand themselves to be the true followers and people of God. Chapters 6 and 10 of *Psalms of Solomon* offer a series of beatitudes for the truly devout who do not stray from God and the statutes of the law. These righteous are persecuted (5:5, 8-14; 8:23ff.), but the faithful will live forever (14:3). However, criminals and sinners will inherit Hades (14:9-10). God is going to gather a holy people who will not tolerate wickedness. These are the children of God.

In the late first century C.E., toward the close of the period being considered, two documents, 4 Ezra and 2 *Baruch*, reflect some of the same sentiments and convictions observed in these earlier documents. Chapters 15-18 of 2 *Baruch* discuss the many who have not followed Torah and the few who have.[19] The few are those of Baruch's community. In 18:1-2 and 48:18-19 Baruch describes his community as "the few" (see also 41-43; 78:7). Most have sinned and cast away the "yoke of the law" (41:3). However, in chap. 84 Baruch renews for his faithful community the covenant which Moses established.[20]

---

[19] G. Sayler, "II Baruch: A Story of Grief and Consolation," in *Society of Biblical Literature 1982 Seminar Papers*, ed. K. H. Richards (Chico, Cal.: Scholars Press, 1982) 488.

[20] F. J. Murphy, *The Structure and Meaning of Second Baruch*, SBLDS 78 (Atlanta: Scholars Press, 1985) 25.

The faithful scribe Baruch and his community become the true covenant people and represent those who have remained faithful to God's covenant and commands.

4 Ezra shares a similar perspective. The "few" of 4 Ezra have been faithful concerning the law and for this reason are God's elect (3:19ff.). The author believes that few people have truly kept the law. There may be individuals who have kept it, but no nations (3:36). This world belongs to the many, but the world to come to the few. Many have been created, but few will be saved (8:2-3). These few are the righteous mentioned throughout 4 Ezra (7:17, 51, 111; 9:14ff.). They are the remnant who have remained faithful to God and God's law. They are contrasted with the wicked or ungodly who will be judged at the time of the vindication of the righteous (8:48; 15:1-8, 23).

Finally, in terms of the sectarian nature of Judaism in the period 165 B.C.E.–100 C.E., the observations of the Jewish historian Josephus should be included. Josephus lists the various Jewish groups active during the period he purports to describe. In *Jewish War* (*J.W.*) 2.8.2 §119 Josephus says that there are three philosophical sects or schools (*haireseis*) among the Jews: the Pharisees, the Sadducees, and the Essenes. In this description the Essenes appear to be the focus. The Pharisees are described at greater length in the parallel passage in *Jewish Antiquities* (*Ant.*) 18.1.2 §11. Here a fourth philosophy is added almost as an afterthought (Josephus says at the outset of 18.1.2 §11 that there are only three sects among the Jews). *Antiquities* 13.5.9 §171 briefly describes the Pharisees, Sadducees, and Essenes in relation to the Hellenistic notion of fate.[21] For our purposes, what Josephus has to say about the Pharisees is of interest when we consider the prominence of the Pharisees in the Gospel of Matthew and in the world of which both formative and Matthean Judaism were a part. In terms of the various factions and parties that comprised the social world of Judaism in this period, it would be important to comment on what Josephus tells us about the Pharisees.

In *Jewish War* the Pharisees are first mentioned because they achieved political power and influence under Alexander Jannaeus's wife and successor, Alexandra.[22] "Now the Pharisees joined themselves to her to assist in her government. These were a certain body (*syntagma*) of Jews that appear more pious than others and seem

---

[21] See G. F. Moore, "Fate and Free Will in the Jewish Philosophies According to Josephus," *HTR* 22 (1929) 374.

[22] A. J. Saldarini, *Pharisees, Scribes and Sadducees in Palestinian Society: A Sociological Approach* (Wilmington, Del.: Michael Glazier, 1988) chap. 6.

to interpret the laws more accurately" (*J.W.* 1.5.2 §108–12). Josephus describes how the Pharisees worked their way into Alexandra's favor. They became the real administrators of public affairs, enjoying royal authority. *Antiquities* 13.15.5ff. §399–417 describes the death of Alexander Jannaeus and the advice he gave to his wife, Alexandra, that she might be successful during her reign. Alexander tells her that if she wishes to remain in power she must put some of her authority in the hands of the Pharisees. They, through their popularity with the people, will reconcile the nation to her. The Pharisees possess the trust of the people and have tremendous influence with them. The start of 13.16.2 §405 describes the steps Alexandra takes to initate this power-sharing arrangement with the Pharisees. "She allowed the Pharisees to do everything; to whom also she ordered the multitude to be obedient. She restored again those practices which the Pharisees had introduced, according to the traditions of their forefathers, and which her father-in-law Hyrcanus, had abrogated" (*Ant.* 13.16.2 §409).

Anthony Saldarini notes that several things can be observed about the Pharisees from these passages. First, the Pharisees appear as an organized, or at least distinct, body (*syntagma*). The term employed here (not *hairesis*) suggests an organized group. It is clear also that as a political force the Pharisees are in existence and are ready to assume political power during the reign of Alexandra.[23] Saldarini insightfully depicts the Pharisees as political "retainers" in a traditional agrarian society. The retainers are in the service of the ruling class, serving the governing class as educators, religious functionaries, and administrators. They would most likely be on the payroll of the ruler as long as they enjoyed his or her favor.[24]

This role of the Pharisees is clear from the passages that describe their relationship with Alexandra. Until they fell out of favor, the Pharisees enjoyed a similar relationship with John Hyrcanus. Josephus records that the Pharisees became jealous at the successes of Hyrcanus. In *Ant.* 13.10.5 §288 the popular support of the Pharisees is mentioned by Josephus. In this passage Hyrcanus, a Pharisee himself, is offended by the comment of one Eleazar, who encourages Hyrcanus to surrender the high priesthood. The Pharisees, when asked whether Eleazar should be given the death penalty for this, responded in the negative; according to Josephus this was due to their leniency. This enraged Hyrcanus, who finally withdrew from

---

[23] Ibid.
[24] Ibid., chap. 3. "Retainer" is a term derived from G. Lenski.

the party of the Pharisees and joined the Sadducees. From this point on, Hyrcanus legislated against the Pharisees and their practices. This is referred to in *Ant.* 13.16.2 §409.

Josephus thus illustrates the precarious position of retainers in ancient societies. They can quickly fall in or out of favor. Whether they are insiders or outsiders depends on the state of their relationship with those in power, because they rely on the support and patronage of the rulers. For example, as quickly as the Pharisees gained political power with the ascent of Alexandra, so quickly did they lose it at her death.[25] A similar depiction of the tenuous nature of the Pharisees' relationship with the rulers is found in *J.W.* 1.29.2 §567. Here it is Herod who is angry with the Pharisees, because he suspects them of being involved in the intrigue and conspiracy to place Antipater, Herod's son, on the throne.[26] Herod accuses his brother's wife of subsidizing the Pharisees to oppose him. The Pharisees are once again mentioned in the context of political affairs and struggles. The story about Herod in *J.W.* 1.29.2 §567 shows how quickly the political fortunes of the Pharisees could change.

The Pharisees' role as a political interest group associated with the political rulers is alluded to in the Gospel tradition as well as in the alliance they make with the Herodians against Jesus (Mark 3:6; 12:13). They are also linked with the chief priests and elders (Mark 8:31; 11:27; 14:43, 53; 15:1) and with the chief priests alone (14:10; 15:3, 10, 11, 31). Supportive for Saldarini's description of the Pharisees as political retainers is the fact that they must defer to these other political bodies while in Jerusalem. Their influence and authority are strongest around Galilee.[27]

According to Josephus, the Pharisees emerged as an organized body and a viable political interest group around the year 100 B.C.E. This would have been sometime during the reign of John Hyrcanus or Alexander Jannaeus. The Pharisees were a distinct enough group that Josephus was able to describe their beliefs and piety for his Roman readers. The Pharisees enjoyed the support of the people. This was their base of power and influence. They enjoyed *de jure* political power when they were able to form an alliance with one of

---

[25] Ibid.; see especially chaps. 5 and 6.

[26] Ibid., chap. 5.

[27] See A. J. Saldarini, "The Social Class of the Pharisees in Mark," in *The Social World of Formative Christianity and Judaism: Essays in Tribute to Howard Clark Kee*, ed. J. Neusner et al. (Philadelphia: Fortress Press, 1988) 69–77.

the ruling body. This relationship, however, was tenuous; consequently, the Pharisees had periods of some political power and other
times when they were clearly in disfavor with those in power. The
Pharisees are mentioned in Josephus for the most part when they are
involved in issues relating to political power or intrigue. Political
power and order are central concerns for Josephus.[28] From Josephus
we learn that the Pharisees, given their role as retainers, were also
involved with struggles for power in, influence with, and recognition
from the parent group. That the Pharisees were competing with
other groups or *haireseis* during this period is attested by their losing
the favor of Hyrcanus when he decided to change from the Pharisaic
party to that of the Sadducees. This competition between the Pharisees and the Sadducees is evidenced also in the Gospels.[29]

The Pharisees, however, were one of many sects or factions active
in this period. We should not assume that Josephus has given us an
exhaustive list of the sects within Judaism at this time. Indeed, these
sects from Josephus represent a small minority of the population in
Palestine.[30] Of course, at certain times these sects may have had
influence far beyond what their numbers might suggest.[31]

Thus, in the period under consideration, we are able to identify
several communities that felt alienated from the dominant power
groups and had developed their own beliefs and hopes as a result of
their experience of alienation and persecution. Unfortunately, we
have no texts that are clearly Pharisaic texts. This makes it difficult to
determine their views, practices, and attitudes. However, we do
know that the Pharisees were one group among many during this
period of fragmentation and factionalism. They too experienced both
favor and alienation and were clearly involved in the competition and
conflict between various groups, parties, and communities.

The sectarian nature of the communities referred to above is clear.
They perceived themselves to be the righteous minority. They
rejected, or were rejected by, the parent group. They would have
been primarily at odds with the religio-political powers in their
setting. These powers could have been the priests in the temple in

---

[28] Saldarini depicts Josephus as being primarily interested in issues involving
political power and stability (*Pharisees, Scribes and Sadducees*, chap. 5). On the piety
and religious practice of the Pharisees, see chap. 2 below.

[29] See, e.g., Matt. 22:34ff.

[30] D. Rhoads, *Israel in Revolution: 6–74 C.E.* (Philadelphia: Fortress Press,
1976) 32.

[31] Josephus gives their numbers as follows: Pharisees 6,000 (*Ant.* 17.2.4 §42),
Essenes 4,000 (*Ant.* 18.1.4 §20), and Sadducees "a few" (*Ant.* 18.1.4 §17).

Jerusalem or the local *boulē*, or authorities who exercised power because they enjoyed the favor of a ruler or Roman client.[32] These sects saw themselves as God's chosen people and agents and so claimed to be what the parent group claimed to be.[33] The sectarian communities developed certain themes and characteristics which helped to define who they were, particularly over against the parent body. It is to these additional themes we now turn. These themes and developments comprise other aspects of the sectarianism from 165 B.C.E. to 100 C.E. and also are important elements in the horizon of formative Judaism and the Gospel of Matthew. Both of these groups came out of this very setting of factionalism and sectarian communities. Matthean and formative Judaism reflect the sectarian nature of their social world in their makeup, the claims they make, their language, and in their relations with one another. This wider horizon of sectarianism in no small way helps to explain some of the developments, claims, and conflicts evident within formative Judaism and Matthew's Gospel.

The Language of Sectarianism

Often individual words can be windows into a wider world of assumptions and implied meaning. Individual words and idioms can represent systems of association that belong not just to the individual mind, but to the community as a whole. These single words have implied meanings of tremendous significance for those who share the horizon or social world of the community.[34] Their meaning and, in particular, their deeper significance, which often lies below the surface, are related to the setting and situation of their world.

The sectarianism of Judaism in this period possessed characteristic language and terms which help to reveal much about the self-understanding of the communities which employed the language. This language also reveals much about how these communties viewed the world around them. This "language of sectarianism" conveys the

[32] It seems the Pharisees during this period would have experienced both power and rejection, and perhaps persecution. Their political fortunes changed several times during this period. At times the Pharisees were probably "sectarian" (they were on the "outs" with the parent group), while at other times they would have enjoyed decisive political power.

[33] See Blenkinsopp, "Interpretation and Sectarian Tendencies," 1.

[34] E. D. Hirsch, Jr., *Cultural Literacy: What Every American Needs to Know* (Boston: Houghton Mifflin, 1987) 64, 68. According to Hirsch, understanding these deeper meanings helps to constitute one's "cultural literacy."

deep social divisions which seem to have characterized this period.[35] The sectarian communities tend to make a sharp distinction between themselves and the majority of those around them. This is particularly true where the leaders of the people are concerned. These communities view the leadership as responsible for the grievous state of affairs they now are experiencing. The terms employed to distinguish between the two groups, the sectarian community on the one hand and those in control on the other, are highly charged and polemical.

Two terms that are characteristic of these sectarian communities and are regularly found in their writings are "lawless" and "righteous." 4 Ezra repeatedly uses the term "righteous" to describe the few who are saved and who will inherit the promises of God. The term "righteous" serves as a designation for Ezra's faithful community. It helps to describe the community and to differentiate it from the unfaithful majority (7:17, 51; 9:14ff.). Often these righteous are directly contrasted with the wicked or ungodly (8:48; 15:23). The righteous are few, but the ungodly abound (7:51). Only the righteous are saved and promised the world to come (7:48). Those who will perish are those who persecute the righteous ones (8:57).

Along similar lines, 2 *Baruch* 14 offers an extended definition and explanation of the reward for the "righteous." These righteous are clearly the faithful community behind 2 *Baruch* (see 15:8). The author writes that these righteous, who have been gathered by God, will be rewarded (85:3-5). The appearance of the righteous in the resurrection is described in 49:1–52:7. Again, as in 4 Ezra, it is only these righteous who will be saved (2 *Bar.* 75:1–77:26).

The "righteousness" of the elect is contrasted with the "wickedness" of the sinners also in 1 *Enoch* (94:1, 4; 103:11-12). The favorite term of the author for those with whom the community struggles is "the sinners" (94:5; 96:1, 4; 99:1ff.). These sinners stand in opposition to the righteous few. The author claims that the sinners oppress people and commit injustices (94:6; 99:15); they encourage other people to engage in their wickedness (94:5). In the woes, the sinners are denounced for their trust in wealth (94:6ff.; 97:1ff.). These sinners persecute the righteous (95:6; 103:11-12). These sectarian communities believe that "the sinners" have no share in eternal life. The righteous will be vindicated and given charge over the sinners at the judgment (99:10; 94:11; 96:1; 97:1; 100:1).

The author of the *Psalms of Solomon* also employs these buzzwords; he refers to the antagonists of his community as "sinners"

---

[35] Donaldson, "Moses Typology," 37.

(1:1; 2:16, 35; 3:11; 17:23). The members of the community are the "righteous" (3:3, 8; 10:3; 14:1-2) and "those who fear the Lord" (3:12; 12:4; 13:12; 15:13). The righteous are described in a number of passages (4:8; 13:6-11; 15:6). The sinners are lawless (*anomia*), a term that occurs throughout (*Pss. Sol.* 1:8; 2:3, 12; 4:1, 8, 12; 17:11). The lawless and the righteous are often placed together and contrasted with one another (9:2; 8:8-9). The lawless sinners are described in scathing terms in *Pss. Sol.* 4. They are profaners. Their hearts are far from God. They live in hypocrisy and only to impress others. They misuse the law and defraud innocent people. Their fate is described with some relish in 4:14ff. These lawless have stolen from the sanctuary (8:11), are impure (8:12), and surpass even the Gentiles in all their sins (8:13). The sinners will perish for all time (15:13). "They will be driven out from their inheritance" (17:23). Conversely, nothing can harm the righteous (13:6). It is those who fear the Lord who will eventually rise up and obtain eternal life (3:12). The sinners will not be remembered by God (3:11).

These sectarian communities reflect enmity toward the parent group in the derogatory names that body is assigned in the literature and in the descriptions of the behavior and attitudes which the authors frequently and freely give of that group. In *1 Enoch* these "sinners" are guilty of idolatry, blasphemy, and cursing (94:9; 95:4; 96:7; 99:7; 104:9). They have altered the words of the law, perverted the covenant, and consider themselves guiltless (99:2). They oppress the poor, abuse their wealth, and misuse the agencies meant to ensure justice, such as the laws and the courts.

The lawless leaders in *Psalms of Solomon* have ignored God and act arrogantly (1:4-8). They have corrupted the cultus and are guilty of all kinds of impurities (2:3-13; 8:11-12). They judge and condemn others, while they are guilty of theft and of abusing God's law and statutes (4:1, 8; 8:9). *2 Baruch* characterizes the sinner as one who despises God's law and has stopped up his ear so as to avoid having to hear it (51:4). Sinners do not love God's law and for this reason are perishing (54:14). They have rejected the understanding of the Most High (54:18). In *4 Ezra* the sinners are those who are separated from and unfaithful to God's law (9:36). These sinners have scorned God's law and covenant (7:82). It is the righteous who have understood and followed God's law.

The language of a number of the documents from this period reflects the bitter factionalism that was characteristic of many of the sectarian communities of this age. The terms carried some significant connotations. The struggle between these sectarian communities and those in power was cast in rather stark, black-and-white terms. The members of the community were righteous, just, faithful to God, and sure to be vindicated by God. Those in the parent group, on the other hand, were corrupt lawbreakers who were far from God, oppressed God's people, and would have no share in the world to come. The attitudes and actions of those in power are frequently described as hypocritical, self-serving, and deceptive.

The exclusive nature of these terms and the judgment they implied on the group in power would certainly have been cause for conflict and tension between communities and parties. The nature of the inflammatory language usually indicates that those who are using it constitute the minority.[36] The language of sectarianism then signals something about the social location of those using it. The sectarian communities of this period felt persecuted. They did not possess political power. They believed that those in power, the parent body, were corrupt and false leaders. The parent group varied from period to period and place to place. The highly charged language employed by these communities reveals the frustration and anger they felt toward those in power. Perhaps most significantly, this language highlights the competitive and caustic setting and the sectarian background out of which both formative and Matthean Judaism came. Matthew freely adopts this language and employs it in his struggle to legitimate the position of his community in the face of the influence and impact of formative Judaism.

Hostility toward the Jewish Leadership

Much of the hostility and highly charged rhetoric coming from these sectarian communities was directed toward the Jewish leadership. The leaders naturally varied from period to period and place to place. For the Qumran community these leaders were the priests in the Jerusalem temple. For *1 Enoch* they were the leaders of the Hasmonean empire during the period of their greatest expansion. For *2 Baruch*, *4 Ezra*, or the Gospel of Matthew, these leaders could have been people allied with and sympathetic to the Romans or simply the

---

[36] L. Kriesberg, *The Sociology of Social Conflict* (Englewood Cliffs, N.J.: Prentice-Hall, 1973) 87. This type of hostility has been referred to as "safety valve" behavior. It vents some of the frustrations and anger the community feels, but at the same time reveals that the community is powerless and constitutes the underdog in this setting (Kriesberg, *Sociology*, 92ff.; and L. Coser, *The Functions of Social Conflict* [New York: Free Press, 1956] 41).

local leaders and elders in a particular setting or community who had gained power following the destruction of the temple. In the view of these sectarian communities, these leaders had betrayed the people, had turned from God, and had brought upon Israel the hardship the people were now experiencing. The struggle and alienation characteristic of these communities, which are clearly reflected in their writings, are largely due, these communities believed, to the corrupt leadership.

2 Baruch 64, for example, speaks allegorically about the wickedness that existed in the days of Manasseh. It was the wickedness of Manasseh the priest and his profaning of the sanctuary which led the Most High to withdraw from the temple (64:2). 4 Ezra tends to attack the corruption of most of Israel. The Jewish leadership and the majority of Israel are lumped together and dealt with in the same manner. In 4 Ezra the leaders and those who follow their teaching constitute the many who have strayed from God's law (8:1, 3, 59; 9:15).

The keys of the temple become a symbol in the post-70 period for the failure of the priests and religious leaders to be faithful and to execute properly their duties. Like some of the terms related to the sectarianism of this period, the keys also appear to carry a series of associated meanings for those who inhabit this social world in the post-70 period. In the lamentation over the destruction of the temple in *2 Bar.* 10:18, the priests are ordered to take the keys of the sanctuary and cast them up to heaven, "because behold, we have been found to be false stewards." The priests ask God to "guard your house yourself." Similarly in the *Paraleipomena Jeremiou* (4 *Baruch*), Jeremiah takes the keys of the temple and casts them toward the sun, saying, "Take the keys of the temple of God and keep them until the day in which the Lord will question you about them. Because we were not found worthy of keeping them, for we were false stewards" (4:4).

This theme concerning the keys is still evident in the late second century in the *Fathers According to Rabbi Nathan* (*'Abot de Rabbi Nathan* [ARN]). In one passage, just as Jerusalem is being destroyed, the high priests throw the keys of the temple up to heaven, saying, "O Master of the Universe, here are the keys which thou didst hand over to us, for we have not been found trustworthy custodians to do the king's work and to eat at the king's table."[37] The relinquishing of

---

[37] *The Fathers According to Rabbi Nathan*, trans. J. Goldin (New Haven: Yale University Press, 1955) 37.

the keys by the priests signals the priests' failure to perform their tasks faithfully and points to the loss of their position of influence and access to God. Other people and agents emerge to fulfill this role. The image of the keys in this period is used by these various authors to draw attention to the failure of the Jewish leadership, their infidelity, and their loss of authority to act as the interpreters of God's law and will on behalf of the people. Interestingly, as is well known, Matthew seizes upon this very image for his own community.

Elsewhere, related to the hostility toward the Jewish leadership in these sectarian documents, *4 Baruch* makes it clear that Jerusalem is a corrupt and sinful place. It is because of this sin that the destruction occurred (1:2; 2:2; 4:4, 7). It is interesting to note that the tearing of the temple veil is described in *Testament of Levi* 10:3 in order to draw attention to the shameful behavior of the priests behind the veil. The people profane the priesthood, defile the altars of the sanctuary, set aside the law, and nullify the words of the prophets with their perversity (*T. Levi* 16:2-4). The priests of the temple plunder the Lord's offering and teach God's commands out of greed for grain (*T. Levi* 14:4, 6). The *Lives of the Prophets* (3:15) similarly speaks of the faithless people in the temple in Jerusalem. It is clear that the Jewish leaders, specifically those associated with the temple, were viewed in many circles in the post-70 period as corrupt and faithless.

This attitude toward the Jewish leadership, however, is not unique to the period following 70 and the destruction of the temple. Indeed, hostility toward and rejection of the Jewish leadership are common characteristics of the sectarian communities throughout the period 165 B.C.E.–100 C.E. The contempt with which the Qumran community viewed the Jerusalem priesthood and leadership is explicitly stated: Israel has forsaken God and has been unfaithful (CD 1). God has deserted the sanctuary. The priests profane the temple and fail to observe the distinction between clean and unclean (CD 5:2ff.). The leaders who misguide the people are "teachers of lies" and "false prophets." They are seers of falsehood who have wickedly schemed to cause the people to exchange the law engraved on their hearts for the "smooth things" which they speak (1QH 4).[38] The *War Scroll*, which describes the final battle of the community with the Kittim, reveals the belief on the part of the community that they, following the victory, will reorganize and reconstitute the temple in its pure and true form.[39] The community is the true temple of God, and

---

[38] See Vermes, *DSS*, 161.
[39] See the first half of col. 2 of the *War Scroll*; cf. Vermes, *DSS*, 122–23.

therefore those in the Jerusalem temple are apostate and false leaders whom God will overthrow.

The attack on the Jewish leadership is unusually strident in the *Psalms of Solomon*. This mid-first-century B.C.E. document, perhaps written in Jerusalem, contains repeated attacks on the Jewish leadership, accusing them of corruption and hypocrisy. This document serves as a prime example of the hostility toward the Jewish leadership during this period on the part of the sectarian communities and the deep divisions which existed within Israelite society.

> Why are you sitting in the council of the devout, you profaner? And your heart is far from the Lord, provoking the God of Israel with law-breaking; Excessive in words and in appearance above everyone, he who is harsh in words condemning sinners at judgement. His hand is the first one against him, as if in zeal, yet he himself is guilty of a variety of sins and intemperance. His eyes are on every woman indiscriminately, his tongue lies when swearing a contract. . . . May God remove from the devout those who live in hypocrisy; may his flesh decay and his life be impoverished. (*Pss. Sol.* 4:1-5)

It is clear from this passage that those being attacked comprise the leadership. They "sit in the council of the devout," are able to dress extravagantly, and have the authority to pass judgments on others. This obviously suggests positions of power and leadership for this group. The *Psalms of Solomon* go on to say that these people twist the law for their own purposes; they are hypocrites who, as in the view of the other sectarian communities, have profaned the sanctuary and the offerings with their lawless acts. They break their oaths and contracts and no longer act on God's behalf. The worst possible fate is wished upon these false leaders.

A theme that is often associated with the condemnation and judgment of the Jewish leadership in these sectarian documents is the leaders' role in the shedding of innocent blood. *2 Baruch* 64:2 describes the wickedness of Manasseh: he killed the righteous and shed innocent blood. The wicked priests in *T. Levi* 16:2-4 have not only defiled the altars, set aside the law, and nullified the words of the prophets, but they persecute just men and take innocent blood upon their heads. *4 Ezra* 15:22 describes the sinners as those who have shed innocent blood upon the earth. The first two chapters of *4 Ezra*, which were redacted by a Christian author and are referred to by scholars as *5 Ezra*, have picked up on this theme. When God is speaking in the appeal to Israel, this theme emerges. "I sent you my servants the prophets, but you have taken and slain them and torn their bodies to pieces; their blood I will require of you, says the Lord" (1:32).

Along with the hostility toward the Jewish leadership, the accusation that they persecute the righteous and have shed innocent blood once again reflects the social location of these sectarian communities. They, the righteous, have been oppressed by those in control. They have interpreted the rejection and persecution they experience in terms of Israel's prophetic history and the fabled persecution of righteous men at the hands of corrupt leaders. These sectarian communities claim an association with the prophets of old, who were by this time widely recognized as righteous men and agents of God who were unjustly persecuted by corrupt leaders. In developing this theme these communities have begun to align themselves with some of the heroic underdogs of Israel's history. At the same time the Jewish leaders are being associated with some of the storied villains of the same history. The claim that the Jewish leaders have slain innocent blood and God's messengers or *righteous* becomes a common, albeit harsh, charge from the alienated communities in this period. It was one of several ways in which the community sought to discredit the leadership and to assert that they, the sectarian community, were in truth God's chosen people.

The rejection of the Jewish leadership during this period within Judaism was widespread among these sectarian communities. These communities viewed the leaders as dishonest and corrupt. They were far from God and did not understand or follow God's laws and statutes. Their inheritance was lost, and their fate had been sealed. The righteous few were the ones truly called by God to lead. They possessed the true understanding of God's law. The horrible events of this period, particularly the destruction of the temple, served as proof of the corrupt nature of the present leadership and the vindication of the righteous few. Rejection of the Jewish leadership was indeed widespread during this period, and so also was the hostility between the parent group and the different sectarian communities. The Matthean community fits easily into this world and reflects much of the same hostility toward the Jewish leadership. It is within this milieu and context that Matthew's Gospel must be read and understood.

The Centrality of the Law

The question which the exclusivistic claims characteristic of sectarian communities provokes is, How do we establish that we are indeed the true covenant community? How is the community able to show that they are truly the elect, in contrast to the group with which they contend? These communities believed that they constituted the righteous few, to the exclusion of the lawless many. Such a claim requires a precise definition of what constitutes membership in the community. The community must also legitimate its claim to be the true people of God in the face of its competition, who would obviously dispute this. The claims and disputes of these communities usually centered on the law and the proper understanding and interpretation of it. The law emerged as both the common ground and battleground between the competing factions and communities during this period.[40] It was by means of the law that the sectarian communities were able to legitimate their own position and denounce that of their adversaries. Faithfully keeping the law became for these alienated communities the condition for remaining in the covenant.[41]

The interpretation of the law was an essential part of the life of the Qumran community. The community saw in the Scriptures prophecies that applied to their own community. The community was the very fulfillment of these prophecies. "The Old Testament text, which originally had a reference to some event in the contemporary scene at the time it was written, nevertheless was vague enough to be applied to some new event in the history of the Qumran sect."[42] J. A. Fitzmyer refers to this interpretive process on the part of the Qumran community as "modernization."[43] In this process of the modernization of the text, the Qumran community saw itself as the subject of a particular passage and understood the elements of the passage as referring to some aspect of how they lived and what they believed in the present. 1QpHab 7:1-5 captures this understanding of the Scriptures.

> God told Habakkuk to write the things which were to come upon the last generation, but the consummation of the period he did not make known to him. And as for what it says, "That he may run who reads

[40] The author owes this expression concerning the role of the law to Dr. David Tiede.

[41] E. P. Sanders, "The Covenant as a Soteriological Category and the Nature of Salvation in Palestinian and Hellenistic Judaism," in *Jews, Greeks and Christians*, ed. R. Hamerton-Kelly and R. Scroggs (Leiden: E. J. Brill, 1975) 40.

[42] J. A. Fitzmyer, "The Use of Explicit Old Testament Quotations in the Qumran Literature and in the New Testament," in *Essays on the Semitic Background of the New Testament*, Sources for Biblical Study 5 (Missoula, Mont.: Scholars Press, 1974) 16.

[43] Ibid., 21ff.

it," this means the Righteous Teacher, to whom God made known all the mysteries of the words of his servants the prophets.

In this passage Habakkuk's oracle is viewed by the Qumran community as referring to their own sect, and not primarily to something in the time of Habakkuk. The meaning of the oracle for the Qumran community is revealed and explicated by the Righteous Teacher, to whom the mysteries of God have been revealed (1QpHab 7:7). Fitzmyer lists some eleven passages from Qumran where this process of modernization is clearly evident.[44] The Qumran covenanters believed that they understood and kept God's law. Others in Israel, particularly those in the temple in Jerusalem, had failed to understand it and had corrupted it through using the law for their own means and gain. 1QS 5 states that "whoever approaches the Council of the Community (for membership) shall enter the Covenant of God in the presence of all who have freely pledged themselves. He shall undertake by a binding oath to return with all his heart to the Law of Moses." "He shall undertake by the Covenant to separate from all the men of falsehood who walk in the way of wickedness."[45] The community claims it has the true understanding of the law of God. God, according to 1QS 9, "has concealed the teaching of the law from the men of falsehood, but shall impart true knowledge and righteous judgement to those who have chosen the Way."[46] The law or the Scripture was used by the community, through its creative interpretations, as the means by which it was able to validate its beliefs and denounce those of its enemies.

The interpretive technique which Fitzmyer has referred to as modernization is a clear example of the community describing and defending its actions through appeal to the law or Scripture. The community believed that the words of the law and Scripture were fulfilled in the history and life of the Qumran community. The true meaning and words of the Scripture were explicated for the community by the Teacher of Righteousness, as the passage from the Habakkuk commentary shows. The people at Qumran constructed an elaborate defense of their community, its beliefs, and actions and an equally elaborate denunciation of the leaders in Jerusalem. Both the defense of the community and the denunciation of the leaders

[44] The Qumran passages Fitzmyer examines are CD 1:13-14; 4:12-18; 6:11-14; 7:15-16, 18-21; 8:9-12, 14-16; 19:1; 4QFlor 1:2-3, 14-16, 16-17.

[45] See Vermes, *DSS,* 79.

[46] Ibid., 88.

were centered primarily on the law and the community's distinctive interpretation of it. This understanding and application of the law were fundamental for sustaining the life and faith of the community.

A number of the other sectarian communities during this period used the law to support and explain their positions as well as to denounce the positions of their opponents. *1 Enoch* describes the oppressive sinners as people who alter the words of truth and pervert God's law (*1 Enoch* 99:2). Chapter 104 goes into considerable detail concerning the way in which the sinners corrupt the Scriptures and the fact that the community of the righteous truly possesses the law and the true understanding of it:

> And I know this mystery: For they (the sinners) shall alter the word of truth and many sinners will take it to heart; they will speak evil words and lie, and they will invent fictitious stories and write out my Scriptures on the basis of their own words. And would that they had written down all the words truthfully on the basis of their own speech, and neither alter nor take away from my words, all of which I testify to them from the beginning! Again know another mystery! that to the righteous and wise shall be given the Scriptures of joy, for truth and great wisdom. So to them shall be given the Scriptures and they shall believe them and be glad in them; and all the righteous ones who learn from them the ways of truth shall rejoice. (*1 Enoch* 104:10-13)

This passage illustrates the polemic concerning the law and Scripture no doubt operative within the setting of the community behind *1 Enoch* 94-108. The charge of true versus false understanding of the law and Scripture is readily seen in 99:10ff. The enemies of the community, the sinners, do not truly follow the law, though they would claim to be doing that. The charge of the author is that they have inserted their own words in place of the words of God. They lead people astray with this false version of the Scripture. The sinners fail to know the whole story (99:11). This is no doubt a serious charge on the part of the community behind *1 Enoch* and would have provoked considerable tension. Those sinners who quote and use the law do so falsely. In fact, it is not really God's law at all that they rely on, but their own words. According to 99:12ff., the Scriptures have been given instead to the righteous and the wise of the community. The author asserts not only that the opponents misuse and fail to understand the law of God but that they no longer possess it. The community has the mysteries of God revealed to them by Enoch, who understands these mysteries and makes them available for the chosen community (92:1; 93:1; 104:10, 12; 108:4, 15).

The law is also a major focus of the attack on the Jewish leadership in the *Psalms of Solomon*. The emphasis in chap. 8 seems to be violations relating to the temple. The lawless leaders have stolen from the sanctuary and defiled the holy temple (*Pss. Sol.* 8:11ff.). However, chap. 4 emphasizes the corrupt way in which the Jewish leadership has handled and manipulated the law. They break the law, and their hearts are far from God (4:1). They misuse the law to condemn others (4:2). They deceitfully quote the law for their own advantage and break it in secret (4:8, 22; 8:9).

The faithful people behind the *Psalms of Solomon* are those who live in the righteousness of God's commandments. Only these faithful have remained true to God's law (14:1-2). For those who have forgotten God and the laws of God, their inheritance is Hades (14:9). The devout few will inherit life (14:10). Had the sinners remembered God and not been so committed to lawlessness, the promises of God would still be theirs. However, God will now gather a holy people who have remembered the law of God (17:26). The law constitutes the ground over which these sectarian struggles are waged during this period. The law serves as a means by which the parent body can be attacked, as well as a means by which the life and beliefs of the sectarian community can be validated.

In *2 Baruch*, from the late first century C.E., the law also plays a central role. Throughout *2 Baruch* it is one's attitude to the law that is the determining factor in guaranteeing salvation or punishment in the coming age (32:1; 44; 48:39; 54:13-14; 84:2-11).[47] The law of God is life (38:2). The law is a lamp for God's people (54:13; 59:12; 77:16). The law is virtually synonymous with wisdom and understanding (44:14; 51:3, 4, 7; 54:13; 38:2-4; 84:1). "In II Baruch all people will be judged according to the degree of their adherence to the law, which is equivalent to the degree of their wisdom."[48] The righteous are those who have guarded the truth of the law and not departed from it (44:14). The wicked are those who have rejected the law and stopped up their ears so as not to hear it (51:4). It is because of their pride that these wicked do not know God's law (48:40). The law is the means by which one determines who are the wicked (41:3; 51:4; 54:14).

Similarly in 4 Ezra, a document that, like *2 Baruch*, was written toward the end of the first century C.E., the law acts as a means to

---

[47] M. Desjardins, "Law in II Baruch and IV Ezra," *Studies in Religion* 14 (1985) 28-29.

[48] F. J. Murphy, "Sapiential Elements in the Syriac Apocalypse of Baruch," *JQR* 86 (1986) 314.

affirm the righteous few and denounce the others. 4 Ezra 9:26ff. describes the abiding glory of the Mosaic law and defines sin as receiving the law but failing to follow it (9:36). Sinners will perish, but the law will abide forever (9:37). The righteous are those who have kept God's commands and law (7:17, 88, 90, 95; 8:30). The wicked who will eventually be rejected by God are those who have failed properly to understand and follow God's law (7:22ff., 37, 72, 80; 8:28). The wicked have scorned the law and denied God's covenants (7:24; 9:11). The law is God's gift to Israel, which they have rejected (3:19ff.). It is the community of the righteous, thanks to the instruction of Ezra, that properly understands and follows the law of God. In fact, it is only the righteous who possess the Scripture. The community has claimed God's law as its own, since, in its view, the majority of the nation has rejected God's law.

These sectarian communities tend to claim that they alone possess the true understanding of the law. God has also disclosed to them the identity of those who have been true to these laws and those who have failed to keep them. An essential element in this claim is the presence of an agent or interpreter who receives understanding from God and in turn imparts this insight and understanding to the community.

In *2 Baruch,* for example, Baruch himself emerges as God's agent, who apprehends God's message and in turn instructs the righteous community.[49] Baruch prays to God and asks for enlightenment (*2 Bar.* 38:1-4). He asks that God make known to him the meaning of the visions. As God's agent, Baruch instructs the community, and in chaps. 44–45 he addresses the teachers of the community on the basis of privileged information and visions he has received from God. These insights must be passed on to everyone in the community, "from the greatest to the least" (77:1). The wisdom which Baruch imparts as God's agent is firmly rooted in the law (chap. 46). It is as a result of this instruction that the community will learn to live (chap. 76).[50]

As F. J. Murphy has observed, Baruch is in fact paralleled with Moses, a connection made explicit in chap. 84. Baruch declares that he reiterates Moses in lifting up God's law and calling God's people to that law. He renews the covenant that Moses established (84:2ff.). Moses and Baruch are the divine intermediaries who reveal to God's people the law and life to which they have been called. "As Moses

[49] Ibid., 321ff.
[50] Sayler, "II Baruch," 495.

left the people and ascended the mountain to receive God's instruction, so also Baruch leaves the people and ascends Mount Zion in order to receive God's instruction."[51] Both Moses and Baruch carry this instruction back to the people. Like Moses, Baruch is portrayed as God's lawgiver. At his death the people wonder to whom they can now go for the law and instruction. Who will distinguish the ways of life and death for them (46:3)? It is Baruch who has been given God's wisdom and instruction, and it is Baruch who relays this divine revelation to the people of the community.

In 4 Ezra 14, Ezra appears as Moses *redivivus* in that he records anew the law for the people. God speaks to Ezra, saying that as he revealed himself to Moses in a bush and spoke to Moses, led him up on Mount Sinai, revealed many secrets and wondrous things to him, and called Moses to declare these things, so now God does the same to Ezra (14:2-8). God calls out to Ezra, who responds, "Here I am Lord." God instructs Ezra "to lay up in your heart the signs that I have shown you, the dreams that you have seen, and the interpretations that you have heard (14:7-9). Ezra is charged to order his house, reprove the people, comfort the lowly, and instruct those that are wise (14:13). God, who has found favor with Ezra, sends the Holy Spirit to him "to write everything that has happened in the world from the beginning, the things which were written in your law, that men may be able to find the path, and that those who wish to live in the last days may live" (14:22).

Throughout 4 Ezra, Ezra is the agent whom God instructs and to whom God discloses visions and secrets. It is as a result of this that the community can be assured that it is fulfilling God's will and following God's law. In the sectarian documents from this period, the struggle to assert the community's superiority and chosenness, particularly in light of all objective evidence to the contrary, was done in part through the appeal to a divine agent who has disclosed God's law and will to the community. This is how the community knows it is the elect and possesses the true understanding of God's law. God's ordained agent has revealed the true understanding of the law to the community.

The law as interpreted within these groups emerged in this period as the means by which the sectarian communities legitimated their position and asserted their status as God's true people, in contrast to their opponents. Their interpretation and application of the Scripture reinforced their exclusive claims. Usually there was a figure in the

---

[51] Murphy, *Structure and Meaning*, 78.

community or in the community's history who served as the agent and revealer of God's law and will for the community. Invariably, revealed insights belonged to the elect few who had faithfully followed God's law, and not the many who had departed from that law. These sweeping and elevated claims on the part of the sectarians no doubt created further tension and struggle. As the tension and conflict increased, these communities continued to look to the law for support for their beliefs and actions and for the eventual vindication of their community by God. During this period the law became perhaps *the* central means by which these sectarian communities attempted to establish the truth of their claims and discredit the claims and position of their opponents.

The Future of God's Covenant People

The issues discussed in this chapter highlight the tension and competition that existed between the various factions within Judaism during this period. The polemical and highly charged rhetoric, characteristic of the sectarian communities discussed above, indicates how seriously these communities viewed their competition. These attacks against "unfaithful Israel" were often aimed above all at the Jewish leadership or parent group. The leaders were held responsible for the rejection by most of the people of God's laws and covenant. Those in the parent group were condemned for being hypocrites and impostors. The sectarians felt oppressed and persecuted by the parent body. They understood themselves to stand in the historic train of Israel's prophets who challenged faithless generations and rulers, were persecuted, and were finally vindicated by God. Each faction viewed itself as God's remnant, "the few" who had remained righteous. They contrasted themselves with "the many" who had "gone the way of the people," the lawless or wicked who had denied the covenants. The sectarians alone had remained true to God's law. "The many" had perverted the law and denied God's commands. The law emerged as the central means by which the sectarians established their faithfulness and proved the apostasy of their opponents.

The sectarian communities interpreted the significant political events of their history as divine vindication of their position and as God's rejection of their opponents. Whether it was the corrupt Jerusalem priesthood and the hellenized Hasmonean rulers (Qumran and *1 Enoch*) or the invasion and destruction of Jerusalem by Pompey (*Psalms of Solomon*) or the destruction of the Jerusalem temple in 70

(*2 Baruch* and 4 Ezra), these events were interpreted as confirmations of the beliefs of the community concerning God's rejection of the parent group. This divine rejection of the rulers and the belief on the part of these communities that most of Israel had denied the law and covenant of their God provoked the question evident in all of these documents: What then is the future of God's covenant people?

The documents from the sectarian communities of this period describe the faithless and rejected majority of Israelites and eventually point to God remaining true to the promises of the fathers through saving an elect few, a remnant. That remnant is, of course, that particular sectarian community and the righteous who comprise the membership. Gwen Sayler has described this as a movement from grief to consolation.[52] These documents express anger and dismay about faithless Israel and its rejection of the commands of God. This rejection is epitomized in the behavior of the leadership, who often seem to emerge as near caricatures of corruption and lawlessness. The consolation in these documents comes in the form of God having remembered his covenant and saving a people who are truly faithful.

The community at Qumran understood itself as the true covenant people. The *Damascus Document* begins by stating that despite Israel's lack of faith and its having forsaken God, God will remember the covenant made with Israel and leave a remnant. This remnant was not delivered up to be destroyed (CD 1:2ff.). That the community considered itself God's elect is evidenced by the standard which they will carry into battle: "The People of God" (1QM 3).[53] Those at Qumran are "the people God has delivered" because "he has kept mercy toward His covenant." They are "the remnant of God's name" (1QM 14).[54] The Qumran covenanters claimed to be the true people of God. The community believed that the day would come when God would drive out the unrighteous and corrupt and restore the true people of God to their rightful place.

The *Psalms of Solomon* also reflect the belief that God will remember the covenant made with Israel. God is faithful to those who themselves remain faithful amid the suffering and persecution the community is experiencing. "God remembers those who live in the righteousness of his commands" (*Pss. Sol.* 14:1-2). The people of this community of the mid-first century B.C.E. believed that in time God would gather a holy people (17:27, 30). The righteous will endure

---

[52] Sayler, "II Baruch," 485.
[53] Vermes, *DSS*, 128.
[54] Ibid., 142.

forever because the Lord has remembered them (10:1; 14:4). However, the fate of those who have forgotten God and rejected the laws
and covenant is judgment and rejection (14:6-10). Despite the
devastating critique of Israel in the *Psalms of Solomon*, there is the consolation that God has not forgotten the covenant with Israel and has
saved a remnant. It is this remnant, these holy few, whom God will
gather. These people, the faithful and righteous of the *Psalms of
Solomon*, will constitute God's true people.

2 *Baruch* and 4 *Ezra* also maintain that God will have mercy and
remember Israel. The true Israelites will find consolation for their
suffering. God will punish their enemies (*2 Bar.* 82:1-2). Baruch
shares with other sectarian communities the belief that those who
will be saved, those who constitute true Israel, are few. Chapters
41–43 ask specifically about the fate of the believers and the wicked.
Those who have cast aside the yoke of the law are doomed. The
righteous who have not been corrupted will be saved.[55] Again, the
true covenant people are a faithful remnant who will finally be vindicated (78:7). Those who live according to the law will be gathered
together. They shall partake in the resurrection (30:1-2). It is the law
that will divide between life and death (46:3).[56] On this day of judgment God also will be vindicated (82:2, 4-9). Similarly, 4 *Baruch* pro-
claims this hope, saying, "God has not left us to grieve over the holy
city which was left desolate and outraged. For this reason the Lord
has taken pity on our tears and remembered the covenant that he
established with our fathers" (*4 Bar.* 6:21).

4 Ezra believes that God will act to judge the wicked and save the
righteous. The righteous, however, are few (4 Ezra 7:60; 8:2, 3; 9:13).
In 12:34, in the interpretation of the fifth vision, it is stated: "But he
will deliver in mercy the remnant of my people, those who have been
saved through my borders, and he will make them joyful until the
end comes, the day of judgement, of which I spoke." This remnant,
the righteous of 4 Ezra, will be in paradise, and the wicked will inherit
Hades (7:36, 78-101). Those who have "gloriously taught the law" are
part of God's true people (8:30-33). In hell are "those who have
despised the Most High and who were contemptuous of his law, and
forsook his ways" (8:56). The lawless perish and no longer are part
of God's chosen people (9:14-25, 32). God's remnant, the righteous
few, will be saved.

---

[55] *OTP*, 1:633–34.
[56] Those who live according to the law of Moses, as the author understands it,
will inherit eternal life. See 2 *Bar.* 32:1; 38:1; 48:22; 51:3, 4-7; 54:15.

The first two chapters of 4 Ezra, known as 5 Ezra, also reveal a preoccupation with this question about the future of God's covenant people and address it directly. Not unlike 4 Ezra, 5 Ezra insists that most of Israel has forsaken the Lord (1:14). Israel failed to cleave to the Rock (1:20). "Because you have forsaken me," says the Lord, "I will forsake you" (1:25). The author refines this point concerning God's rejection of Israel, however: "It is not as if I have forsaken you; you have forsaken yourselves" (1:27).

According to the author of 5 Ezra, as a result of the sin and obduracy that have characterized Israel, the Lord says, "I will turn my face away from you, and turn to other nations and I will give them my name, that they may keep my statutes" (1:24). G. Stanton has drawn attention to this aspect of 5 Ezra. Here the question of the future of God's covenant people is answered by saying that the promises heretofore associated with Israel will now be passed on to other nations or people, "a coming people," who will not forsake God and who will keep God's statutes.[57] The author of 5 Ezra is in agreement with other sectarian communities that Israel has been unfaithful to the laws and statutes of God. They have strayed from God's commands and forsaken the covenant. God is turning to another people, people who bear fruit (1:33-40). These people who bear fruit constitute, in the author's view, the future of God's covenant people.

The question of the future of the covenant people was perhaps the most important issue within Judaism during this period. Each aspect of what we have been calling sectarian Judaism points toward this issue. The denunciation of the leadership, the judgment of God on the people in the form of the events that occurred in their particular setting, and the conviction on the part of these communities that most of Israel had rejected the way of the covenant begged the question, Who then constitutes God's true people?

All the documents referred to above reflect the fact that the groups which produced these documents perceived themselves to be the true heirs of God's promises. These communities believed they were God's remnant. They alone constituted the future of God's covenant people. Despite their exclusivistic claims, these groups would have agreed in several respects. They would have agreed that many in Israel had turned from truly following the laws of God. They would have agreed also about the corrupt and faithless nature of the Jewish leadership. They shared an unmistakable hostility toward those in

[57] G. Stanton, "5 Ezra and Matthean Christianity in the Second Century," *JTS* 28 (1977) 67–83.

power. No doubt the parent group at almost any point during this period would have been struggling for control and acceptance on many fronts. The opposition to the leadership would have taken many forms. This period of factionalism produced several groups that appeared to be hostile toward the leadership.

But because of the exclusive nature of the claims made by these communities, it is doubtful that they would have agreed on the question of the future of God's covenant people. Each group appears to have believed that it alone represented God's true and faithful people. These documents scarcely allow the possibility that anyone outside the sectarian community also might belong to God's true people. It was clearly the conviction of these communities, however, that God had not forgotten the covenant people. On the contrary, the sectarian community was God's true covenant community. Matthean Judaism also shared this point of view and indeed held much in common with these very communities.

The factionalized and fragmented atmosphere of Judaism leading up to and just following the destruction of the temple produced a number of divergent communities, each of which claimed to constitute God's true people. They all seemed to agree on the question, and each seemed to view its own community as the answer to that abiding and essential question. So many different claims and competing groups obviously made for a highly charged, even volatile atmosphere. The tensions and conflicts between the parent group and various sectarian communities continued well into the first and second centuries of this era. The inevitable attempts to bring some sort of order and orthodoxy out of this competitive context in the post-70 period appear to have increased the struggles and tensions within certain communities.

This attempt at consolidation in the post-70 period in Palestine bears directly on Matthew's setting and on our understanding of his Gospel. A pronounced and important dynamic in Matthew's context is the attempt to forge some unity out of this fragmented, sectarian setting. The beginning of the protracted process, which had as its aim the consolidation of Judaism in Palestinian society, is manifest in Matthew's Gospel and accounts for many of the features of that community. The Matthean community witnessed, and was itself obviously involved in, this process of consolidation within Judaism in the post-70 period, represented initially by so-called formative Judaism. It is to these attempts at consolidation and legitimation within Judaism in the post-70 period and the conflicts and competition this process provoked that we now turn.

2

Consolidation and Legitimation in Formative Judaism

THE DESTRUCTION OF JERUSALEM and the temple was not only a political setback for the people of Israel. It meant also the destruction of the cultural and religious center for the people. Indeed, these realms converge and coalesce in the institution and symbol of the temple. The temple constituted both the social and the cosmic structure of Israelite society. A new religio-cultural synthesis was now required if Judaism was to survive. This synthesis and the process of its construction and emergence in the post-70 period are referred to as *formative Judaism*.[1] This term emphasizes the fluid nature of Judaism in this period, as well as the fact that for some time Judaism was in the process of *becoming*, that is, of consolidating, organizing, and obtaining a structure to ensure its existence.

The Pharisees were well positioned for the events of 70 C.E. The program of the Pharisees, the basic pattern of which had been worked out well before 70, placed them in a good position to gain influence following the destruction of Jerusalem and the temple. Among the many things the work of Jacob Neusner has highlighted about the Pharisees, one is clearly the manner in which the beliefs and organizational structure of the Pharisees made them the most viable option for many of the Jews in the post-70 period.[2] The Pharisees already possessed a comprehensive program for social and religious identity which did not require the temple. The Pharisaic activity, which has been summarized as the re-creation of the temple in the home or at table fellowship, while utilizing temple imagery, did not

---

[1] As is widely recognized, Jacob Neusner coined this term. See "The Formation of Rabbinic Judaism: Yavneh from A.D. 70–100," in *ANRW* II.19.2, 3–42; idem, "Judaism after Moore: A Programmatic Statement," *JJS* 31 (1980) 141–56.

[2] See especially J. Neusner, *A Life of Yohanan ben Zakkai: Ca. 1-80 CE* (Leiden: E. J. Brill, 1970) 198ff.

require a temple as such. The Pharisees developed a system centered on the application of the laws of purity around the home and table. Tithing, Sabbath observance, and Torah study were central features of the movement. Temple imagery and issues were employed by the Pharisees; a temple, however, was not required for the execution of their program.[3] The Pharisaic belief in the doctrine of resurrection, retribution, and vindication offered a meaningful form of consolation in the wake of the disaster of 70. The Pharisees had already formulated a hermeneutical program based on their application of Torah, and, according to our sources, they seemed to enjoy the support of the people.[4]

When Jewish groups in the post-70 period were looking for a way of life that could replace what had been destroyed and could be applied to all of Israel, they looked to the Pharisaic system.[5] The Pharisees had already articulated a means of guiding life and relationships through their development of the laws regarding ritual purity. The regulations which the pre-70 Pharisees stressed actually were intended to instruct the members of the sect in their daily life and relations. The purity laws provided a social structure for the sect and guided the life of the sect and its members in that they provided a means of group definition, restricted contact with outsiders, and regulated the internal life of the community.[6] The laws of purity used by the pre-70 Pharisaic sect to regulate their internal relations and

---

[3] See J. Neusner, "Two Pictures of the Pharisees: Philosophical Circle and Eating Club," *ATR* 64 (1982) 525–38; see also "Formation," 41; and *A Life of Yohanan ben Zakkai*, 166ff.

[4] Neusner, *A Life of Yohanan ben Zakkai*, 63ff., 198.

[5] Neusner has defined this "coalition" in "Formation," 3–42, as a combination of scribal and Pharisaic influences. In *Method and Meaning in Ancient Judaism*, vol. 2 (Chico, Calif.: Scholars Press, 1981) 2:94ff., Neusner fills this coalition out further by specifically drawing attention to the element within formative Judaism that would indicate landowners and merchants. "Mishna is the voice of the head of the household, the pillar of society, the model of the community, the arbiter and mediator of goods of this world, fair, just, honorable, above all, reliable." The precise makeup of this coalition is difficult to establish, particularly in this pre-Mishnaic period. However, that this coalition included these landowners and arbiters is supported by the persecution and lack of power felt by certain other factions, for example, the Matthean community. This coalition is discussed by S. Cohen; see n. 12 below.

[6] See J. Neusner, "The Fellowship in the Second Jewish Commonwealth," *HTR* 59 (1960) 125–42; idem, "The Idea of Purity in Ancient Judaism," *JAAR* 43 (1975) 17. The work of the anthropologist Mary Douglas serves as the foundation for much of this; see especially *Purity and Danger* (London: Darton, Longman & Todd, 1966). See also J. Riches, *Jesus and the Transformation of Judaism* (London: Darton, Longman & Todd, 1980) 112–45.

define themselves in relation to the rest of the world were adopted by this post-70 coalition or synthesis. They tried then to apply these laws in a much broader manner to all of Israel.[7] This was a long process. At the close of the first century we can see this process of consolidation in its initial stages.

The process of reorganization and consolidation of Judaism was a protracted one. The period from the events of 70 and the beginning of so-called formative Judaism to the time when there finally existed a dominant form of Judaism was perhaps several hundred years in length. The earliest document which represents the later and far more consolidated rabbinic Judaism, the Mishnah, edited c. 200 C.E., still evidences factions and struggles.[8] It would be anachronistic to assume that there was a direct correlation between the later rabbis and the Pharisees of the late first and early second century. Rabbinism is related to Pharisaism, but it is not simply an extension of it.[9] The Pharisees did certainly play a role in what eventually became rabbinic Judaism. Moreover, the rabbis do claim a strong connection with the Pharisees in the reconstruction of their history.[10] This would seem to confirm the survival and considerable influence of what was once only Pharisaic sectarian beliefs and practices during the later first and subsequent centuries.[11] There is then a strong Pharisaic element in the synthesis of post-70 formative Judaism. However, the institutionalization of Judaism in the post-70 period is probably best described in terms of a coalition. Various elements and streams flow out from the highly sectarian environment of Judaism to begin to form a new synthesis.[12]

[7] See A. Segal, *Rebecca's Children: Judaism and Christianity in the Roman World* (Cambridge, Mass.: Harvard University Press, 1986) 117.

[8] See D. W. Halivni, "The Reception Accorded to Rabbi Judah's Mishnah," in *Jewish and Christian Self-Definition*, ed. E. P. Sanders (Philadelphia: Fortress Press, 1981) 2:204–12. Further, had the Mishnah enjoyed a complete and enthusiastic reception and carried with it implicit authority, what need would there have been for a Tosefta (additions) to the Mishnah? This reveals that the content and the text of the Mishnah were not fixed, but were still rather fluid c. 200.

[9] See A. J. Saldarini, *Pharisees, Scribes and Sadducees in Palestinian Society: A Sociological Approach* (Wilmington, Del.: Michael Glazier, 1988) chap. 10, "Pharisees and Sadducees in Rabbinic Literature."

[10] Ibid. See Mishnah *'Abot* 1:1 and the role the Pharisees play in the rabbinic chain of tradition.

[11] S. Freyne, *Galilee from Alexander the Great to Hadrian* (Wilmington, Del.: Michael Glazier, 1980) 305.

[12] Shaye Cohen envisions a grand coalition within Judaism in this post-70 period: "The Significance of Yavneh: Pharisees, Rabbis and the End of Jewish Sectarianism," *HUCA* 55 (1984) 42.

The established forms of government, along with the bureaucratic apparatus and institutions of Judaism, had been severely disrupted, if not destroyed, with the events of 70. The sociological process of constructing procedures and institutions and the establishing of authorities to guide and protect those institutions had to begin virtually anew. Jacob Neusner has described the coalition which constitutes the driving force behind formative Judaism as a combination of pre-70 Pharisaism and the scribal profession.[13] The Gospel of Matthew, with its rather indiscriminate lumping together of scribes and Pharisees as a formulaic way of referring to the Jewish leadership in that setting, would seem to confirm Neusner's assertion.[14] Regardless of the precise makeup of the coalition that sought to reorganize and reconstitute Jewish life in Palestine after 70, it is clear that this coalition faced the inevitable challenge of defining, establishing, and legitimating their way of life for the people. The task of regulating that life and asserting and maintaining their own authority would inevitably confront them. The aim of this chapter is to chart some of the indications of the attempts at institutionalization and legitimation within formative Judaism. The import of some of these developments for the Matthean community will be spelled out more specifically in the following chapter.

The Symbol of Yavneh:
The Beginning of the End of Sectarianism

The so-called council of Yavneh (Jamnia) has been viewed by many as the most significant event in the institutional development of Judaism in the post-70 period. Yavneh, a Roman center west of Jerusalem near the Mediterreanean coast, is said to have been the location of a Jewish "council" around 90 c.e. Yavneh has been viewed as a watershed in the history of Judaism in that it established the rabbis as the authoritative body and marked the emergence of rabbinic Judaism as the normative form of Judaism. The alleged council of Yavneh has often been seen as the official parting of the ways for early Christianity and Judaism. Within this century W. D. Davies, in his seminal work *The Setting of the Sermon on the Mount*, argued forcefully for the importance of Yavneh and what transpired at the council

---

[13] See Neusner, "Formation," 22.

[14] See R. Hummel, *Die Auseinandersetzung zwischen Kirche und Judentum im Matthäusevangelium*, Beiträge zur evangelischen Theologie 33 (Munich: Kaiser, 1963) 17ff.

in order to understand Jewish Christianity, and Matthew's Gospel in particular.[15]

Two recent treatments of the story of the founding of the academy at Yavneh by Johanan ben Zakkai in the wake of the destruction of Jerusalem, while differing in detail, agree in substance that the account is a rabbinic legend being read back into the events that surrounded the destruction of Jerusalem.[16] There are four accounts: *The Fathers According to Rabbi Nathan*, one from version A (ARNA), and another from version B (ARNB); another version from the Babylonian Talmud (*b. Giṭṭin* 56a and b); and the fourth version from *Lamentations Rabbah* (*Lam. Rab.* 1:5, 31). The legend about Yavneh and the establishment of a school there by Johanan ben Zakkai is derived from these four sources.

A. Saldarini has posited a common *Vorlage* for the four stories. This was a basic, original escape story which developed first into two traditions, then into four. ARNA and ARNB are related to one another, as are *b. Giṭṭin* and *Lamentations Rabbah*.[17] Saldarini makes the important observation that the focus of attention in two of the traditions shifts from Yavneh to Jerusalem.[18] At the end of *Lamentations Rabbah*, Johanan asks that Jerusalem, not Yavneh, be spared. Saldarini and P. Schäfer also acknowledge close affinities between the rabbinic traditions about Johanan, his escape, and subsequent appeal to Vespasian to save Yavneh for a school, and Josephus's own account of his approach to Vespasian and his prediction that Vespasian would become emperor (*J.W.* 3.8.9. §401). In this story, which is similar to the one about Johanan ben Zakkai, Josephus makes an escape, is brought to Vespasian, and predicts that the general will become emperor. We may be seeing a particular genre, involving threats and unusual escapes followed by prophecy. It would certainly seem that both the story by Josephus and the rabbinic traditions about Johanan give the message that the respective heroes enjoy the favor and blessing of the emperor and therefore of the Romans.[19]

---

[15] W. D. Davies, *The Setting of the Sermon on the Mount* (Cambridge: Cambridge University Press, 1964) 256–315.

[16] A. J. Saldarini, "Johanan ben Zakkai's Escape from Jerusalem: Origin and Development of a Rabbinic Story," *JSJ* 6 (1975) 189–204; P. Schäfer, "Die Flucht Johanan b. Zakkais aus Jerusalem und die Gründung des 'Lehrhauses' in Jabne," in *ANRW* II.19.2, 43–101.

[17] Saldarini, "Johanan," 190.

[18] Ibid., 193. Specifically ARNA and *Lamentations Rabbah*.

[19] See the discussion in Schäfer, "Flucht," 80–82. Neusner suggests that the story of Jeremiah, his escape, and the subsequent favor of Nebuchadnezzar may lie behind the Johanan legend (Jeremiah 37–39) (*Life of Yohanan*, 159).

The rabbinic traditions about Johanan ben Zakkai and the founding of Yavneh are highly stylized and, as we said, do not agree on certain significant elements. One such element, important for our purposes, is the question of the centrality of Yavneh itself for these traditions. The traditions have been developed and filled out over time and are completed much later in the rabbinic period.[20] The escape story itself is common to all four, and this is probably the origin and purpose of the original tradition (*Vorlage*). It sought to explain the escape of Johanan from Jerusalem and did so in a manner in accordance with his later reputation as a hero. If Johanan was indeed associated with Yavneh in the post-70 period, then the story also answers any question about how that came to be.

While these traditions are stylized and contain some obvious apologetic aims concerning both the Romans and the figure of Johanan ben Zakkai himself, and while they should not be taken as straightforward historical reflections of what actually transpired, we would still like to inquire about the very presence of the name *Yavneh* in the tradition. A reasonable hypothesis is that some Jews, including Johanan, were quartered in Yavneh during or following the seige of Jerusalem. During this time Johanan started teaching and doubtless acquired a following and, we can see from the traditions about him, a substantial reputation.[21]

With P. Schäfer, we would characterize the traditions about Johanan and the establishment of the academy at Yavneh as a foundation myth (*Grundungslegende*).[22] The specific events in the legend cannot be trusted as being historically factual. The aim of the legend, however, is to address questions that have ramifications far beyond simply the question of what literally happened between Johanan and Vespasian and between Jerusalem and Yavneh. This legend has over time been reworked and utilized by the rabbis to explain their origin as teachers and their role as the recognized carriers of Rome's *imprimatur*. The story not only emphasizes the significance of the figure of Johanan ben Zakkai, but also explains the unusual, if not miraculous,

---

[20] Schäfer, "Flucht," 98. He says, however, that these "späte Quellen können auch historisch wertvolle Nachrichte enthalten."

[21] Schäfer, "Flucht," 98; see also Saldarini, "Johanan," 204. The process and struggle to obtain authority within the early rabbinate are treated by M. Goodman, *State and Society in Roman Galilee A.D. 132–212*, Oxford Centre for Postgraduate Hebrew Studies (Totowa, N.J.: Rowman & Allanhead, 1983).

[22] Schäfer, "Flucht," 98. See also the discussion on myth and its function in N. Perrin and D. Duling, *The New Testament: An Introduction* (2d ed.; San Diego/New York: Harcourt Brace Jovanovich, 1982) 50.

origins of nascent rabbinic Judaism. It serves to legitimate the early rabbis in their role as the teachers and authorities in the post-70 period. This is the symbolic import of Yavneh and the traditions surrounding it. Historically the founding of a school and the establishing of clear lines of authority, including with it the sanction of Rome, took much longer. Only gradually did rabbinic schools become authoritative for Judaism. "The story of the meeting [of Johanan] with Vespasian explains this gradual development by means of one, crucial meeting."[23]

S. Cohen has described the function of Yavneh and whatever occurred there as an attempt to bring some sort of unity out of the fragmented setting of Judaism in the post-70 period. The aim of Yavneh, according to Cohen, was the end of sectarianism and the forging of a unified coalition within Judaism.[24] In a similar spirit, later rabbis enjoined their followers, "Do not make separate factions, but make one faction all together" (*Sifre Deut.* 96).[25] While the events of 70 must have exacerbated the problem of factions and sectarianism within Judaism in this period, the fragmentation cannot be attributed to these events alone. As we have seen, sectarianism was a central feature of Judaism in this period, as the documents and communities discussed above indicate.[26] The protracted process of social reconstruction and order in the post-70 period, expressed in legendary fashion in the traditions concerning Yavneh, had as its aim the creation of a stable and enduring Jewish society. The legendary symbol of Yavneh reflects the *beginning* of the task of social reconstruction in the wake of the destruction of Jerusalem.

To speak of the beginning of the end of sectarianism is not to suggest that an authoritative body suddenly appeared which was able to impose an orthodoxy, however vague, on the various groups and factions within Judaism. It is true that the Yavneh tradition gives this impression, but this is a sociological improbability. The formation and establishment of guidelines and authoritative figures or bodies would be part of a lengthy process of social construction within formative Judaism. The task of social construction is summarized in these words: "Be deliberate in judgement, raise up many disciples,

---

[23] Saldarini, "Johanan," 204.

[24] Cohen, "The Significance of Yavneh," 42.

[25] A marvelous illustration of the unifying aim of the later rabbis is captured in the traditions concerning the figure Akabya ben Mahalaleel. See A. J. Saldarini, "The Adoption of a Dissident: Akabya ben Mahalaleel in Rabbinic Tradition," *JJS* 33 (1982) 547–56.

[26] See the discussion in chap. 1.

and make a fence around the law" (*m. 'Abot* 1:1). This reflects how later rabbis understood their predecessors' task following the destruction of the temple. The post-70 period was the time when the Jewish community in Palestine was beginning the process of social construction and of ordering their life. Naturally this took time and involved struggles. Some communities were uncomfortable with or were caught in the middle of this process. Such is the case with the Matthean community. The process of social reconstruction and the unification of various factions within formative Judaism did not happen in a single event or at one specific point in time. Some of the initial institutions and offices that resulted from this process of consolidation took a generation to appear. Matthew's community is beginning to contend with the emergence of some of these institutions. We will discuss the Matthean responses further in the next chapter.

It is important to recognize the beginning of social order and construction within so-called formative Judaism. The story of Yavneh represents the beginning of that process, and by no means its conclusion. We should reiterate also that when formative Judaism was contending with the Matthean community it was one of several options for the people in the post-70 period. Only over time did formative Judaism have the influence to speak for and represent a sizable portion of the people. In the Matthean community we encounter a nascent formative Judaism, beginning to consolidate and attempting to gain influence and control in its immediate setting. Matthew and his community felt the effects of some of these initial developments.

Even in later rabbinic literature there is no tradition about a *council* at Yavneh. The euphemism for the gathering at Yavneh is not "council," but "on that day."[27] The rabbinic literature speaks about an academy or school, denoting the beginning of instruction by the teachers, but they do not use the terms "synod" or "council." These are terms which scholars have used to designate the gathering at Yavneh, and they are inappropriate. J. P. Lewis is correct in saying that this view of Yavneh by subsequent scholars is anachronistic and imposes an authoritative and official shape to the gathering at Yavneh which is inappropriate.[28] The traditions about Yavneh focus on Johanan, the sanction of Rome upon Johanan and his successors,

---

[27] See *b. Berakot* 28a: "Eduyoth was formulated on that day." See S. Leiman, *The Canonization of Hebrew Scripture: The Talmudic and Midrashic Evidence* (Hamden, Conn.: Archon Books, 1976) 120–24.
[28] J. P. Lewis, "What Do We Mean by Jabneh?" *JBR* 32 (1964) 128.

and the founding of a school where the teachers of formative Judaism could instruct and interpret Torah for the people.

There may well have been a gathering of some sort at Yavneh following the destruction of Jerusalem.[29] This would account for the presence of Yavneh in the tradition at all. For now the most we can say about Yavneh is that it symbolizes the beginning of the end of sectarianism, and the initial efforts at forging a new coalition to perpetuate and reshape Judaism in the wake of the tragedy of 70. At the level of myth the symbolic import of Yavneh is not to be underestimated. The foundation myth about Yavneh, as retold by successive rabbis, confirms them as the carriers of authority and legitimates them as the institution which would provide for learning and atonement henceforth.[30] The coalition that emerged from the events of 70 took on the task of unifying Jewish society and constructing institutions and authorities to maintain and perpetuate that society. We turn now to some of those institutions and the attempts to legitimate and maintain them with the period of formative Judaism.

Institutional Developments
within Formative Judaism

After the first revolt against Rome, Jews in Palestine were confronted with the task of building new institutions and structures for the future. Formative Judaism began to reorganize the social, religious, and communal life of the Jewish community.[31] J. Neusner fixes the date for some of these institutional and political developments within formative Judaism around the time of Gamaliel II (c. 90).[32] However, fixing the precise date of any particular development within formative Judaism is notoriously difficult. A number of problems, not least of which is the late date of the rabbinic literature, obscure any clear picture of the development of this and other features within formative Judaism. What is significant for our purposes is the evidence of the beginning of some of these institutional developments within the Gospels and in the material culture of first-century Palestine. Here

---

[29] As Saldarini suggests ("Johanan").

[30] This is the point of ARNA 3 with regard to Johanan and the temple.

[31] See L. S. Levine, "The Jewish Patriarch (Nasi) in Third Century Palestine," in *ANRW* II.19.2, 649; see also S. Cohen, "Patriarchs and Scholarchs," *PAAJR* 48 (1981) 57–85, for some illuminating suggestions about the origins of these institutions.

[32] J. Neusner, "Formation," 42.

we can see evidence of the beginning of the process of institution building within formative Judaism.

One is able to speak with greater certainty and clarity if the focus becomes the social and institutional developments apparent within formative Judaism, instead of an attempt to fix specific dates and people to these developments. Our focus here will be on some of the institutional developments within formative Judaism and whatever evidence there might be that these developments are making their presence known within their world and setting. One can observe along broader lines the period in which these institutions began to appear and have an impact. One cannot say, however, precisely when and where these developments first appeared. But that is not our concern. We are concerned with the initial institutional developments within formative Judaism and the impact they may have had on the Matthean community and its world.

The Rabbi

The term *rabbi* did exist prior to formative Judaism's application of it to its leaders and authorities. The word itself is found in a fifth-century B.C.E. Aramaic fragment from Elephantine. It appears also in the Hebrew Scriptures (2 Kgs. 18:17, 19, 27; Isa. 36:2, 4, 11-13).[33] But the rabbi first emerges as the central, authoritative figure in rabbinic Judaism. The rabbis settled disputes and delineated the rules or way of living and were the interpreters of the law. When did this office and function appear within post-70 Judaism? When did formative Judaism organize itself to the extent that authoritative teachers of the law and a subsequent *office* of the same began to emerge?

We have no evidence that the term "rabbi" refers to an official office and function by the end of the first century. E. Lohse claims that an inscription from a Jerusalem ossuary bearing the common Greek word for teacher, *didaskalos*, is evidence of the term "rabbi" being a technical term within Judaism in the first century.[34] However, the archaeological evidence Lohse cites is later than the first century.[35] The inscription from the Jerusalem ossuary which Lohse mentions does not constitute any evidence about the title Rabbi in the first century. The inscription contains the word "teacher" (*didaskalos*), not

[33] Ibid., 19.
[34] E. Lohse, "Ra'ab," *TDNT*, 6:961–65.
[35] See N. Avigad, "The Excavations at Beth She'arim," *IEJ* 4 (1954) 98, 104; idem, "The Excavations at Beth She'arim," *IEJ* 7 (1957) 249.

"rabbi." Lohse has mistakenly assumed that the two terms are synonymous. That rabbis were to function as teachers is true. However,
the presence of the term "teacher" on the ossuary does not indicate
by any means the application of the notion or office of rabbi in the
first century. There is absolutely no evidence that the term *didaskalos*
in the inscription represents a translation of "rabbi."[36]

Clear evidence for the use of "rabbi" as a technical term referring
to the office and function of teacher and authority within formative
and emergent rabbinic Judaism comes from the necropolis at Beth-
She'arim in Galilee, where there are numerous sarcophagi bearing
the *title* "rabbi." The remains from Beth-She'arim "constitute the
single most important resource for understanding the culture of the
rabbinic world."[37] According to N. Avigad, catacombs 13, 14, and 20
at Beth-She'arim all contain inscriptions referring to various rabbis,
including one that reads, "This is the tomb of Rabbi Gamaliel."[38] The
earliest tombs and inscriptions at Beth-She'arim, however, come
from the end of the second century C.E. We thus possess clear archaeological evidence of the use of "rabbi" as a technical and authoritative
title for Jewish leaders in Galilee by the end of the second century.[39]

Most important for our purposes is the use of the term "rabbi" as
an unofficial but honorific title in the Gospels. The term is used
essentially to connote honor or respect. H. Shanks has tried to show
that the use of the term "rabbi" in the Gospels is not anachronistic,
that is, inserted later once the term carried its *official* meaning.[40]
According to Shanks it represents a stage in the development of the
word which predates its use as a *terminus technicus* for an authoritative leader in emergent rabbinic Judaism.[41]

The Gospels do provide some important information concerning
the evolution of the term "rabbi" as it developed into an authoritative
and essential institution within formative and later rabbinic Judaism.

[36] H. Shanks, "Is the Title 'Rabbi' Anachronistic in the Gospels?" *JQR* 53 (1963)
344.

[37] See E. M. Meyers and A. T. Kraabel, "Archaeology, Iconography, and
Nonliterary Written Remains," in *Early Judaism and Its Modern Interpreters*, ed.
R. A. Kraft and G. W. E. Nickelsburg (Philadelphia: Fortress Press, 1986) 180–81;
see also Avigad, "Excavations at Beth She'arim," 239–55.

[38] Avigad, "Excavations at Beth She'arim," 104.

[39] The title could also have been in use elsewhere. After all, Beth-She'arim was
a desired burial spot for faithful Jews from the Diaspora.

[40] H. Shanks, "The Origins of the Title 'Rabbi,'" *JQR* 59 (1968) 152–57.

[41] S. Zeitlin, Shanks's detractor on this point, did not seem to understand the
distinction Shanks was making; see Zeitlin, "The Title Rabbi in the Gospels Is
Anachronistic," *JQR* 59 (1968) 158–59.

Mark and John (Luke does not use the term) are obviously familiar with the term and employ it frequently as an address of honor and respect. In Mark, Peter calls Jesus "rabbi" during the transfiguration scene (9:5), depicting Jesus as equal in stature and importance to Moses and Elijah. Peter refers to Jesus again as "rabbi" in Mark 11:21 when questioning Jesus about the withered fig tree. Judas calls Jesus "rabbi" in 14:45 just prior to the betrayal.

John employs the term more often and with greater freedom. Two of John the Baptist's disciples follow Jesus and call him "rabbi" (John 1:38), which John translates for his audience "teacher" (*didaskalos*). Nicodemus, however, calls Jesus "rabbi" and "teacher" in the same verse (3:2). Here "rabbi" is distinguished from "teacher" as a term of honor and not merely one of a function, such as teaching. Nathanael calls Jesus "rabbi" in 1:49, as do other disciples in 4:31; 9:2; and 11:8. In 3:26 John the Baptist is addressed as "rabbi" by his disciples. Mary addresses Jesus with the related honorific term *rabboni* in John 20:16, as does the blind man in Mark 10:51.

This evidence from the Gospels concerning the use and meaning of the term "rabbi," together with the archaeological evidence from Beth-She'arim, provides us with two chronological poles within which we can place the development and trajectory of an important institutional development within formative Judaism, namely, the title and office of rabbi. The Gospels reveal a general, honorific, and nontechnical understanding of the term. "Rabbi" is a form of address revealing respect and honor. It does not necessarily indicate a function, and it certainly does not indicate an official, established office and role. On the other hand, the much later evidence from Beth-She'arim does reflect an understanding of the term that is technical in nature. These inscriptions refer to authoritative and revered teachers from emergent rabbinic Judaism. Thus, the hundred years between the writing of the Gospel of John and the dating of the Beth-She'arim catacombs at the close of the second century is the period in which the term "rabbi" developed from a general term of honor to a specific, technical term referring to the central authorities of the early rabbinic period.

The Gospel of Matthew signals some interesting developments concerning the term "rabbi." Matthew reflects a degree of resistance to this title and office. Matthew is clearly not opposed to the central *function* of the rabbi, namely, teaching. The disciples are expected to be teachers (5:19; 28:20). There are scribes who surely perform a closely related function in the community (13:51; 23:34), and the elaborate instruction and *halakah* concerning the law is reminiscent of the role of teacher/rabbi (9:12ff.; 12:1ff.; 15:1ff.). So the function of teaching and the importance of instruction are in no way diminished in Matthew; indeed, this activity is stressed in the Gospel. Matthew, however, does show signs of dislike for the *title* "rabbi."

Only Judas addresses Jesus as "rabbi" in Matthew's Gospel (26:25, 49). Matthew has altered Peter's "rabbi" in Mark 9:5 to Lord (*kyrios*) in Matt. 17:4. In chap. 23 Jesus says that the scribes and Pharisees love "respectful greetings in the market places" (*agoras*) and being called "rabbi" by others. Matthew charges his community not to be called "rabbi" (23:8), for one is your teacher (*didaskalos*). They should not be called father, and they should not be called leaders (*kathēgētēs*), for one is their leader, that is, Christ (23:10). Matthew 23 cannot be read solely as a polemic against the title "rabbi," though it does include that. The passage 23:7ff. represents Matthew's concern with a hierarchy in the community. He is aiming at a "brotherhood" based on mutuality and therefore encourages his community to eschew such titles and prerogatives. However, as E. Schweizer has pointed out, the fact that Matthew has included this passage presupposes the presence within the community of these functions and those members who assume these titles.[42] Matthew has related the desire to be called "rabbi" with the Jewish leadership in his setting, whom he refers to in shorthand manner as the scribes and Pharisees. They are the ones who like to be greeted as "rabbi." For Matthew that is reason enough to avoid it.

The title "rabbi" for the scribes and Pharisees in chap. 23 can be related to other institutional developments within formative Judaism in Matthew's setting. Matthew applies the symbolic authority of "sitting in the chair of Moses" to the scribes and Pharisees (23:2), and therefore people should do what they say.[43] The phrase in 23:13 that the scribes and Pharisees are able to lock up the kingdom of heaven from humans portrays an authoritative role for them within that setting. The woes about the oaths of the scribes and Pharisees (23:16-22) and about tithing (23:23-26) suggest also more official and

---

[42] E. Schweizer, "Matthew's Church," in *The Interpretation of Matthew*, ed. G. Stanton (Philadelphia: Fortress Press, 1983) 139; W. Trilling, *Das Wahre Israel: Studien zur Theologie des Matthäus-Evangeliums* (Munich: Kösel, 1964) 36ff.

[43] "The seat of Moses" is a symbolic expression of authority. The actual seat as part of the synagogue architecture develops later; see E. Sukenik, *Ancient Synagogues in Palestine and Greece*, The Schweich Lectures (Oxford: Oxford University Press, 1934); also I. Renov, "The Seat of Moses," in *The Synagogue: Studies in Origins, Archeology and Architecture*, ed. J. Gutmann (New York: KTAV, 1975) 233–38.

institutional roles for the scribes and Pharisees. Matthew has employed the proselytizing activity of the scribes and Pharisees in a technical sense referring to the activity of obtaining converts (23:15). This can be distinguished from Luke's use of the term, which, not surprisingly, parallels the understanding of *prosēlytos* as it is found in the Septuagint. A *prosēlytos* is a foreigner, sympathetic to or allied with the Jewish community, like the *gēr* of Israelite history.[44] Here Matthew uses *prosēlytos* in the sense of a convert. This is more in keeping with the use of the term in later rabbinic literature, and distanced from that of the Septuagint.[45]

Matthew's dislike for the term "rabbi" reveals a development not seen in the other Gospels. Matthew equates "rabbi" with the Jewish leadership in his setting. For this reason he has tended to avoid the term. He has encouraged disdain for the title by connecting it with Judas. The title Rabbi can be correlated with some of the other institutional developments within the Jewish leadership evident in chap. 23 of Matthew. The term "rabbi" was beginning to be associated with the leaders of the newly developing movement, formative Judaism. These leaders were acquiring functions, authority, and a title. They were the teachers and arbitrators within Matthew's setting. This development concerning the role and title of Rabbi in Matthew is the beginning of an essential institution which comes to fuller expression in later rabbinic Judaism.

The Blessing upon Dissenters

We are concerned here with the institutional development within formative Judaism of the practice of banning or excluding from the community those who do not conform to the life and practice of the movement. Within the fluid period which gave birth to formative Judaism, a number of factions competed for influence and control. It is accurate to claim, however, that a decisive stage in the process of communal self-definition is reached when a community sets criteria for exclusion.[46] The ability to exclude dissenters indicates that those

---

[44] See J. A. Overman, "The God-Fearers: Some Neglected Features," *JSNT* 32 (1988) 17–26; K. Lake, "Proselytes and God-Fearers," in *The Beginnings of Christianity*, vol. 1, ed. K. Lake and F. J. Foakes Jackson (reprint, Grand Rapids: Baker, 1979) 83.

[45] See H. C. Kee, *The Origins of Christianity: Sources and Documents* (London: SPCK, 1980) 155ff., for some of the salient rabbinic passages.

[46] R. Kimelman, "*Birkat Ha-Minim* and the Lack of Evidence for an Anti-Christian Jewish Prayer in Antiquity," in *Jewish and Christian Self-Definition*, 2:226–44.

doing the excluding possess a degree of authority within the setting where the ban is applied. The group which practices the excluding must also have a sufficiently well-defined identity to be able to agree on what constitutes a violation grave enough to warrant exclusion. A number of the sectarian communities within Judaism had clearly reached this decisive stage of self-definition and organization. For means of internal protection and for clarification of what the group stands for, some procedure for expulsion from the group is often adopted. The community in one way or another has reached a consensus, usually subconsciously (it is "taken for granted"), concerning what the community is about and what it stands for when banning is practiced. Formative Judaism developed the institutional practice of banning, which both protected and defined the group. Where this development of banning is concerned formative Judaism was not alone.

The Qumran community, for example, possessed its own form of expulsion, which was aimed at purifying the offender, if the ban was for a limited period of time. If one lied about property at Qumran, that person was excluded from the "pure meal" of the community for a year (1QS 6).[47] Falling asleep during the community's service, leaving during the service, being seen naked, and slandering one's companion all resulted in bans of varying degree and severity (1QS 7). Sins against individuals and lapses in personal purity could be atoned for through limited bans and exclusion from the communal gatherings. However, it is interesting to note that according to 1QS 7, "whoever has slandered the Congregation shall be expelled from among them and shall return no more."[48] To slander the community or its authorities resulted in permanent expulsion from the sect. According to Josephus, such expulsions were extremely harsh because those Essenes who were cast out from the community "often died after a miserable manner" (J.W. 2.8.8 §143).[49]

In 1 Corinthians 5 the apostle Paul advocates the expulsion of a member guilty of *porneia*, both for the individual's salvation and for the purification of the community.[50] Paul seems to presuppose the

[47] G. Vermes, *The Dead Sea Scrolls in English* (New York: Penguin, 1975) 82.

[48] Ibid., 84.

[49] See G. Forkman, *The Limits of Religious Community: Expulsion from the Religious Community within the Qumran Sect, within Rabbinic Judaism, and within Primitive Christianity* (Lund: Gleerup, 1972) 39–78. See also T. Beall, *Josephus' Description of the Essenes Illustrated by the Dead Sea Scrolls*, SNTSMS 58 (Cambridge: Cambridge University Press, 1988) 19.

[50] Forkman, *Limits of Religious Community*, 150–51.

presence of a procedure at Corinth which served the purpose of expelling those who threatened the community. Paul expresses consternation in 5:2 with the Corinthians because they have not already put him out of their midst. They should have "grieved" over this situation and removed the sinner, rather than allowing the matter to persist.[51] The Gospel of Matthew also evidences within the community a procedure for expulsion (18:15ff.). As we will see below, Matthew comes to this position reluctantly.[52] Nevertheless, we see here also the development of procedures and criteria for expulsion and community discipline.

So it is clear that there existed a number of communities in the first century of this era which possessed procedures designed to expel those who would threaten the community, or who in some way did not appropriately conform to the values and life of the community. As we have stressed, after the destruction of Jerusalem and the loss of institutional leaders and thereby the processes by which the collective life was regulated, new procedures needed to be developed. This process took time. Such a procedure evolved within emergent rabbinic Judaism and was called the *Birkat ha-Minim*, literally, "the blessing on the heretics." This represents the twelfth of eighteen benedictions pronounced in the synagogue, the so-called *Amidah*, and many have maintained that it originated at the council of Yavneh. The benediction read:

> For apostates let there be no hope.
> The dominion of arrogance do thou speedily
>   root out in our days.
> And let the *Nazareans* and the *Minim*
>   perish in a moment.
> Let them be blotted out of the book of the living.
> And let them not be written with the righteous.[53]

Some have maintained that the *Birkat ha-Minim* is a sanction directed specifically against Christians and that *Minim* is really a catchword for "Christians."[54] However, several recent treatments of

---

[51] Ibid., 139. Forkman suggests that being "puffed up" refers to the Corinthians' having "winked" at the offender. That is to say, they turned the other way.

[52] See chap. 4, where this measure within the Matthean community is discussed further.

[53] Forkman, *Limits of Religious Community*, 91.

[54] See G. D. Kilpatrick, *The Origins of the Gospel according to St. Matthew* (Oxford: Oxford University Press, 1946) 109ff.; W. H. C. Frend, *The Early Church* (Philadelphia: Fortress Press, 1982) 35ff.

this subject have drawn attention to the lack of evidence for any specifically anti-Christian prayer in early rabbinic Judaism.[55] Rather, the "Minim prayer was a defensive measure against Jewish dissenters," who denied any number of elements which were, or were becoming, essential to developing formative Judaism.[56] This might include the denial of the resurrection, the rejection of Torah, pronouncing the Tetragrammaton, or healers who use the Scriptures.[57] As F. Manns has observed, in later rabbinic literature the *Min* is often mentioned in the context of debates concerning Scripture, which suggests tensions over the evolving, *orthodox* interpretations that the controlling body was beginning to enforce.[58]

As we have mentioned, there were numerous Jewish groups and factions in this period of formative Judaism. The effort to consolidate and forge a coalition in the period after 70 would have to contend with many factions and competing points of view. It is important not to overestimate anachronistically the impact of Christianity upon Judaism in the first two centuries of this era.[59] The *Birkat ha-Minim* was directed basically against schismatics or dissenters. That is to say, the benediction in question was aimed at any person or group that would disrupt the coalition that formative Judaism was struggling to forge in this period. There were many groups that would have fit into this category. Most likely, the followers of Jesus were one of these groups. This benediction is indeed an important stage in the consolidation and definition of formative Judaism. There is no conclusive evidence, however, that the early Christians were the sole focus and aim of the banning practice within formative Judaism. Early Christians would have most likely felt the impact of this development along with many other groups in their setting, but the blessing was not directed against them as such.

Discussions concerning the "blessing upon dissenters" have regularly suffered from some of the same uncritical scholarly assumptions as have those about Yavneh. The traditions about Yavneh, as we observed, were developed over time. In a rather legendary fashion

[55] Kimelman, "*Birkat Ha-Minim*"; S. Katz, "Issues in the Separation of Judaism and Christianity after 70 C.E.: A Reconsideration," *JBL* 103 (1984) 49–75; A. Finkel, "Yavneh's Liturgy and Early Christianity," *JES* 18 (1981) 231–50.

[56] Finkel, "Yavneh's Liturgy," 240.

[57] Ibid., 240–41.

[58] See F. Manns, "Un centre judéo-chrétien important: Sépphoris," in *Essais sur le Judéo-Christianisme* (Jerusalem: Franciscan Printing Press, 1977) 165–90. See, for example, *m. Berakot* 10a; *Gen. Rab.* 82:10.

[59] Kimelman, "*Birkat Ha-Minim*," 233.

those traditions describe the establishment of the first rabbinic academy, depict the unusual authority of Johanan, and reflect the favor of Rome which the rabbis enjoyed. We stressed that these traditions had been fashioned over a considerable period by subsequent rabbis to explain their origins, position, and authority. Yavneh is a foundation myth which depicts the gradual and protracted process of the development of the rabbinic school and functionaries in one crucial meeting.

Similarly, the process of communal self-definition and the criteria for expulsion from the community developed over a considerable period of time. It did not happen in a single event within the history of formative Judaism. The sociological process of defining the community and adapting a process by which dissenters could be expelled would naturally be a protracted one. It would be quite unlikely that the group seeking to do the expelling would enjoy the same authority everywhere, uniformly. This was doubtless a long process that would have varied from place to place and would have been dependent on local situations.[60]

K. Kohler and, more recently, P. Schäfer have described the evolution and development involved in the composition of the Eighteen Benedictions.[61] Schäfer has drawn attention to the changes in the wording of petitions 11 and 12, which are more properly referred to as maledictions. The wording and the subjects of the maledictions in the tradition have fluctuated.[62] Kohler has suggested that the first three and last three benedictions belong to an earlier version of seven benedictions.[63] Benedictions 10 and 11 refer to the nationalistic hopes for Israel in the future. They were originally eschatological in nature. In the same fashion, Kohler asserts that the doom of the evildoers (*Minim*) also referred originally to the messianic future. In time this twelfth benediction, like the eleventh benediction concerning the national hopes of Israel, underwent changes and was transformed into its present state.[64] While we are unable here to engage in a complete study of the complex history of the tradition of the *Amidah*, it will suffice simply to observe that the benedictions themselves are

[60] Ibid., 244.

[61] K. Kohler, "The Origin and Composition of the Eighteen Benedictions," in *Contributions to the Scientific Study of the Jewish Liturgy*, ed. J. Petuchowski (New York: KTAV, 1970) 52–90; P. Schäfer, "Die sogenannte Synode von Jabne," in *Studien zur Geschichte und Theologie des rabbinischen Judentums* (Leiden: E. J. Brill, 1978) 45–64.

[62] Schäfer, "Die sogenannte Synode."

[63] Kohler, "Origin and Composition," 56.

[64] Ibid., 66.

products of a long process of formation and development. They did not suddenly appear *in toto* at a specific point in time. The act of banning in nascent rabbinic Judaism may have had its roots in the sectarianism of the period prior to 70 and Jerusalem's destruction. C. H. Hunzinger has postulated a pre-70 Pharisaic background for the rabbinic practice of banning.[65] Hunzinger's argument may be correct; however, his discussion is for the most part flawed by his lavish use of later rabbinic texts. As we noted above, many Jewish groups possessed procedures of limited and total exclusion from the sect. Each could have played part in the background and evolution of this practice in later rabbinic Judaism. It would be correct, however, to assert that the practice of exclusion and communal punishment we see come to full flower in the liturgical development of the *Birkat ha-Minim* in emergent rabbinic Judaism possessed a background and historical setting out of which it developed. Here Hunzinger is certainly correct. Over a period of time these procedures would have been adapted and transformed to fit the new situation and support the new and developing authoritative body. Again, this would have been a gradual process and would not have happened at once.

This institutional development of a procedure for exclusion within formative Judaism would not have been felt uniformly across Palestine or even Galilee, and it is unlikely that it would have been applied in precisely the same manner in each locale or situation. It would be uncritical and anachronistic to impose a well-fashioned and formal liturgical development like the twelfth benediction and the banning procedure it contains upon the fluid period which is our concern, namely, that of formative Judaism. The institutional development of exclusion and the self-definition involved in knowing who to exclude would take time. This did not take place at one meeting, or through the offices of one person.

What one encounters in the early period of formative Judaism (c. 70–100) is the *beginning* of the process of consolidation and, where this specific practice of banning or exclusion is concerned, the imposition of authority and discipline by the new post-70 synthesis. The

[65] C. H. Hunzinger, "Spuren pharisäischer Institutionen in der frühen rabbinischen Überlieferung," in *Tradition und Glauben: Das frühe Christentum in seiner Umwelt*, Festschrift K. G. Kuhn (Göttingen: Vandenhoeck & Ruprecht, 1971) 147–56; see also I. Elbogen, *Der jüdische Gottesdienst in seiner geschichtlichen Entwicklung* (Hildesheim: G. Olms, 1962) 33–35, 50ff., who tries also to trace the development of the benedictions in later material.

Gospel of John reflects an initial stage of banning within formative Judaism. J. L. Martyn has drawn attention to this in his influential book *History and Theology in the Fourth Gospel*.[66] In particular, Martyn has discussed the process of being excluded from the synagogue in John (*aposynagōgos*, 9:22; 12:42; 16:2). Martyn has tried to relate this development within the Fourth Gospel to the *Birkat ha-Minim* based on the apparent reformulation of the synagogue benedictions by Gamaliel (c. 80–115), around the time that John was written.[67] The evidence and process he has described in John's community are important for our understanding of this institutional development within formative Judaism. We do not agree that the process of being put out of the synagogue in the Fourth Gospel possessed a formal correspondence with the *Birkat ha-Minim*. With Wayne Meeks we believe that *Berakot* 28a, where the story of the reformulation of the benediction is told, depicts as a punctiliar event in Gamaliel's life something that was surely a linear development occurring over an extended period of time, *culminating* in the formulation of the *Birkat ha-Minim*.[68]

Our aim is not simply to identify the exclusion from the synagogue associated with the twelfth benediction but to draw attention to the protracted sociological process in which formative Judaism was engaged c. 80–90 C.E. Attempts to connect the phenomenon of "being put out of the synagogue" in John (9:22) directly with the *Birkat ha-Minim* can lose sight of the broader and more significant social and institutional development within formative Judaism which this episode betrays. Morton Smith's judicious comment is helpful here: "The *Birkat ha-Minim* is useable as an indication of *the sort of thing John had in mind*, but no more, and certainly not as a fixed point for dating."[69] Martyn has anachronistically imposed a shape and uniformity to the practice of banning which did not emerge until much later in the development of rabbinic Judaism. The Johannine community reflects an initial stage of banning that comes to fuller expression much later in the formulation of the twelfth benediction. In John we see a reflection of the process by which the Jewish community and leadership in that particular setting have set the criteria for exclusion.

---

[66] J. L. Martyn, *History and Theology in the Fourth Gospel* (2d ed.; Nashville: Abingdon, 1979) especially 37–63.

[67] Ibid., 50ff.

[68] Ibid., 54–55.

[69] Cited by Martyn, *History and Theology*, 57 n. 75.

Earlier Gospel traditions mention persecutions and floggings (Matt. 10:17), or being cast out (*ekballō*) from the synagogue (Luke 6:22ff.). The presence of *ekballō* in the early Gospel tradition very likely reflects some of the opposition which the Jesus movement met with initially and the heated debates and struggles in which they were involved. Some early followers of Jesus probably were thrown out of their gathering places. However, the story in John 9 has several aspects that set it apart from these earlier Gospel accounts and indicate its setting in later formative Judaism around the end of the first century. First, John 9:22 reveals that an issue concerning one's confession about Jesus may now constitute exclusion from the synagogue. The Johannine community believes that confession in Jesus as *Christos* is grounds for exclusion from the synagogue, as the parenthetical narrative comment makes clear. This surely reveals a development removed in time from the early struggles in and around the gathering place depicted in other Gospel accounts, both for the Jesus movement and formative Judaism.[70] Further, the evangelist betrays his own anachronism in referring to the "disciples of Moses" in v. 28. The opponents of Jesus during his ministry would not have understood themselves in this manner, nor would they have juxtaposed themselves in this way to "the disciples of Christ," as John has done.[71] The debate between the two rival parties, each of which has disciples and its own authorities and leaders, is portrayed in this passage. Here we see the party with the upper hand, the "we" of v. 28 who are disciples of Moses, instituting the process by which schismatics may be removed from the gathering place. All this suggests a setting in time much closer to the end of the first century—not a story taken from the ministry of Jesus himself.

Of course, one is unable to determine precisely what transpired historically in and around the Johannine community. The people behind John's Gospel are deeply involved in a conflict with the Jewish community in that setting. Polemic colors much of what we read in John, including the account of exclusion from the synagogue.[72] Turning from the specific issue of the *Birkat ha-Minim*, we

---

[70] R. E. Brown, *The Gospel According to John*, Anchor Bible 29, 29A (2 vols.; Garden City, N.Y.: Doubleday, 1966, 1970) 1:380.

[71] Ibid., 1:379–80.

[72] See R. E. Brown, *The Community of the Beloved Disciple* (New York: Paulist, 1979) 66ff., for the "Jews" in the Fourth Gospel. See especially W. Meeks, "Breaking Away: Three New Testament Pictures of Christianity's Separation from the Jewish Communities," in *"To See Ourselves as Others See Us": Christians, Jews and*

are able to see the broader and more significant sociological development which this story represents.[73] Like Matthew, the Johannine community has its own gathering place but is still in close contact with the Jewish community. Members of the Johannine community still go to synagogue (one must *go there* to get thrown out), though the two communities have apparently parted company. Though Matthew's community has separated from the synagogue, the members nevertheless seem to keep close ties with it (see Matt. 23:1ff.). In both settings the Jewish leadership has gained the upper hand. They possess more influence and authority. Matthew and John have at least this much in common. What emerges clearly in John is the significant institutional development, due to the increased authority of the Jewish leadership, of a procedure to remove and exclude from their community gatherings those who dissent, through action or belief.

In John 9 we can see a concrete example of how this institutional development "might have worked" in the day-to-day life of one early Christian community. In dismissing the formal correspondence between this and the *Birkat ha-Minim* we avoid having to impose anachronistically a character and unity on this procedure, which is a product of later rabbinic literature and its authorities.[74] The *Birkat ha-Minim* is a formal expression from a later period in rabbinic history which depicts in far too succinct a manner the significant institutional development within earlier formative Judaism of the process of excluding dissenters and schismatics from the community. The Johannine community in particular, and very likely others in and around that setting, is beginning to feel the pressure of that new development within formative Judaism.

The Gathering Place

When we speak about the beginnings of institutional developments within formative Judaism, we would expect to find evidence that the new movement was developing liturgies, authoritative functionaries, and communal procedures for the definition and defense of the community. One might also expect to see evidence of places where the new movement in its varied shapes and forms could meet and carry

---

"Others" in Late Antiquity, ed. J. Neusner and E. Frerichs (Atlanta: Scholars Press, 1985) 102–3.

[73] Meeks, "Breaking Away," 102.

[74] Ibid., 120.

on its business and rituals, however modest. Indeed, this is the case with late first-century formative Judaism. We have evidence from material culture of modest, late first- and early second-century gathering places for formative Judaism. These places are understandably simple and thereby reflect the simple and small beginnings of formative Judaism prior to its finally establishing itself as the dominant form of Judaism in the third and subsequent centuries.

The search for first- and second-century gathering places has suffered from anachronistic attempts to discover synagogues as they are known to us in the later fourth through sixth centuries, with their ornate and distinctive architecture and art, in the soil of the late first and early second centuries.[75] This is particularly true concerning our understanding and translation of the term for the meeting place of formative Judaism, *synagōgē*. Etymologically this term means simply "gather together." We should not envision a full-blown, sophisticated institution when we encounter this word in first- and second-century documents. The simple roots of this term in fact reflect the nature of these gatherings and the gathering places themselves in the period of formative Judaism. The highly stylized and developed synagogue institutions, such as those found in places like Tiberias and Capernaum, came much later, and at a time when rabbinic Judaism was well articulated and constituted the undisputed orthodoxy of Judaism.[76]

The actual beginnings of these institutions were far more modest and only later developed into more complete houses of worship. However, the beginning of this development in the late first and early second centuries is significant for our purposes, because it indicates an initial stage of organization and institutionalization within formative Judaism. This is a development which makes its presence felt within the Matthean community.

At present, there are first-century buildings interpreted as synagogues (i.e., gathering places) at Herodium, Masada, Gamala in Gaulanitis, Magdala, and perhaps Chorazin.[77] (E. M. Meyers and

[75] See H. C. Kee, "The Transformation of the Synagogue after 70 C.E.: Its Import for Early Christianity," *NTS* 36 (1990) 1–24.

[76] For a review of the Capernaum material, see the review article by J. Strange, *BASOR* 226 (1977) 65–73. For Tiberias, see D. Edwards's article in *Harper's Bible Dictionary*, ed. P. Achtemeier (San Francisco: Harper & Row, 1985) 1069–70; and *The Princeton Encyclopedia of Classical Sites*, ed. E. Stillwell (Princeton: Princeton University Press, 1976) 920.

[77] J. Strange, "Archeology and the Religion of Judaism in Palestine," in *ANRW* II.19.1, 656.

A. T. Kraabel, however, have drawn attention to some of the debate concerning the Magdala synagogue.[78]) These buildings are unusually plain, reflecting the nature of these communities and the approximate stage of their social development. At this stage formative Judaism relied on simple, purely functional buildings for their communal gatherings. There is no raised platform (*bema*) for Torah reading, no trace of a shrine for the Torah, and no artwork or cultic representations.[79] There is no evidence of sophisticated procedures and rituals or of a highly developed liturgy or worship.

The small building at Magdala (8.16 m. x 7.25 m.) stood at the intersection of two well-paved Roman roads. It contained five stone benches, two aisles which ran the length of the building, and an aisle at the back. The building at Gamala in the modern-day Golan Heights is like the one in Magdala. It is a simple assembly hall, containing four rows with benches and one single entrance.[80] Here we have evidence of a Jewish community alongside of, but separate from, important Christian and pagan sites. This simple first-century structure provides an insight into the nature of the early Jewish gatherings after the temple's destruction but prior to Judaism's establishing of more formal worship when it enjoyed greater self-definition and authority.

L. M. White has made discoveries along similar lines in the Diaspora during this period. His study of the synagogue at Delos reveals that this gathering place was originally a house. As the movement which met in it developed and grew, the walls were knocked out, additions were made, and the house gradually developed into a more complete and formal place of worship.[81] The original movement found a simple and informal gathering place to carry out the communal functions. In time the movement became larger, more sophisticated, and more expressive in its worship and procedures. At this early stage, however, only the beginning of this long process is evident. Delos represents a form of communal identity and nascent institutionalization parallel to several locations in Palestine.[82]

Mention should be made also of the first-century site of Capernaum (*Tell Hum*), located on the northern coast of the Sea of Galilee.

[78] Meyers and Kraabel, "Archaeology, Iconography," 179.

[79] See Strange, "Archeology," 656.

[80] Meyers and Kraabel, "Archaeology, Iconography," 179.

[81] L. M. White, "The Delos Synagogue Revisited: Recent Fieldwork in the Graeco-Roman Diaspora," *HTR* 80 (1987) 133–60; see also idem, "Scaling the Strongman's 'Court' (Luke 11.21)," *Forum* 3 (1987) 3–28.

[82] White, "Delos Synagogue," 155.

While many aspects of this site excavated by the Franciscans remain clouded in uncertainty, several comments can be made which are supportive for our interest in the development of the gathering place as an institution in this period of formative Judaism. The synagogue at Capernaum is probably from the fourth or fifth century, but the date has been a bone of contention.[83] More important for our purposes is the discovery of an earlier first-century structure directly underneath the later synagogue.[84] The building, which utilizes the common black basalt that was used for the first-century residences at Capernaum, appears also to be a common building for general use. Its purpose and identity are not precisely known. It may have been part of previous private residences.[85] However, since more elaborate synagogues were often built on earlier simpler synagogues, this building may have been a gathering place for the community in Capernaum in the first century.[86] It reflects the same basic simplicity as those found at Magdala and Delos, providing above all a functional building for public gatherings and communal activities.

There is a direct analogy between the evolution of the synagogue or gathering place and the church, or *ekklēsia*. The octagonal church across the street from the synagogue in Capernaum is a Byzantine church from the fourth or fifth century. Beneath the church is a house dating from the first century B.C.E. Between the lowest floors of the largest room of the house underneath the church (7.0 m. x 6.5 m., which would have been large for an ancient house), early Roman pottery and coins were sealed. This indicates that the house was founded in the first century B.C.E. Sometime in the late first or early second century, in a manner strikingly similar to the house at Delos, this room received extensive remodeling.[87] The room was plastered three times near the end of the first century, "which may suggest conversion to a public building rather than a remodeling of a house."[88] There is an absence of plain pottery, which points more to public than to private, domestic use. Since the graffiti from visitors on the plastered walls of room 1 of the house date from the second and third

---

[83] See Meyers and Kraabel, "Archaeology, Iconography," 179.

[84] Ibid.; see also E. M. Meyers and J. Strange, *Archaeology, the Rabbis, and Early Christianity* (Nashville: Abingdon, 1981) 58–60.

[85] Meyers and Strange, *Archaeology*, 58–60.

[86] Ibid., 60.

[87] A helpful chart and explanation of the house can be found in I. Mancini, *Archeological Discoveries Relative to the Judeo-Christians* (Jerusalem: Franciscan Printing Press, 1970) 102.

[88] Meyers and Strange, *Archaeology*, 129.

centuries it is reasonable to conclude that the Christian community had converted this room into a house-church (*domus-ecclesia*) which in time (by the second and third centuries) became known to Christian pilgrims.[89]

If this reconstruction of the Christian house at Capernaum is plausible, then we see here an institutional development within early Christianity that parallels—and at Capernaum may even be across the street from—a similar development within formative Judaism. What exactly to call these two gatherings and how they would have understood themselves are good questions. The lines between "Jew," "Christian," and "Jewish Christian" may not have been as distinct then as we often portray them now. J. Strange rightly cautioned the excavators at Capernaum and all the students of this site that these lines are blurred.[90] Capernaum itself was culturally diverse, and there existed greater fluidity between these groups than we often imagine.[91]

By examining the archaeological remains of Capernaum one can observe indications of the establishment of a gathering place where formative Judaism could begin to fashion its beliefs, shape a community, and articulate the way of life according to Torah which would preserve the community in the wake of 70 and in time cause it to prosper and grow. The establishing of a gathering place is an important institutional development. This constitutes an essential step in forming a collective identity and is the beginning of a process which finally culminated in the ornate and sophisticated structures of the Byzantine period.

Matthew's Gospel reflects that this small and initially simple, but nevertheless crucial, institutional development within formative Judaism is taking place in his setting. Among the Gospel writers, Matthew is the one who most clearly indicates the establishment of gathering places for the Jewish community, a group with which the Matthean community is clearly contending. Matthew speaks of "their" (*autōn*) synagogues (see 4:23; 9:35; 10:17; 12:9; 13:54; and *hymōn* in 23:34).[92] Only in Matt. 6:2, 5; 23:6 is synagogue not followed by the pronominal genitive. Matthew understands that there are specific gatherings of the Jewish leadership and their followers, toward whom the Matthean community is feeling such animosity.

[89] Ibid.
[90] Strange, *BASOR* 226 (1977) 69.
[91] Ibid.
[92] Kilpatrick, *Origins*, 110.

Matthew 10:17 and 12:9, and 23:34 in particular, give the impression of entering a synagogue building.[93] However, it is clear from Matthew's general treatment of the Jewish leadership and community in his setting that they have formed their own offices and institutions and have started also to establish their own gathering places. Matthew's own community seems to have responded in kind with its selection of "church" or *ekklēsia* as a designation for their own gathering place.[94]

Mark also refers to "their" synagogue (see 1:23 and 1:39). Both of these verses present textual problems; the *autōn* is omitted by several manuscripts. Luke's lone use of the genitive with "synagogue" in 4:15 has the same textual problem.[95] In Mark 1:21, 29; 3:1; 6:2; 12:39; 13:9 "synagogue" appears without the genitive pronoun. Mark 1:23 tells of Jesus' first visit to the synagogue in that Gospel, and it betrays the evangelist's own hand with the characteristically Markan use of "immediately" (*euthys*) and the participle "entering" (*eiselthōn*).[96] Mark 1:21-23 seem to be redactional verses. It is likely that 1:23 and the reference to "their" synagogues can be attributed to the author. This is perhaps the only indication of such a development in Mark's setting. Mark, however, is not consistent enough on this point to warrant further attention. He and his community are far less concerned about the consolidation and development of the Jewish community within its midst than is Matthew. The Markan community provides us with almost no indication whatsoever of possessing community structures or any institutional developments.[97]

Matthew consistently makes the distinction between the Jewish gathering places and the gathering of his community. Matthew regularly accompanies *synagōgē* with the genitive plural of a personal pronoun. This is not so in the other Gospels. It appears then that there is a place in Matthew's setting where the Jewish leadership and their followers gather. Matthew reveals this with telling regularity. Similarly, and supportive for the development of separate institutions for formative Judaism and Matthew's community is Matthew's use of "their" (*autōn*) to describe the scribes of the opposition (Matt. 7:29; compare Mark 1:22).

In Matthew one can see indications of the institutional development of the gathering place within formative Judaism attested to in

[93] As does Mark in 3:1; "go into" (*eiselthen*).

[94] Developed by H. C. Kee in "The Transformation of the Synagogue."

[95] Kilpatrick, *Origins*, 110.

[96] J. Gnilka, *Das Evangelium nach Markus*, EKKNT (Zurich: Benziger, 1978) 1:77.

[97] H. C. Kee, *The Community of the New Age* (London: SCM, 1977) 152.

the archaeological findings from the late first century. In Matthew's setting a modest, functional gathering place or assembly hall was recognized as the center of the collective life of the religious body and leadership with whom the Matthean community was so clearly at odds. This place was making its presence known and felt within the Matthean community. This initially small institutional development is important because it indicates two separate communities growing up alongside of, and over against, one another. Formative Judaism was organizing to the extent that it was developing its own identifiable places of meeting and worship and acquiring the institutional roles and officials to go along with these modest structures, which in time grew into impressive and prominent edifices across the Palestinian landscape.

"The Paradosis *of the Fathers":* *Traditionalizing the New Movement*

It was noted above that the social constructions which communities and movements engage in often ultimately serve the purpose of legitimating the movement, its leaders, and its beliefs.[98] These constructions are of a tenuous nature. The truth of how a community lives and what they believe does not forever appear as a given. The institutions, positions of authority, and beliefs and values that a movement develops are shaped in part by the need to protect the movement from attacks from the outside.[99] The movement, however, must also make what are initially tenuous social constructions designed to guide the life of the community and allow the movement to appear more permanent and stable to its members. These constructions serve as an apology to outsiders, and they are a means of instruction and training for the insiders. Part of the process of making these beliefs appear more plausible, particularly to ensuing "second-generation" members, involves giving them a status and pedigree they initially did not possess.[100] These social institutions and human constructs must begin to appear grounded in something far more established and permanent.

The beliefs and life of the community cannot continue to be seen as *de novo* and as innovative human constructions. For the beliefs of

---

[98] See P. L. Berger, *The Sacred Canopy: Elements of a Sociological Theory of Religion* (Garden City, N.Y.: Doubleday, 1969) 30–31.

[99] This notion is expressed in Berger, *Sacred Canopy*, 47.

[100] The term "second-generation" comes from Berger, *Sacred Canopy*, 30–31.

the community to remain plausible they must begin to be seen as part of a much greater system and tradition. What is actually new and innovative must be portrayed as having its origin in a higher order. The philosopher Arnold Gehlen dealt with this notion in the context of the process of institutionalization. If institutions and the beliefs and values they represent are to be accepted and remain plausible, these beliefs and patterns must be pushed into the background and take on the appearance of being traditional, accepted, and legitimate. Gehlen referred to this process as "filling in the background."[101] Max Weber similarly spoke about the need for a charismatic movement to be traditionalized or rationalized if it were ever to take on a permanent character and not be simply transitory.[102] The process of traditionalizing the movement, then, is an attempt to legitimate the beliefs of the group in the hope that these beliefs will in time take on a more sacred frame of reference.[103] In order for the movement to survive, people must gradually forget that this social order was established by people and continues to be dependent on the consent of people. These social constructions within the movement must come to be identified with a greater, more established and traditional authority.

Formative Judaism and Matthew's community both were concerned with legitimating their beliefs and behavior. They too had to present their respective movements as traditional, acceptable, and legitimate. In a manner strikingly similar to what both Gehlen and Weber have described, formative Judaism and the Matthean community sought to traditionalize their new movements, in order to legitimate the convictions and actions of their communities. We will discuss Matthew's attempts at traditionalization below.[104] Here we wish to focus on this process within formative Judaism.

Josephus tells that the Pharisees observe traditions (*paradosis*) not recorded in the law of Moses (*Ant.* 13.10.6 §297). These traditions were banned when Hyrcanus deserted the Pharisees for the Sadducees, following his being offended by the Pharisees. Josephus describes the traditions thus:

> What I would now explain is this, that the Pharisees have delivered to the people a great many observances by the tradition from their Fathers,

---

[101] A. Gehlen, *Urmensch und Spätkultur* (Bonn: Athenäum, 1956) 56ff.

[102] Discussed in M. Weber, *Economy and Society*, ed. G. Roth and C. Wittich (Berkeley: University of California Press, 1978) 241–48.

[103] Berger, *Sacred Canopy*, 33.

[104] See chap. 3 (under "Scripture, Interpretation, and Tradition in Matthew") for a discussion of the so-called fulfillment citations.

which are not written in the law of Moses; and for this reason the Sadducees reject them, and say that we are to honor those observances which are in written word, not observing those which are derived from the tradition of our forefathers. Concerning these things great disputes and differences have risen among them. (*Ant.* 13.10.6 §297)

These traditions, banned by Hyrcanus, were later restored under Alexandra, the wife of Alexander Jannaeus. The Sadducees rejected the traditions which the Pharisees claimed they had received. This was a bone of contention between these two factions. Josephus records that the two groups had controversies and serious differences over this. The Sadducees accepted only those laws written down in the law of Moses. The *paradosis* of the Pharisees was not written down.[125] A. I. Baumgarten, in his illuminating study of the Pharisaic *paradosis*, suggests that there may have been others who also took issue with the claim of the Pharisees.[106] Josephus records that the Pharisees value themselves and their skill in "the law of their forefathers" (*Ant.* 17.2.4 §41). They make people believe that they are highly favored by God. Josephus accuses the Pharisees of "pretending to observe the laws of which God approves."[107] It is implied here that the traditions which the Pharisees claim are from God are nothing but their own creation. Here is another instance of contention over the Pharisaic traditions, which are said to be nothing more than human traditions. This accusation is similar to that of the Sadducees in *Ant.* 13.10.6 §297.

The apostle Paul claims that his persecution of the church as a Pharisee was a result of his zeal for "the traditions (*paradosis*) of my ancestors" (Gal. 1:14). In 1 Corinthians Paul the convert uses *paradosis* in a way to legitimate his version of the resurrection in the face of the contrary views which he is encountering (1 Cor. 15:1-3). Here Paul wishes to overrule the exploited tradition of the resurrection at Corinth through appeal to the apostolic tradition, of which he claims to be a part. How can Paul substantiate the version of the

---

[105] A. I. Baumgarten, "The Pharisaic Paradosis," *HTR* 80 (1987) 70. This insightful article provided much of the impetus for this chapter. The author expresses his debt to Professor Baumgarten for this and other illuminating studies of this period of formative Judaism.

[106] See the discussion about Nicolaus of Damascus as a source for *Antiquities*, books 13–17, in A. I. Baumgarten, "The Name of the Pharisees," *JBL* 102 (1983) 411–28.

[107] See Baumgarten, "Pharisaic Paradosis," 70. The comments by R. A. Marcus are included there.

resurrection to which he appeals? He attempts to identify this para-dosis with the paradosis of the apostles.[108] For both Paul the Pharisee and Paul the apostle, tradition (*paradosis*) served the purpose of legiti-mating his beliefs and was the means by which others could poten-tially be convinced.

From Josephus we can see that the Pharisaic claim that their unique beliefs and practices are derived from the ancient traditions of the fathers met with opposition. The Pharisees attempted to derive power and influence from their use of these distinctive traditions — above all, the claim that these traditions were ancient and estab-lished. In book 13 of *Antiquities* it is clear that this attempt was succeeding. Josephus adds that the Sadducees are able only to con-vince some of the wealthy of their point of view, while the Pharisees have the multitude on their side. The claim on the part of the Pharisees that their beliefs were in actuality grounded in the ancient traditions of the fathers lent credence and pedigree to their move-ment. While this claim did serve to legitimate their beliefs to the people, and apparently successfully so, it also provoked conflict and dispute.

The Gospels give evidence of disputes between Jesus and the Phari-sees concerning the "traditions of the elders." Matthew and Mark record just such a dispute between Jesus and the Pharisees and scribes. Both evangelists equate these traditions with humans and not God. The Pharisees have found a way to reject the traditions of God in order to hold to their own traditions (Matt. 15:6; Mark 7:8).[109] It is important to see the confrontation in the Gospels over the Phari-saic *paradosis* which is also found in Josephus. The claim by the Pharisees that their distinctive traditions were derived from the fathers was well known. It is also clear that this claim of tradition and antiquity by the Pharisees met with considerable resistance.

In both the Markan and Matthean traditions the scribes are also lumped together with the Pharisees. This would seem to suggest a later stage, around and after 70, when these originally Pharisaic prac-tices were being applied to a broader group. That the conflict over the Pharisaic traditions in Mark and Matthew (called "your traditions" in Matt. 15:6 and Mark 7:9) refers to the practices of scribes and Phari-sees in an immediate post-70 period accords well with Jacob Neusner's treatment of this passage. "The stress on maintaining temple purity

---

[108] J. H. Schütz, "Apostolic Authority and the Control of the Tradition: I Cor. 15," *NTS* 15 (1968–69) 453.
[109] This passage will be discussed further in chap. 3.

in the eating of meals outside of the temple, and the larger concep-
tion that the ordinary folks should behave as if they were priests, was
an innovation coming probably at the turn of the first century."[110]
Formative Judaism in the post-70 period adopted this claim and
employed it to establish its beliefs and position in this period between
70 and 100. Mark and Matthew dispute these claims. Mark dismisses
the *traditions* in abrupt fashion (Mark 7:19). Matthew also rejects the
Pharisaic traditions, but he engages the argument more fully and
tries to justify the behavior of the disciples in light of the law. In
Josephus we see that there indeed is opposition to the Pharisaic claim
of tradition for their practices. However, the popularity of the Pharisees' practices with the people is mentioned by Josephus. While the
Sadducees reject these traditions, the Pharisees and their traditions
are not necessarily portrayed in a negative light in this passage from
Antiquities.[111]

The Pharisaic *paradosis*, which formative Judaism adopted and inte-
grated into their system, was a subject of dispute. The Sadducees
rejected it. In *Ant.* 17.2.2 §41-45 and in the Gospels of Mark and
Matthew the Pharisees are accused of pretending to follow the laws
of God. Their traditions are really of their own creation, to suit their
purposes and ends.[112] While this claim clearly has its roots in Pharisaic sectarian practices, in the period in which Matthew, Mark, and
Josephus are writing we can see that this claim by emerging formative Judaism to possess the tradition of the elders and to embody
those traditions in their practices is hotly contested. This traditionalization of the new movement was a move to establish and to legitimate these rather novel beliefs on the part of first the Pharisees in the
pre-70 period and then the coalition of formative Judaism in the
period from 70 on.

This claim was finally accepted and became associated with a
greater and more sacred frame of reference, as *m. 'Abot* 1:1 attests.
One senses in this later rabbinic passage precisely what we said must
take place in order for the social constructions and institutions of the
movement to be sustained. These institutions must begin to appear
more permanent and stable. These originally new beliefs and practices

---

[110] J. Neusner, "First Cleanse the Inside," *NTS* 22 (1975–76) 494.

[111] See the discussion in S. Cohen, *Josephus in Galilee and Rome: His Vita and
Development as a Historian* (Leiden: E. J. Brill, 1979) 236–38.

[112] Baumgarten, "Pharisaic Paradosis," 70–71; see also D. Schwartz, "Josephus
and Nicolaus on the Pharisees," *JSJ* 14 (1983) 157–71. See also the reaction of the
Sadducees in ARNA 5; here the *paradosis* of the Pharisees is seen by the Sadducees
as a needless burden.

must acquire a pedigree and a status. What were once human constructions must come to be seen as having their origin in a higher order. In time, these novel practices and interpretations take on a more sacred frame of reference.

This claim on the part of formative Judaism that its beliefs and practices are not new but are traditional, going back to the fathers, would serve the purpose of convincing outsiders of the validity of their claims and at the same time would explain and reinforce their practices for members who in time might come to question the plausibility of some of their beliefs. Matthew's community endeavored to accomplish the same thing through its use of Scripture, particularly the fulfillment citations.[113] Both Matthew and formative Judaism claimed great antiquity for their beliefs and traditions.

For formative Judaism, the prestige of association with the fathers would have been considerable. Initially this claim was resisted. The period under consideration here, c. 70–100, the time at which both Josephus and Matthew were writing, was the period when formative Judaism was first seeking to assert the antiquity of its new movement in the face of several other options and movements. Matthew's community was one such group which opposed this claim by formative Judaism. In time, however, the attempt to traditionalize the new movement and some of its innovative beliefs and practices succeeded, as the final emergence of rabbinic Judaism as the dominant form of Judaism attests. As A. I. Baumgarten observes, the process of traditionalization is a deliberate attempt to attain a pedigree and credibility. While initially creating opposition and conflict, the attempt within formative Judaism to traditionalize the new movement was something which eventually proved successful.[114]

Viewing the claim to represent the traditions of the elders as a means of traditionalizing and legitimating the new movement reinforces a claim made by J. Neusner concerning formative Judaism. The success of formative Judaism was due, among other things, to its capacity to claim that things in the post-70 period really had not changed at all. This new synthesis of formative Judaism and its emerging new authorities simply and effectively claimed to be representing the traditions and heroes of Israel's past.[115] They were the heirs of the great tradition and the bearers of God's revelation to the

[113] See chap. 3, under "Scripture, Interpretation, and Tradition in Matthew."
[114] Baumgarten, "Pharisaic Paradosis," 77.
[115] Neusner, "Formation," 22.

people of God. In time this claim was established, and the leaders and practices of the movement were accepted as authoritative.

"The Most Accurate Interpreters of the Law": *The Law and Legitimation*

Claiming antiquity and the traditions of the fathers was not the only means by which the new movement could establish itself as an acceptable and authoritative body in the post-70 period. Formative Judaism inherited from pre-70 Pharisaism a concern for the law and the accuracy of its interpretation which served it well in this initial period of formation and definition following 70.

After the destruction of the temple, study and interpretation of Torah became the central ritual and activity for many within Judaism. The temple cult was replaced by study of Torah.[116] This development is an important reason why Pharisaism was so well placed following the destruction of the temple to move into a position of power and influence. As was noted above, the Pharisaic program, articulated prior to 70, did not require an actual temple. As formative Judaism took shape and articulated its beliefs and practices, the study and ritual of Torah were already in the heritage of Judaism. Leaders developed and utilized study of the law as a means of establishing their position as the authoritative interpreters of the law.

Josephus describes the Pharisees as "the most accurate interpreters of the law" (*J.W.* 1.5.1 §110; 2.8.14 §162; *Life* 38.191).[117] *Antiquities* 17.2.4 §41 claims that the Pharisees "pride themselves on the accuracy (*akribeia*) of their adherence to ancestral tradition." This is from a section that is somewhat negative toward the Pharisees, but even here Pharisaic accuracy concerning the traditions and laws is recognized.[118]

In his speech before Agrippa in Acts 26:5, Paul the apostle describes the Pharisees as "the strictest party" (*akribestatēn hairesin*). In Acts 22:3 Paul claims that he studied at the feet of Gamaliel and was "trained in the exact observance (*kata akribeian*) of the law of our

---

[116] Ibid., 38.

[117] See also *Ant.* 20.9.1 §43; *peri tous nomous* most likely refers to the Pharisees, particularly in that this deals with a group opposing an action of a Sadducean high priest. See Baumgarten, "Name of the Pharisees," 413.

[118] Baumgarten, "Name of the Pharisees," 415. Baumgarten is interested in connecting the name of the Pharisees with this accuracy concerning the law. This is not our concern; we are interested in the potential power and prestige that would result from this reputation for those who claimed it.

ancestors." Here is another reference to Pharisaic training as being the strictest and most accurate concerning the Jewish law. The term *akribeia* in these passages from Josephus and Luke thus refers to the accuracy of Pharisaic teaching and interpretation of the law.

For pre-70 Pharisaism, the claim to represent the most accurate interpretation and teaching of the law was one significant way influence and power could be achieved. There were times when the Pharisees enjoyed power through the support and sanction of the ruler.[119] However, even when they did not enjoy the support of the political powers, the Pharisees did seem to enjoy popularity with the people. This is clear in the story about Alexander Jannaeus's death. Even though Alexander opposed the Pharisees during his reign, they did nevertheless enjoy the support of the people. It is for this reason that Alexandra is encouraged to befriend the Pharisees and share her power with them (*Ant.* 13.15.5 §399). In *Ant.* 13.10.6 §297, Josephus explains that the teachings of the Sadducees have only convinced a few of the wealthy, while the Pharisees have convinced the multitudes. Finally, at the conclusion of *Antiquities*, Josephus explains that the Jewish people truly value and respect someone who is fully acquainted with the laws and able to interpret their meaning. There have been many who have tried to master this, but only a handful have succeeded (*Ant.* 20.11.2 §268). One source of the Pharisees' popularity and influence with the people no doubt was their reputation as the most accurate interpreters of the law.

This privileged position and reputation became all the more crucial in the post-70 period following the destruction of the temple. The law now emerged as the central symbol for post-70 Judaism. Who was recognized as the authoritative interpreters had a great deal to do with who emerged as the accepted and established movement. The Pharisees had learned to obtain power through Torah interpretation, and not the temple system.[120] With the temple in ruins, this influence and reputation concerning the law would prove vital for the success of formative Judaism following 70.

Torah became the agent and means of revelation in the period following 70. Authority was derived from and confirmed through Torah

---

[119] The political fortunes of the Pharisees are discussed by Saldarini in *Pharisees, Scribes and Sadducees*. See the discussion in chap. 3.

[120] S. Isenberg, "Power Through Temple and Torah in Greco-Roman Palestine," in *Christianity, Judaism, and Other Greco-Roman Cults*, ed. J. Neusner (Leiden: E. J. Brill, 1975) 2:42.

and Torah interpretation.[121] God's will is expressed in Torah. With the destruction of the temple, God's will as expressed in Torah becomes the foundation of authority within Judaism. Naturally, in the immediate post-70 period there were other options, such as the re-creation of a third temple or the popular Zealot option, as manifested in the Bar Kochba revolt of 133. However, formative Judaism pursued the option that was prefigured in pre-70 Pharisaism, namely, the understanding and fulfilling of God's intentions for Israel through the study of the law and the application of it to their daily lives.[122]

Once the centrality of the law is recognized and accepted as the focus and primary ritual for many within post-70 Judaism, the position of interpreter of the law becomes a critically important one. Those who possess the true, accurate, and authoritative interpretation of the law are those who will emerge as the leaders and dominant force in this period. Herein lies the important relationship between the law and its interpreter. Formative Judaism and those within the movement who constituted its leadership took their lead from pre-70 Pharisaism and claimed to be the most accurate interpreters of the law.

However, within the post-70 period there were some who would contest the claim made by formative Judaism that they possessed the authoritative understanding and interpretation of the law. Matthew's community debated with this movement over issues of the law. They held the conviction that they completely understood and fulfilled the law. They maintained that those with whom they were contending, namely, formative Judaism, distorted and corrupted the law.[123] Both Matthew's community and formative Judaism agreed on the importance of the law for daily living. They differed, however, on how to interpret that law and on who should do the interpreting. Matthew is unique among the Gospel writers in the degree to which he enters into debate over issues of the law with the Jewish leadership. The conflict stories within the Gospel of Matthew reflect that community's interpretation of the law over against that interpretation offered by formative Judaism.

Both Josephus and the Acts of the Apostles associate the claim of "most accurate interpreters of the law" with the Pharisees. However,

---

[121] J. Neusner, "Religious Authority in Judaism: Modern and Classical Modes," *Interpretation* 39 (1985) 373–87.

[122] Ibid., 383ff.

[123] This issue will be discussed in chap. 3.

both of these writers, while reflecting a claim about pre-70 Pharisaism, also reveal something about the reputation of the emerging Jewish leadership in the post-70 period concerning their interpretation of the law. Even Matthew, for all his contention with formative Judaism and its leaders, seems to reveal that he too is aware of their position of authority and reputation concerning the law (Matt. 23:2-3; 5:21).

Formative Judaism adopted several traditions about the Pharisees in the pre-70 period and applied them to the new movement. One example is the claim that what they believed and practiced was not new but was passed on to them by their ancestors. Formative Judaism also adopted the reputation of being the most accurate intepreter of the law in order to legitimate the role of the leaders of the people in the post-70 period. Both of these claims would initially create competition and conflict. This is the case with the Matthean community. However, in time, both claims would serve to establish the movement as the dominant and authoritative body upon which the people would depend and to which they would look for guidance and instruction.

The Social Development of
the Matthean Community

WITHIN THE FLUID AND FRAGMENTED setting of post-70 Judaism, both the emerging formative Judaism and the Matthean community struggled to establish, order, and define their beliefs and life. Both were influenced by the wider setting of the sectarian nature of Judaism, and indeed both adopted certain patterns and procedures characteristic of this period, transforming them for their own use in the post-70 period. The social and institutional developments within the Matthean community we are now to consider serve as the evidence for this process of self-definition and development within that community after 70. Like formative Judaism, the Matthean community was struggling to survive and make its way through what was doubtless an uncertain and unstable period in Palestine following the destruction of the Jerusalem temple. These developments helped to ensure the perpetuation of the community and, like all roles and institutions, helped to guide the members of the community in their life and behavior concerning fellow members as well as those outside the group.[1]

The Matthean community developed roles within the group, positions of authority, and articulated a defense of their position regarding the Jewish law, the future of God's people, and the Jewish leadership in their setting. These procedures and developments served the purpose of instructing and defending the community. These developments, however, are not *sui generis*, rising out of thin air. As we noted

---

[1] It was Arnold Gehlen who said that institutions "unburden" (*Entlastung*) people and societies. By this Gehlen meant that decisions, actions, and patterns of behavior are determined for members by institutions. Gehlen defined "institution" rather broadly. The term represents any pattern of behavior within society as well as structures and roles or figures of authority. See A. Gehlen, *Urmensch und Spätkultur* (Bonn: Athenäum, 1956).

in chap. 1, a fundamental insight of the sociology of knowledge is that these constructions and institutions are responses to threats and challenges to the community and its life from the outside or from potentially disenchanted members.[2] The social developments within the community constitute an answer to the competition and conflict the community is experiencing. The legitimating formulas, procedures, and institutions explain the movement and have been shaped largely in response to the most immediate threat faced by the community. As we will see, many of the social developments within the Matthean community can be understood best as responses to the most immediate threat that community faced, namely, formative Judaism, which was developing and gaining the upper hand in the Matthean setting. In this chapter we will analyze the role of Scripture and the law in Matthew, the behavior and ethics encouraged in the community, the roles and positions of authority, and institutional procedures evident within Matthew. Finally, we will discuss Matthew's stance toward Judaism and the Jewish leadership in his setting.

Scripture, Interpretation, and Tradition in Matthew

The Matthean community, like formative Judaism, was a new movement. The beliefs and procedures which each movement possessed were in time presented as established and traditional. We saw above that formative Judaism presented its traditions and procedures as having their origin in the *paradosis* of the ancestors. In a similar manner, Matthew attempts to traditionalize the beliefs of his community concerning Jesus' life and ministry—to give a pedigree and legitimacy to the figure of Jesus and the community's belief in him that it might not otherwise possess. One of the most striking ways in which Matthew ascribes a higher, more sacred and traditional frame of reference to the career of Jesus and thereby to the beliefs of his community is through his application of the notion of fulfillment (*plērōma*). The theme of fulfillment is most obviously expressed in the so-called fulfillment citations, found primarily in the Matthean birth story.[3]

---

[2] P. L. Berger, *The Sacred Canopy: Elements in a Sociological Theory of Religion* (Garden City, N.Y.: Doubleday, 1969) 30–31. To endure and remain plausible, these constructions will have to take on a more sacred frame of reference. This is in part what the process of legitimation intends to accomplish.

[3] The term "fulfillment citation" is thought to have originated with W. Rothfuchs, *Die Erfüllungszitate des Matthäus-Evangeliums* (Stuttgart: Kohlhammer, 1969).

The Fulfillment Citations

The term "fulfillment citation" refers specifically to an application of a prophecy from the Hebrew Bible by Matthew with the claim that a certain event took place "in order to fulfill" something which was predicted by a prophet. In Matthew more than half of the fulfillment citations come from Isaiah. There are some fourteen fulfillment citations, though not all commentators agree on what precisely constitutes a Matthean fulfillment citation.[4]

These fulfillment citations are explanatory notes from the author Matthew to clarify or make explicit that something which happened in the life and ministry of Jesus was intended to happen and transpired precisely to fulfill what one of the prophets of old had predicted. As R. E. Brown observes, "these citations emphasize that the whole of Jesus' life, down to the last detail, lay within God's foreordained plan."[5] These fulfillment passages are not spoken by a character in the story; Jesus does not make the connection between his actions or events that happen to him and the prophetic predictions. These are explanatory comments added by the narrator Matthew[6] and so take on the character of a commentary by the author.[7] In short, these fulfillment citations were added by Matthew in order to emphasize something about Jesus and belief in him.

The Matthean preoccupation with *explicitly* grounding events in the ministry of Jesus in Scripture is not a pronounced feature of the Gospel of Mark. This is not to say that Mark may not be interested in some sort of "promise–fulfillment" schema. Mark, however, does not resort to this overt and studied use of Scripture.[8] On the relatively rare occasions that Scripture is overtly cited in Mark or the

---

This particular term is to be preferred over the older "reflection citations" because it draws attention to the function of the citations, i.e., fulfillment.

[4] See R. E. Brown, *The Birth of the Messiah* (Garden City, N.Y.: Doubleday, 1979) 98; and U. Luz, *Matthew 1–7: A Commentary* (Minneapolis: Augsburg, 1989) 156–64. The passages are 1:22; 2:5, 15, 17, 23; 3:3; 4:14; 8:17; 12:17; 13:14, 35; 21:4; 26:56; 27:9.

[5] Brown, *Birth of the Messiah*, 96–97.

[6] K. Stendahl, "Quis et Unde? An Analysis of Matthew 1-2," in *The Interpretation of Matthew*, ed. G. Stanton (Philadelphia: Fortress Press, 1983) 60.

[7] Luz, *Matthew 1–7*, 156.

[8] H. Anderson, "The Old Testament in Mark's Gospel," in *The Use of the Old Testament in the New and Other Essays: Studies in Honor of W. Stinespring*, ed. J. Efird (Durham, N.C.: Duke University Press, 1972) 280–306; see also H. C. Kee, "Scripture Quotations and Allusions in Mk. 11-16," in *Society of Biblical Literature 1971 Seminar Papers* (Missoula, Mont.: Scholars Press, 1971) 475–502.

notion of fulfillment is explicitly mentioned, it is done by Jesus or another character in the story and not stressed by the author Mark in terms of an editorial comment (cf. Mark 1:15; 14:49). By contrast, Matthew does not appear to be comfortable with mere references or allusions to Scripture but wants to make overt and clear the connection between the life and ministry of Jesus and the traditions and promises of Israel's history.

K. Stendahl has correctly observed that these citations in Matthew have an apologetic aim.[9] They explain and justify events that occurred in the life of Jesus which may perhaps have been problematic for those maintaining belief in him as Messiah. At first glance these citations may appear pedantic, perhaps as a Matthean obsession with mere details. For example, the effort put into explaining the *patria* of the Jesus family being in Nazareth (2:23ff.) or the time spent in Egypt (2:15ff.) or the riding on the ass (21:4) may all seem rather tangential to the story. However, the effect of these claims by Matthew is far greater than simply tying up a few loose ends in the biography of Jesus the Messiah.

The effect of these events, depicted as they are in Matthew as the fulfillment of God's timeless, foreordained plan as prophesied through the prophets, is above all a confirmation that Jesus is God's chosen agent. The belief the community has placed in him is not erroneous. The peculiar events in the life and ministry of Jesus and in the community which follows Jesus are intended to happen and are in fact proof that they are God's people, following God's agent, Jesus. The mention of specific passages and prophets from the Hebrew Scriptures is an attempt by Matthew to supply support for his story of Jesus and to explain that these events and beliefs are not new, innovative, or repudiating of Israel's past. Rather, they are the fulfillment of that same history and heritage.

Both G. Strecker and K. Stendahl are correct in saying that these fulfillment citations are a result of a kind of scribal activity. These elaborate and creative applications of prophecies are a result of some informed study and use of Scripture.[10] Such a detailed application of Scripture, designed to create a unity between the life and ministry of Jesus and the Old Testament, reflects a sophisticated understanding of Scripture.[11] Certainly these citations would have instructed the

---

[9] Stendahl, "Quis et Unde," 59.

[10] G. Strecker, *Der Weg der Gerechtigkeit* (Göttingen: Vandenhoeck & Ruprecht, 1962) 83; K. Stendahl, *The School of St. Matthew and Its Use of the Old Testament* (Philadelphia: Fortress Press, 1968) 195.

[11] Strecker, *Weg*, 84.

community; however, this elaborate and explicit use of Scripture suggests also a defense against Judaism, which is another apologetic aim of these citations.[12] One reason Matthew is so careful to ground actions and events in the life of Jesus explicitly and obviously in Scripture is to present a challenge to his Jewish opponents.

Matthew lays claim to the same tradition and Scripture as the community's Jewish opponents. We will see below that this is a distinction between Matthew and Mark. In so obviously aligning the story of Jesus and the events in his ministry (sometimes down to a seemingly obscure detail, cf. 21:4) with the ancient traditions and promises of Israel, Matthew claims that the beliefs of his community are not new or misguided but rather established and traditional. They have their ground in the very promises and traditions of the history of Israel. Matthew has tried to traditionalize the beliefs of his new movement through the use of the fulfillment citations. His use of Scripture in this way would defend the beliefs and behavior of his community to members who might have started to doubt the legitimacy of the group's peculiar interpretations and actions. Also, as has often been observed, this would be a clear challenge and response to the Jewish leadership, which Matthew perceives as the opposition to his community. H. Frankemölle is correct in seeing in this use of the fulfillment citations a struggle over *tradition* between the Matthean community and Judaism.[13]

The fulfillment citations do not primarily clarify "historical events" in the life of Jesus.[14] These citations emphasize the Matthean community's claim to the very traditions formative Judaism was lifting up and claiming as its own. This would obviously lead to competition and conflict. While the traditions and Scriptures of Israel were something the Matthean community and formative Judaism held in common, Matthew's claim that these traditions and promises are fulfilled exclusively in the person and action of Jesus of Nazareth would provoke certain tension and struggle between these two movements.

Matthew, not unlike the Qumran community, was interested in finding in Scripture support and evidence for the beliefs and practices of his community, over against the group with whom they were contending.[15] Matthew was interested in these prophecies from

---

[12] Luz asserts that the citations are a defense (*Verteidigung*) against Judaism (*Matthew 1–7*, 161).

[13] H. Frankemölle, *Jahwebund und Kirche Christi* (Münster: Aschendorff, 1974) 306, 389. Also Luz, *Matthew 1–7*, 162.

[14] Strecker, *Weg*, 72, 85.

[15] See above, chap. 1, under "The Centrality of the Law."

Scripture insofar as they could be used to confirm the authority and position of Jesus and, at the same time, confirm the beliefs and life of the Matthean community against the Jewish community, which was attempting to claim the same traditions and promises.[16]

The birth story plays a special role in Matthew's attempt at traditionalizing the new movement. Roughly half of the fulfillment citations are concentrated in the Matthean birth narrative. This highlights the importance of explaining that the origins of Jesus lay within the divine plan and therefore confirm his being chosen by God to "save his people" (1:21). R. E. Brown has emphasized the parallels in the Matthean birth story with the story of Moses in Exodus. This is something widely recognized, but bears repeating in light of our concern with the traditionalizing of the beliefs of the Matthean community in the face of competition from formative Judaism.[17]

As pharaoh sought to do away with Moses, so Herod tried to do away with Jesus (Matt. 2:13; Exod. 2:15). Herod massacred all the boys under age two in Bethlehem in the same manner that pharaoh killed every male born to the Hebrews (Matt. 2:16; Exod. 1:22). Both Herod and the king of Egypt died (Matt. 2:19; Exod. 2:23). Jesus' father Joseph and Moses are commanded to return either to Israel or to Egypt because it is now safe (Matt. 2:19; Exod. 4:19; Matt. 2:21; Exod. 4:20).[18]

The story of the birth of Moses according to Josephus, however, may contain even further parallels to Matthew's version of Jesus' birth (*Ant.* 2.9.2–2.10.1). In Josephus the giving of the name *Moses* is emphasized in a manner analogous to the Matthean story (*Ant.* 2.9.6).[19] The remarkable nature of the child Moses, including even his "divine form," goes beyond that of the account in Exodus and has certain similarities with the Matthean birth story (*Ant.* 2.9.7; Matt. 1:23; 2:11). Josephus emphasizes the birth of Moses as the fulfillment of prophecy and prediction through the figure of the "sacred sage" who divines the meaning of all the events in this account and who figures so prominently in the Josephus version.[20] Visions, foretelling, and prophecy figure prominently in the Josephus version and are, as Stendahl observes, particularly important vehicles of revelation for Matthew.[21]

---

[16] R. S. McConnell, *Law and Prophecy in Matthew's Gospel* (Basel: Friedrich Reinhandt, 1969) 138.

[17] Brown, *Birth of the Messiah,* 113ff.

[18] Ibid.

[19] Stendahl, "Quis et Unde," 65.

[20] Discussed by Brown, *Birth of the Messiah,* 14 n. 41.

[21] Stendahl, "Quis et Unde," 57; see *Ant.* 2.9.2, 4, 7.

The unmistakable parallels between Jesus and Moses in the section containing half the fulfillment citations (parallels which are in some respects even more prominent when comparing Josephus's version of Moses' birth) are clear attempts by Matthew to lend credibility and stature to the figure of Jesus. The portrayal of Jesus as in some way Moses *redivivus* and the obvious parallels between their respective origins defend the life of the Matthean community by claiming continuity with the heroic figure of Moses and the authoritative traditions associated with him.

The particular use of the notion of fulfillment, as it is expressed in the fulfillment citations, is an attempt by Matthew to lend antiquity and authority to the beliefs and life of his community. The use of Scripture and the interpretation of certain prophecies in light of the history of Jesus of Nazareth make the claim, in the face of contention and competition from the Jewish leadership in Matthew's setting, that the beliefs and actions of his community are neither spurious, new, nor innovative. Rather, the figure of Jesus and therefore the beliefs of the Matthean community about Jesus are the fulfillment of God's foreordained plan. The life of the Matthean community is in continuity with the Scripture, promises, and traditions of the history of Israel.

As Matthew attempts to do elsewhere in his Gospel, so here he draws parallels between Jesus and Moses.[22] As God chose Moses to be the divine agent and liberator of the chosen people, so God chose Jesus as the agent who "will save his people." The life and ministry of Jesus are no aberration, and neither is the life of the Matthean community. All that took place "was in order to fufill what God had predicted through the prophets." Jesus and the life of the Matthean community are in continuity with the traditions and promises of Israel's history. Indeed, as a result of this distinctive use of Scripture by Matthew, Jesus—and through him the Matthean community—is depicted as the fulfillment of that very history and tradition. This constitutes both a defense of Matthew's community and a challenge to the opposition.

The Conflict Stories

What the conflict stories reveal about Matthew's use of the law is significant, especially Matthew's defense of his community's

---

[22] Matthew's attempt to portray Jesus as Moses *redivivus* is seen most clearly in the Sermon on the Mount; see W. D. Davies, *The Setting of the Sermon on the Mount* (Cambridge: Cambridge University Press, 1964).

interpretation of the law before the opposition.[23] What is most characteristic about the Matthean conflict stories is that these stories portray Jesus as an accurate and true interpreter of the law.[24] This helps to distinguish Matthew's treatment of the conflict stories from that of Mark. Matthew, through his reworking of these traditions, justifies his community's interpretation and application of the law over against the accusations offered by the opponents. We will focus on three conflict stories: (1) the Sabbath controversy in Matt. 12:1-8; (2) Matt. 15:1-20, which deals with issues of ritual purity; and (3) the debate in Matt. 22:34-40, which culminates in the so-called love command.

We may note the following regarding the Matthean conflict stories generally: Matthew has formulated three additional conflict stories. Matthew 12:39-42 is a conflict with the scribes and Pharisees concerning their demand for a sign from heaven. This request from the Pharisees is found in Mark 8:11. However, Jesus, in a fashion not uncharacteristic of Mark, dismisses the request. In Mark 8:11 Jesus simply sighs and offers no sign. Jesus provides no real response to the request of the Pharisees. Here the request is treated as misguided, even trivial, and consequently the Markan Jesus does not engage the Pharisees.

Matthew has developed this pericope much more fully. Though Jesus claims no sign will be given (Matt. 12:39//Mark 8:12), a sign is in fact given—that of Jonah—which is derived from Q (Matt. 12:15ff.// Luke 11:30ff.). Matthew, unlike Luke, is explicit about the meaning of the sign. It refers to the resurrection of Jesus, which is as certain a sign to Matthew's contemporaries as was Jonah to the people of Nineveh (Matt. 12:41//Luke 11:30). People have little excuse for their unbelief in Matthew's view. Matthew repeats the story, though in abbreviated fashion in 16.1ff.[25]

Matthew 22:41-46 is a story about the question concerning David's son. In Matthew, as in the parallels, Jesus poses this question about the sonship of the Christ (cf. Mark 12:35//Luke 20:41). In Matthew this question is asked of the Pharisees, who are unable to answer. In Mark and Luke—but not in Matthew—the question is posed in the context of Jesus' teaching in the temple. This passage serves as

---

[23] The term "conflict story" is all the more appropriate for Matthew where the conflict and competition with the Jewish leadership are so keenly portrayed.

[24] A. Hultgren, *Jesus and His Adversaries: The Form and Function of the Conflict Stories in the Synoptic Tradition* (Minneapolis: Augsburg, 1979) 187.

[25] Matthew's repetition or "doubling" of stories is a literary device of his; see, e.g., 17:24ff.; 22:17ff.; 16:19; 18:18.

another occasion to show Jesus' superiority over the Pharisees, particularly where the Pharisees' grasp of Scripture is concerned. This passage in fact follows on the heels of another display of Jesus' understanding of Scripture in contrast to that of the Pharisees. The third conflict story added by Matthew is 22:34-42, the love command, which is discussed below.

Matthew also has a tendency in his conflict stories to depict the Pharisees as the opponents of Jesus. While this tension is present in the tradition which he has inherited (cf. Mark 2:16; 3:16), Matthew has expanded on it considerably. Matthew often has the Pharisees in place of Luke's more general "crowd" (*ochloi*) (Luke 3:7; 11:14, 29; Matt. 3:7; 12:38). R. Hummel observes that on at least six occasions outside of chap. 23, Matthew has specified the Pharisees as the opponents of Jesus.[26] The central tension in the Matthean conflict stories—one that is pointedly emphasized—is the contrast of Jesus' interpretation with that of the Pharisees. We now turn to a closer look at three of these conflict stories, inquiring particularly into what these stories reveal about the Matthean community's view and interpretation of the law.

Matt. 12:1-8. Matthew took over this story from Mark, as did Luke. This is a controversy between Jesus and his disciples over against the Pharisees. Matthew, in contrast to Mark and Luke, explains that the disciples were hungry and for this reason plucked grain while passing through the field and began to eat, though it was the Sabbath. Luke and Mark offer no explanation for the disciples' actions. Matthew adds the point about the disciples' hunger to make a clearer and more cogent connection between the actions of the disciples and that of David in the temple, which is the analogy used by all three evangelists. Both the disciples in Matthew and David in the temple were hungry and therefore ate on the Sabbath. Matthew reiterates the point by describing the actions of the priests on the Sabbath who "profane the Sabbath," yet are "guiltless."[27]

Following the claim that the priests who do work in the temple on the Sabbath are guiltless, Matthew adds a citation from Hosea which explains the scriptural foundation for Jesus' understanding and the

---

[26] R. Hummel, *Die Auseinandersetzung zwischen Kirche und Judentum im Matthäusevangelium*, Beiträge zur evangelischen Theologie 33 (Munich: Kaiser, 1963) 17.

[27] The priests were required to do some work on the Sabbath, thereby profaning it, but they remained "guiltless"; see Lev. 24:8; Num. 28:8. See A. H. McNeile, *The Gospel according to Matthew* (London: Macmillan, 1915) 169.

behavior of his followers. Prior to citing Hos. 6:6, Matthew records Jesus saying, "If you had known what this means . . . you would not have condemned the guiltless." Matthew stresses that the disciples of Jesus are guiltless and have not violated the law. The problem is that the Pharisees do not understand the law properly. This is made explicit by the application of Hos. 6:6 in this context by Matthew.

Jesus and his disciples do not break the law. They break with the Pharisees over interpretation of the law, but not with regard to its validity or importance.[28] The law and its application, in Matthew's view, are to be understood primarily in terms of Jesus' demand for compassion. It is this "core value" that guides the application of the Sabbath laws.[29] This is emphasized by Matthew in 12:9-14, which continues with the same theme. In this passage Jesus goes on to heal a man with a withered hand on the Sabbath. Verse 12 provides a summary for the whole section starting in 12:1. That is, it is lawful to do good on the Sabbath. Those people in the Matthean community who are being accused of breaking the Sabbath law are really not doing so. Their detractors fail to understand what the Lord really requires, as expressed in Hos. 6:6.

This passage from Hosea, "I desire compassion and not sacrifice," is important for Matthew. He is the only Gospel writer to cite this prophetic verse, and he does so twice. In 9:13 the passage is used in response to another accusation from the Pharisees. This time the legal issue at stake is Jesus' dining with tax gatherers and sinners. Hosea 6:6 is used to justify the actions of Jesus—and, we may assume, the followers of Jesus—in light of a particular application and understanding of the law.[30] Hosea 6:6 is directed against Matthew's opponents with respect to the law.[31] Matthew applies this verse in a manner that summarizes his community's view and interpretation of certain laws. More than once the Matthean community must have had to answer for what appeared to be a lax disposition toward the law.

For our purposes it is important to see the way in which Matthew has transformed his tradition in order to show that Jesus and his disciples do not break the law. What is at stake is the *interpretation* of

---

[28] See the discussion of 5:17-20 below.

[29] For the notion of the "core value" as a hermeneutical principle, see J. Neyrey, "The Idea of Purity in Mark's Gospel," *Semeia* 35 (1986) 91–128.

[30] *The Fathers according to Rabbi Nathan*, trans. J. Goldin (New Haven: Yale University Press, 1955) 34.

[31] R. Guelich, "Not to Annul the Law, Rather to Fulfill the Law and the Prophets" (Diss., Hamburg, 1967) 46.

the law. Here Matthew stands in contrast to Mark. In his version of the same Sabbath controversy, Mark makes no attempt to absolve Jesus or the disciples of any guilt. First, the priests in the temple are not "guiltless" (cf. Matt. 12:5); they broke the law (Mark 2:26). However, this is not a concern for Mark. These laws are no longer an issue for the faithful. Mark offers a rather sweeping summary statement which puts the issue to rest: "The Sabbath is made for man, not man for the Sabbath" (Mark 2:27). The disciples did break the law, but this law does not abide. Matthew strikes this Markan summary statement; this is far too radical a view of the law for him. His community still maintains the validity and application of the law for their life. E. Schweizer is right in saying that the Matthean community still practiced Sabbath observance.[32]

Matthew's treatment of this conflict story takes seriously the accusation made by the Pharisees. He offers an explanation of why his community's view of the Sabbath laws is consistent with the Law and the Prophets. Again Matthew attempts to make the case that the beliefs and behavior of his community are not erroneous or a radical break with Israel's laws and traditions. The followers of Jesus are "guiltless" (cf. Matt. 12:7). Matthew asserts that his community is lawful and, indeed, possesses the true interpretation of the law.

Matt. 15:1-20. Many of these same objectives and aims that were present in the Sabbath controversy in 12:1ff. can be seen in the dispute about purity and unwashed hands in 15:1-20. Matthew has taken this story over from Mark 7 and transformed it accordingly so as not to conflict with his view of the role and meaning of the law in his community. A story which Mark uses to set aside the laws and traditions of the Jewish leaders in his setting is applied by Matthew in a manner that articulates and defends the interpretation of these purity laws within his setting.

In this story Mark and Matthew both have Pharisees and some scribes coming to ask Jesus why his disciples break with the "tradition of the elders." The disciples eat with unwashed hands and therefore do not observe the appropriate laws of purity (Matt. 15:2; Mark 7:5). In both Mark and Matthew Jesus responds that the Pharisees and scribes have forsaken the commands of God for their traditions (Matt 15:3; Mark 7:8). Jesus sets the traditions which the Pharisees and scribes follow over against the commands of God. In following their tradition they have neglected the law of God. Both

---

[32] E. Schweizer, "Matthew's Church," in *The Interpretation of Matthew,* ed. G. Stanton (Philadelphia: Fortress Press, 1983) 129.

Matthew and Mark seem to agree that this is because the Pharisees and scribes have focused on external matters, failing to realize that it is really internal matters, issues relating to one's thoughts, attitudes, and desires which cause defilement (*koinoi*) in a person (Matt. 15:18; Mark 7:21).

Matthew, however, uses this occasion to develop the misguided nature of the Pharisees and their teaching further. The Pharisees (the scribes are not mentioned here) are blind guides and plants which God will uproot (Matt. 15:13-14). This has no parallel in either Mark or Luke. What is most striking about the Matthean treatment of this material is the manner in which he summarizes Jesus' argument. For Mark, since purity is an internal matter, relating to issues of the heart, one need not worry any longer about the rules of ritual purity.[33] Mark, therefore, in a sweeping fashion reminiscent of his view of the Sabbath law (2:27), declares that "all foods are clean." His community, in light of this particular understanding of Jesus' teaching about the Jewish law, is no longer bound by these "traditions." Even though the Markan version of this episode is probably more historically accurate and closest to the pre-70 situation and application of these traditions, Mark nevertheless seems to dismiss completely these concerns about ritual purity.[34]

Once again Mark's response to the accusations of the scribes and Pharisees is far too extreme for Matthew. Matthew has deleted the Markan summary statement, "therefore, all foods are clean" (Mark 7:19). The culmination of the Matthean response is quite different. Matthew argues that, since defilement is a result of what is inside someone ("it is not what goes into the mouth that defiles, but what comes out of the mouth"), eating with unwashed hands does not defile. In 15:19 Matthew lists the things that defile a person, thereby making that person impure. But to eat with unwashed hands, as the disciples have just done, according to Matthew, does not violate the traditions, despite the claims of the Pharisees and scribes.

According to Matthew, Jesus and the disciples do not play fast and loose with the law or the Pharisaic *paradosis*. Matthew and his community are very sensitive to this charge. In this passage Matthew

---

[33] The Gospel of Mark liberates its audience from these legal concerns. "Die Einsicht in das menschlichen Herz als dem Quelle des Bösen sollte hellhörig machen für das Wort des Evangeliums, dass Befreiung verheisst" (J. Gnilka, *Das Evangelium nach Markus*, EKKNT [Zurich: Benziger, 1978] 1:289). For Matthew the human heart is a source of sin or lawlessness, but this does not do away with certain legal issues and requirements.

[34] See J. Neusner, "First Cleanse the Inside," *NTS* 22 (1975–76) 486–95.

responds to any accusation from the community's partners in debate that his community has set aside the law. Quite to the contrary, Matthew offers a subtle and reasoned explanation for the disciples of Jesus—and those in his community who behave in a similar fashion—asserting that they have neither broken this law nor violated the traditions. This is in stark contrast to Mark, who responds that the concern for purity in the manner in which the Pharisees raise it is no longer a concern of his community.[35]

Matt. 22:34-40. This brief encounter between Jesus and the Pharisees is significant for several reasons. First, as noted above, Matthew has made this pericope into a conflict story. In the parallel passages in Mark and Luke the person asking the question (a *grammateus* or scribe in Mark, and a *nomikos* or lawyer in Luke) comes off in a rather positive light and is praised by Jesus (Mark 12:34; Luke 10:28). In Matthew the Pharisees have gathered together and sent one of their own, a lawyer, to ask a question of Jesus to test him. The Pharisees' antagonistic response in 22:34ff. is clearly contrasted with the enthusiastic response of the crowd in the preceding verse.[36] The lawyer asks, "Teacher (*didaskalos*), which is the greatest commandment in the law?" (Matt. 22:36). That the question involves Jesus' interpretation of the law is clear in all accounts. However, the question goes beyond this in that it asks about the controlling feature or core value by which the rest of the law is understood. Matthew, in contrast to the other evangelists, is explicit about this. Jesus responds by citing the so-called love command, which is a combination of Deut. 6:5 and Lev. 19:18. Only Matthew then adds, "On these two commandments depend all the laws and the prophets" (Matt. 22:39). This Matthean addition emphasizes his belief that the law, while still valid, must be understood and applied in light of this, the greatest commandment.

Matthew has used this occasion of the encounter between Jesus and an apparently well-meaning lawyer or scribe, clearly well established within the Gospel tradition, to set up another confrontation with the Pharisees over the interpretation of the law. Matthew took this opportunity to lay out the distinctive interpretation and application of the law which his community practices. In this passage

---

[35] Contrary to McConnell, who maintains that the laws discussed in Matt. 15:1-20 are no longer binding for Matthew, thereby missing the subtle but important distinction between Mark and Matthew here (*Law and Prophecy*, 82).

[36] R. Gundry, *Matthew: A Commentary on His Literary and Theological Art* (Grand Rapids: Eerdmans, 1982) 447ff.

Matthew states quite clearly the hermeneutical principle that informs the Matthean community's understanding and use of the law. Gerhard Barth understands this passage as yet another attempt to make the principle of the "love command" stand out as the controlling force in the community's understanding of the law in contrast, Matthew believes, to that of the Pharisees.[37] This command to love is prominently placed in other parts of the Gospel (Matt. 5:43ff.; 7:12; 19:19; 24:12; 27:34ff.). The love command in Matthew, according to G. Bornkamm, emerges "as the canon for the Interpretation of the whole Torah."[38] "For Matthew it serves as a shortened formula for the Torah."[39] The Law and the Prophets depend (*krematai*) on this one command. This command to love is the community's "authoritative, interpretive priniciple."[40] This in no way dismisses the law for the community. It does mean, however, that one's understanding and application of the law are now shaped in light of the love command. In Matthew's view Jesus did not break the law. Instead, he offered a particular interpretation of it which the Matthean community practices and which Matthew is at obvious pains to show is superior to that of the Pharisees.

Matthew thus has significantly altered the material in the conflict stories he took over from the tradition. Matthew's redactional work aims at offering a response to, and a defense against, the accusations of the Jewish opponents in his setting who take issue with the Matthean view and use of the law. "The preponderance of the Matthean *Streitgespräche* seek to legitimate the *halacha* of the first Gospel over against the claims of Pharisaism."[41] In contrast, the Markan community reveals a clear attitude of freedom from the law. The Markan community is free from the Sabbath command (2:28) and rejects the traditions of the elders as "the traditions of men" (7:8). Mark seems to know little of the extended *halakah* and the legal disputes characteristic of the Matthean setting. Mark portrays Jesus as a powerful and innovative figure who overrules or dispenses with the traditions and laws of Israel. Jesus can repudiate these laws and traditions in favor of the presence of the kingdom as he has announced it.

---

[37] G. Barth, in *Tradition and Interpretation in Matthew,* by G. Bornkamm, G. Barth, and M. J. Held; trans. P. Scott (Philadelphia: Westminster, 1963) 76–78.

[38] G. Bornkamm, "Das Doppelgebot der Liebe," in *Neutestamentliche Studien für R. Bultmann* (Berlin: Walter de Gruyter, 1957) 93.

[39] H. Frankemölle, *Jahwebund,* 302–3.

[40] Hummell, *Die Auseinandersetzung,* 52.

[41] Ibid., 55.

This is not Jesus' view of the law as seen through the Matthean community. According to Matthew neither Jesus nor those who follow him are lawbreakers. In response to this charge Matthew, through his reshaping of the conflict stories, offers a reasoned argument aimed at demonstrating that the actions of his community are consonant with the Law and the Prophets. Those who would undo the law—and those who accuse the Matthean community of doing so—do not correctly understand and interpret the law. The conflict stories in Matthew's Gospel offer examples of that correct interpretation, which came to them through Jesus. This interpretation is repeatedly placed over against that of the Pharisees, whom Matthew regularly imports as Jesus' partners in debate. The Matthean understanding of the law, informed by love and compassion (5:44; 9:13; 12.7; 22:39), is depicted as the true interpretation.

Matthew is contending with and responding to claims from his Jewish opponents that his community fails to follow the law. Matthew has engaged his opponents, claiming that they, not the Matthean community, fail to understand the law. What has shaped the Matthean conflict stories is a struggle with a Jewish group that claims Matthew's community is not law-abiding. Matthew has used these stories to defend his community's view of the law and to assert the truth of their interpretation over that of his opponents.

Matthew 5:17-20

> Think not that I have come to abolish the law and the prophets; I have come not to abolish them but to fulfill them. For truly, I say to you, till heaven and earth pass away, not an iota, not a dot, will pass from the law until all is accomplished. Whoever then relaxes one of the least of these commandments and so teaches men so, shall be called least in the kingdom of heaven; but he who does them and teaches them shall be called great in the kingdom of heaven. For I tell you, unless your righteousness exceeds that of the scribes and the Pharisees, you will never enter the kingdom of heaven. (RSV)

This passage from the beginning of the Sermon on the Mount warrants particular attention because of the scrutiny it has received over the years from commentators. Many have claimed that this is the *crux interpretum* concerning Matthew's view of the law.[42] Although we cannot here provide an exhaustive review of the wide range of opinions that this pericope has provoked from scholars, this passage

---

[42] See the helpful discussion and review article by R. Guelich, "Interpreting the Sermon on the Mount," *Interpretation* 41 (1987) 117-30.

is unavoidable when assessing Matthew's view of the law and the application of the law within his community. We will inquire particularly about how these verses relate to Matthew's view of the law in general and what this understanding of the law would mean for the ethics and behavior of the Matthean community.

Interpretations of this passage from Matthew have often become lost in questions concerning the authenticity of certain verses and the editorial activity of Matthew. These studies have failed to take seriously the wider context of Matthew's Gospel and the illustrations of how the law is understood in other parts of Matthew.[43] (The conflict stories, discussed above, would be just such examples.) This is an unfortunate result of certain redaction-critical studies.[44] The isolation of this passage from the rest of the Gospel can lead to some contrived interpretations of 5:17-20. As E. Käsemann has said, "While this passage is the subject of lively controversy, it is essentially unambiguous, and commands obedience to the whole Torah."[45]

We would agree with Käsemann's assessment, albeit in a qualified manner. Matthew does maintain the enduring validity of the law. And, as we saw above, Matthew believes that both Jesus and his community, which enacts the teaching of Jesus, are followers and fulfillers of the law. They do not break the law, but understand it and fulfill it completely (Matt. 5:19, 48). What is essential is that the fulfilling of the law is determined by one's interpretation of the law. It is entirely possible to be zealous concerning the keeping of the law and still be lawless (*anomos*) (Matt. 23:28). The correct understanding of the law provides for its fulfillment. The conflict stories illustrated the correct understanding and application of the law as far as Matthew is concerned. These stories provide some concrete examples of how the legal debate was carried on in the Matthean setting. These stories also made explicit the principles upon which Matthew's understanding of the law is founded.

This distinction between violating the law and fulfilling it through a different interpretation is an important one. Matthew 5:17-20 introduces the so-called antitheses, which occupy the rest of chap. 5. In these antitheses Jesus could be viewed as doing away with certain laws, even setting himself over the law with his own *lex nova*.

---

[43] For example, R. Banks, *Jesus and the Law in the Synoptic Tradition*, SNTSMS 28 (Cambridge: Cambridge University Press, 1975) 203–26.

[44] As observed by G. Stanton in "The Origin and Purpose of Matthew's Gospel: Matthean Scholarship from 1945-1980," in *ANRW* II.25.3, 1895.

[45] E. Käsemann, "The Beginnings of Christian Theology," in *New Testament Questions of Today* (Philadelphia: Fortress Press, 1969) 85.

However, 5:17-20 warns against this conclusion. "Do not think," begins v. 17, "that I have come to annul the law and the prophets. I have come rather to fulfill them." In the teaching of Jesus that follows, no part of the law, however small, will be done away with.[46] If Matthew were not struggling to maintain this distinction between violating the law and fulfilling it through the proper and true interpretation, he would not have included this section 5:17-20 at all. The entire pericope betrays his hand and distinctive vocabulary;[47] it provides a prolepsis of the Matthean view of the law. The tension that develops throughout the Gospel over the Matthean understanding of the law and the conflict with the Pharisees over that interpretation are summarized in these verses.[48] Jesus and his followers do not break the law; they fulfill it. Their application of the law surpasses that of the scribes and Pharisees, who represent the opponents and who charge the Matthean community with destroying (*katalysai*) the law.

The beginning of v. 17 ("Do not think") as U. Luz observes, indicates that a perception exists that the Matthean community does not follow the law.[49] Matthew responds to this accusation. The fact that the scribes and Pharisees are once again identified as the contending party suggests that they represent the accusers, namely, the Jewish leadership in Matthew's setting.[50] Matthew's understanding of the law is closer to that of his Jewish antagonists than is Mark's, for example. This, however, is what is provoking the conflict.[51] The proximity (both geographically and ideologically) has caused this tension and struggle between the Matthean community and the Jewish leadership. The fact that both of these parties assert their

---

[46] The phrase "until all is fulfilled" refers not to the arrival of Jesus, but rather to an eschatological event in the future. It is at this time when the righteous will be separated from the *anomia* on the basis of "what they have done" (Matt. 25:45).

[47] Contrary to H. D. Betz's unusual claim that Matthew 5–7 is entirely pre-Matthean. The phrase "the law and the prophets," *plērōma*, and the concern about outdoing the scribes and the Pharisees are all Matthean additions and preoccupations (H. D. Betz, *Essays on the Sermon on the Mount* [Philadelphia: Fortress Press, 1985] 90; see also C. Carlston, "Betz on the Sermon on the Mount: A Critique" *CBQ* 50 [1988] 47–57).

[48] E. Schweizer claims that 5:17-20 is explicated in what follows (*Matthäus und seine Gemeinde*, SBS 71 [Stuttgart: Katholisches Bibelwerk, 1974] 84).

[49] Luz, *Matthäus*, 232.

[50] See U. Luz, "Die Erfüllung des Gesetzes bei Matthäus (5.17-20)," *ZTK* 75–76 (1978–79) 404, 412.

[51] See L. Coser, *The Functions of Social Conflict* (New York: Free Press, 1956) 82; see also J. Gager, *Kingdom and Community: The Social World of Early Christianity* (Englewood Cliffs, N.J.: Prentice-Hall, 1973) 80ff.

adherence to the law and accuse the other of failing to follow it has set the stage for struggle and conflict.

The Jewish leadership is alluded to in 5:19a with the reference to the authoritative role of teaching. Those who teach (*didaxē*) others to do away with the law are least in the kingdom. For Matthew teaching the law is bound up with "doing" it (5:19). On other occasions Matthew claims that this is a distinction between his community and the Jewish leadership (see 23:3, 23). Matthew's community understands, teaches, and does the law. This is the *fulfillment* of the law and the righteousness which surpasses that of the Matthean antagonists. If you not only teach the law but *do* it, applying the dominant principles of love and compassion, you have fulfilled the law and properly enacted the will of God in heaven (7:12; 12:50; 21:31). Love and mutuality, as seen in the antitheses, guide the interpretation of the valid and enduring law.[52]

Law in the Matthean Community

The Jewish law emerged as an important and essential issue in the struggle between the Matthean community and the opposition. This alone should tell us much about the setting and provenance of the Gospel, as well as the identity of the Matthean opponents. Both parties maintained a high view of the law. The law itself was in no way optional. Both groups laid claim to the law and accused the other of distorting it. The law served as the means both of discrediting one's opponent and of vindicating one's position.

Matthew took his stand in the midst of the laws and traditions of Israel and defended the beliefs and actions of his community. Indeed, according to Matthew, the beliefs and actions of his community constitute the fulfillment of Israel's traditions and promises, as Matthew asserts in the fulfillment citations. Further, and contrary to the claims of the Matthean opponents, Matthew's community accurately lives out the law. They are not lawbreakers who destroy the law; instead, they fulfill the law of Israel through their distinctive interpretation and application of it. The conflict stories provide concrete illustrations of the application of the Matthean interpretation of the law. These stories, reworked by Matthew, claim that Jesus and his followers do not break the law. Matthew provides an elaborate defense of his community's view of the law in these stories. Matthew

---

[52] Schweizer, *Matthäus*, 84: "Für Matthäus gibt es aber keine rechte Lehre ohne des entsprechende Tun." This is the law guided by love, the golden rule (Matt. 7:12). Schweizer asserts that this is what guides Matthew's hermeneutic.

5:17-20 can be read as a sort of programmatic statement about the community's view of the law. This passage responds to charges leveled against the community.[53] This view of the law and its interpretation is explicated in the antitheses that follow 5:17-20.

As in formative Judaism, the Matthean community was developing a means by which the law was to be interpreted and applied. As Frankemölle has noted, this developing orthodox interpretation in Matthew is closely related to orthopraxis: a true understanding of the law involves *doing* the law.[54] Action accompanies one's understanding and interpretation. This, Matthew suggests, is the fulfillment of all righteousness. The enacting of the law is informed by the values of love and compassion. The conflict stories and the examples concerning the law in chap. 5 are intended to illustrate this point.

In contrast to the Markan community, the law still did function within the Matthean setting, where the Gospel tradition was modified and shaped by Matthew to explain and teach the community's view and use of the law. Matthew also used these reworked traditions to defend his community against accusations that they did not understand or adhere to the law. In the face of this challenge from the developing Jewish leadership in his setting, Matthew articulated his community's distinctive understanding of the law, which was designed to defend and instruct the community as well as to respond to—and perhaps challenge—their opponents.

Ordering the Life of the Community

As the Matthean community continued to feel pressure and competition from the developing, dominant Jewish body and increasingly felt themselves separated from that Jewish group, they responded by developing their own rules, values, and norms by which their community could be guided. The development of social, community values and ethics also provided guidance and meaning for the individual. The values which the community established as a result of its own developing self-definition instructed the individual members concerning their own "role expectancy."[55] As the Matthean community

---

[53] Luz, "Erfüllung," 426.

[54] Frankemölle, *Jahwebund*, 279.

[55] "Role expectancy" is discussed by B. Holmberg, *Paul and Power: The Structure of Authority in the Primitive Church as Reflected in the Pauline Epistles* (Philadelphia: Fortress Press, 1978) 168–69. Holmberg acknowledges his debt to P. L. Berger and T. Luckmann, *The Social Construction of Reality* (Garden City, N.Y.: Doubleday, 1967) 53–57.

increasingly became isolated from the group that was emerging as dominant in their setting, the need for the community to provide its own structures and procedures emerged. The Matthean community responded to the conflict and antagonism that characterized its relationship with its world, and particularly the dominant body in that world, by constructing its own society, however small that society may have been. Such an undertaking, which no doubt would have been a gradual process over a protracted period, would require guidelines for behavior, means by which deviance could be handled, and an articulation of the stance of the members toward those outside the Matthean community.

These values and norms, which are an essential part of the process of social development and community definition, arise out of a need for the community to explain and defend itself to members or opponents. This would have been required of the Matthean community if it was to survive as a community or movement distinct and separate from formative Judaism. The values and self-identity of the community and its members became essential for them to withstand the pressure and conflict with the opponents. In the ongoing life of the community, however, these values tend also to serve the purpose of legitimation. These values and norms, as they are expressed and repeated, begin to effect a consensus.[56] That is to say, the values and behavior espoused by the community quickly develop into accepted parts of the community's life and world. These values become part of the community members' generalized understanding of who they are and how they are to live. This process is essential for the development of the community, and it is essential if the community is to survive from generation to generation.[57] We will discuss this process within Matthew's Gospel in terms of "the ordering of the Matthean community," specifically Matthew's instruction to his community concerning communal life, the behavior of its members, the disciplining of errant members, and the community's response to those outside the community and in the civil realm.

Righteousness in Matthew

If one were to focus simply on the number of times the term "righteousness" (*dikaiosynē*) appears in Matthew's Gospel, one might

---

[56] See N. Luhmann, "Institutionalisierung: Function und Mechanismus in socialen System der Gesellschaft," in *Zur Theorie der Institution*, ed. H. Schelsky (Düsseldorf: E. Diederich, 1970) 30; P. L. Berger, *The Sacred Canopy: Elements of a Sociological Theory of Religion* (Garden City, N.Y.: Doubleday, 1969) 29.

[57] Berger, *Sacred Canopy*, 30–31.

conclude that this is not a very important notion for Matthew. The term "righteousness" appears seven times in Matthew, though the corresponding adjective "righteous" (*dikaios*) occurs seventeen times.[58] These statistics, however, can be misleading. "Righteousness" emerges as the all-embracing notion for the actions, behavior, and disposition of the disciples and followers of Jesus[59] and therefore of the members of the Matthean community.[60]

The thought that Matthew intends to express the demands placed upon the community members and the actions expected of them through his use of *dikaiosynē* has not been universally accepted by scholars. Some have sought to see the term righteousness as referring to a gift from God and not necessarily the behavior and response expected of a disciple. Such approaches, however, may project the apostle Paul and his distinctive notion of *dikaiosynē tou theou* onto Matthew.[61] J. Reumann is correct in warning against "Paulinizing" Matthew.[62] Matthew was interested in forming and reforming the behavior, beliefs, and attitude of his community.[63] Matthew stresses the behavior and actions (*praxis*) expected of his community throughout his Gospel. This can be seen, for example, in his redaction of Mark 8:38. Here Matthew, apart from Mark and Luke, has stressed the actions (*praxis*) of a person in his version of this Markan passage reported in Matt. 16:27. In this passage Matthew has emphasized that the actions of a person have a direct bearing on the response of the Son of man when he judges people in his glory. The versions appearing in Mark and Luke lack this emphasis. Similarly, when the angels in Matt. 13:49 separate the righteous from the wicked at the judgment the criterion is conduct that corresponds to the will of God.[64] Matthew's treatment of the judgment presupposes the possession of *dikaiosynē* for entry into the kingdom.[65] In Matthew the

---

[58] *Dikaiosynē* occurs in 3:15; 5:6, 10, 20; 6:1, 33; 21:32.

[59] Bornkamm, in *Tradition and Interpretation*, 30.

[60] Strecker, *Weg*, 153.

[61] Such an attempt can perhaps be seen in G. Künzel, *Studien zum Gemeinde-verständnis des Matthäus-Evangeliums* (Stuttgart: Calwer, 1978) 70ff.

[62] J. Reumann, *Righteousness in the New Testament* (Philadelphia: Fortress Press, 1982) 135.

[63] W. Meeks, *The Moral World of the First Christians* (Philadelphia: Westminster, 1987) 136.

[64] See Bornkamm in *Tradition and Interpretation*, 31.

[65] See W. Trilling, *Das Wahre Israel: Studien zur Theologie des Matthäus-Evangeliums* (Munich: Kösel, 1964) 184. See also Matt. 25:31ff. and the description of the final judgment. The import of one's actions is emphasized there.

kingdom may perhaps be described accurately as a gift from God.[66] However, righteousness (*dikaiosynē*) emerges in the Gospel as the demand placed upon humans and the response expected from members of the Matthean community.[67]

Nowhere do the behavior and the response of the members of the Matthean community receive more attention and emphasis than in the Sermon on the Mount. There Matthew stresses "behavioral tests" for false prophets within the community (7:15-23). The distinctive Matthean notion of "knowing someone by their fruits" is one way Matthew repeatedly emphasizes certain behavior and action for the true follower of Jesus.[68] The parable of the wise and foolish builder also stresses the connection between hearing and *doing* (7:24ff.). The close connection in Matt. 5:19 between teaching and *doing*, in order to be "great in the kingdom of heaven" has already been noted. When Matthew speaks of righteousness within the Sermon on the Mount he is referring to the behavior and actions expected of those within the community.

Righteousness in the Sermon is a goal for the members of the community to pursue. Those who will be satisfied are those who hunger and thirst after righteousness (Matt. 5:6). Here righteousness refers to the desire and effort of the members to live in a manner to which Matthew feels they were called. Matthew 5:10 seems to refer to those members who have been persecuted in some way for their obedience to the demands of the life of righteousness. Righteousness is a goal the members should aim at obtaining in their actions and attitudes. A similar sentiment concerning righteousness is seen in 5:20 and 6:33. Righteousness refers both to actions and to attitudes on the part of the members which surpass those of the scribes and Pharisees (5:20) or the Gentiles (6:32). Matthew explicitly speaks of "doing righteousness" in 6:1, highlighting the *praxis* which is bound up with the term *dikaiosynē*. The members of the Matthean community are not already righteous, but rather are called to aim at a better righteousness in their actions and attitudes.[69]

Dikaiosynē is significant for our purposes in that it serves a distinguishing function for the Matthean community. Matthew has chosen "righteousness" as a key term for designating the proper behavior

---

[66] Reumann, *Righteousness*, 135.

[67] B. Przybylski, *Righteousness in Matthew and His World of Thought* (Cambridge: Cambridge University Press, 1980) 113–14.

[68] See Meeks, *Moral World*, 136.

[69] See Bornkamm, in *Tradition and Interpretation*, 30.

and disposition of the members of his community, in contrast to those with whom the community contends. This is one important way Matthew has attempted to assert the identity and distinctiveness of his community and its life in a hostile setting.[70] Righteousness in the Gospel of Matthew is, as Bornkamm observed, an all-embracing symbol that denotes the actions and attitudes required of the community members.[71] Viewed in this way, the notion of righteousness plays a powerful and important role in ordering the community and instructing the members concerning the proper conduct and behavior expected from them. "Righteousness designates the standard of behavior for the community and the kingdom."[72] The actions and attitudes Matthew has in mind for the members of the community when he speaks of *dikaiosyne* are developed further in the Sermon on the Mount, and we will discuss this below. Here it is important to see that Matthew seized upon the notion of righteousness and developed it into a word that represented the conduct and disposition expected from the members of the community. To be part of the Matthean community and the kingdom of heaven, a certain conduct and attitude were expected. It was to surpass the Gentiles and the scribes and Pharisees. The members were to make this behavior their goal. They were to strive for this righteousness, which distinguished them from the world and helped to order their internal life.

Community Life in Matthew 5-7

The specific content of the behavior and attitude expected from the community member, represented and summarized as we said above in the term *dikaiosyne*, is spelled out in more concrete fashion in the Sermon on the Mount (Matthew 5-7). W. Meeks's comment that Matthew's Gospel constitutes "community-forming literature" is an insightful one.[73] Nowhere is the community-forming activity within Matthew more evident than in chaps. 5-7. This section of the Gospel has as its primary focus the ordering of relationships and behavior within the community. The personal traits and characteristics of the members are made explicit. There is significant material in this portion of the Gospel which is devoted to the subject of maintaining

---

[70] See J. Riches, *Jesus and the Transformation of Judaism* (London: Darton, Longman & Todd, 1980) 113

[71] See n. 59 above.

[72] See Frankemölle, *Jahwebund*, 75.

[73] Meeks, *Moral World*, 136ff.

relationships and resolving disputes within the community. Matthew 5-7 amounts to something like a constitution for the community, which instructs and guides the members.

Matthew's community has been accurately described as a "brother-hood."[74] Matthew alone among the Synoptic Gospels employs the term "brother" (*adelphos*) extensively in a metaphorical sense to denote a fellow member of the community (see 5:22, 23, 24, 47; 7:3, 4, 5; 18:15, 21).[75] While the crowd is mentioned at the start of the Sermon (5:1), it is the disciples who join Jesus on the mountain for the extended teaching. That chaps. 5-7 is instruction intended for the community is evidenced by the high concentration of the term "brother" in this section. If Matthew attempted to portray the Sermon as an event in the public ministry of Jesus he betrayed his true intention through his use of this special Matthean term. The Sermon is intended to instruct the Matthean community on how they are to act, treat one another, and order their internal affairs. The presence of the teaching on prayer and piety, the liturgical form of the prayer in 6:9ff., as well as the warning about false prophets within the group in 7:13-16 all make clear the purpose of the Sermon as a means of communal instruction and guidance.

The opening beatitudes (5:3-12) describe in ideal terms the traits and characteristics of the members of the community. The members are to be humble and intent on pursuing acts of mercy. They should make righteousness their goal. These members are pure in heart and people eager to "make peace" (*eirēnopoioi*; cf. 5:9). Like the prophets of ancient Israel, the Matthean community will be persecuted for their commitment to righteousness and the will of God. This, however, they are told, is cause for joy, because of the great reward which is theirs in heaven. Verses 13-16, which describe the community as salt and light for the world, teach that the members and their behavior play an important role in the mission of the community. The good work (v. 16) which the members engage in is noticed by the world—or at least should be (vv. 15-16)—and this results in the observers' giving glory to God.

In light of our overall view of the Sermon as a document that instructs and orders the life of the community, Matt. 5:21ff. is best understood in terms of specific examples of just how that life within

---

[74] J. Gnilka, "Matthäusgemeinde und Qumran," *BZ* 7 (1963) 51; Trilling, *Das Wahre,* 212.

[75] Mark and Luke use "brother" in a literal sense, except for Mark 3:34 and Luke 6:42; 8:21.

the community is to be different from the world around them. These verses are distinctive Matthean material and find only occasional parallels with the other evangelists. Here Matthew provides concrete examples of how this ethic of righteousness is to be executed. Matthew 5:21-22 deals with the subject of anger "toward a brother" and states that such anger constitutes a violation of the law. Related to this, vv. 23-24 provide advice about reconciliation in the event that a schism does erupt between members or factions within the community. That 5:21-24 should comprise part of the Sermon at all suggests that these problems were not simply hypothetical, but rather were concrete issues within the life of the Matthean community. Verses 25-26 also deal with the theme of reconciliation, but not necessarily between two contending members, or *adelphoi*. These verses may also apply to reconciliation between a community member and someone outside the community who wishes to initiate legal proceedings against the member. In vv. 25-26 the aim of this reconciliation is to avoid being brought into court, which is not an institution that has served the Matthean community well (see 5:26).

Matthew 5:27-30 deals with the subjects of lust and adultery. Like the first antithesis in 5:21, v. 27 begins with a legal citation obviously familiar ("you have heard") to Matthew's audience. The discussion, however, centers on the disposition of one's heart, not the actual act of adultery. The focus on the attitudes of those in the community is significant because it stresses the conduct and spirit of the relationships within the community.[76] The *disposition* of the members toward one another was as much a concern for Matthew as their actions. In 5:33-38 Matthew discusses oaths and vows which have no place in the community (5:34); 5:39-42 also takes up the theme of forgiveness and reconciliation; 5:43-48 emphasizes the need for love, particularly for those who would not seem to deserve it. The love of which Matthew speaks is intended also for those whom the members might hold to be enemies or outsiders, and not just fellow members of the community.

This instruction from chap. 5 is clearly ideal in its content and tone. After all, as we will see shortly, Matthew's own treatment of both enemies and outsiders did not at every point measure up to the standard expressed in 5:21ff. The strident attacks on the Pharisees and the sectarian attitude which presupposes membership in the (Matthean) community as a prerequisite for membership among the called (*eklektoi*) and the true people of God (21:43) do conflict with

[76] Gundry, *Matthew*, 194.

the substance of 5:21ff. The community is, as noted above, "called forth" to a greater righteousness. The community possessed goals about their life and relationships. There were no doubt many times those goals were unfulfilled, as one can easily infer from the content of the Gospel itself. Nevertheless, Matthew does mean throughout chaps. 5–7 to instruct the members about the behavior and attitudes which now should characterize relationships within the community. As Meeks has asserted, Matthew is interested in shaping the behavior, beliefs, and attitudes of his community. Matthew 5–7 aims above all at doing just that.

The same can be said about the function of 6:19-34. These verses also encourage a certain order and set of values for the community and its members. These verses constitute teaching about possessions within the community. They attempt to draw the focus of the audience away from possessions and things and toward trusting in God and the life of righteousness the community is called to pursue. Again, this is suggestive about the social location of the community. This heightened concern about possessions has led some to see a wealthier community behind the Gospel of Matthew.[77] Within the Matthean community were some who could afford to trust in possessions and "treasures on earth." Righteousness and the pursuit of righteousness are lifted up as the goal of the members of the Matthean community (6:33). This alone should be their focus.

Matthew 7:1-5 warns against judging and accusing other members (*adelphoi*; see 7:3, 4, 5). Avoiding or resolving conflict within the community emerges as a pronounced theme of the Sermon. The members of the Matthean community are "peacemakers" (5:9). They are not to insult each other (5:22) but are to be reconciled to one another (5:24). They are to offer the left cheek to those who slap them

---

[77] The suggestion that Matthew represents a wealthier community has been made by G. D. Kilpatrick (*The Origins of the Gospel according to St. Matthew* [Oxford: Clarendon, 1946] 124–25), followed by J. D. Kingsbury ("The Verb *Akolouthein* as an Index of Matthew's View of His Community," *JBL* 97 [1978] 67ff.), *contra* Schweizer (*Matthäus*, 13, 17–19, 42–60, 138–40). Schweizer seems to follow G. Theissen in viewing the Matthean community as itinerant, wandering charismatics (see Theissen, "Wanderradikalismus: Literatursoziologische Aspekte der Überlieferung von Worten Jesu im Urchristentum," *ZTK* 70 [1973] 248–51). There are inherent problems with this reconstruction in light of the social and cultural setting of first-century Galilee; see J. A. Overman, "Who Were the First Urban Christians? Urbanization in Galilee in the First Century," in *Society of Biblical Literature 1988 Seminar Papers*, ed. David J. Lull (Atlanta: Scholars Press, 1988) 160–68. Lower Galilee, the sphere of the Jesus movement, cannot be characterized as a number of isolated rural villages.

on the right (5:39), and are to love friends and enemies alike (5:43-44). All of this suggests a situation of tension and struggle within the community. It is clear that the Matthean community struggles with an opponent in the form of the Jewish leadership. However, the elaborate concern and concentration within the Sermon (as well as in chap. 18) with dissension and conflict suggest tension within the Matthean community as well.

This tension within the Matthean community cannot, however, be attributed to the presence of a specific group which Matthew refers to as those who are "lawless" (*anomos*).[78] The term *anomia* belongs to the realm of highly charged sectarian language typical of Matthew's time and setting, as noted above.[79] This is not distinctive Matthean language; the term is common in the literature from the groups who feel pressure from the dominant, or "parent," group in their setting. The accusatory rhetoric and highly charged language on the part of the sectarian group were ways in which the party in power could be discredited and the sectarian group vindicated. In fact, it was typical in this period within Judaism to juxtapose "righteous" and "lawless." These are two *Stichwörte* which help us to recognize that we are reading sectarian literature. Matthew has adopted and employed "the language of sectarianism" well known within the literature of his time and place. Matthew shares with other sectarian groups of the late first century a strong disdain for the dominant Jewish leadership, and he expresses this through the application of this stock and highly charged language. Both "righteous" and "lawless" are terms that figure largely in the sectarian literature from this period. Matthew's hostility toward and alienation from the dominant Jewish group have stimulated the regular use of these terms. The persecuted minority (Matt. 5:9-10) is the righteous, who will be vindicated, while the more dominant body is the lawless, who corrupt God's law and will (see Matt. 23:28).

Matthew applies the term *anomia* to anyone who deviates from the will of God or fails to produce "good fruit" (see 7:17; 12:33; 21:43). For this reason both the enthusiastic prophets of 7:15ff. and the scribes and Pharisees can be called *anomia* (7:23; 23:28).[80] These groups could not be more different in terms of makeup and practice;

---

[78] The most recent treatment of this is J. Davidson, "Anomia and the Question of an Antinomian Polemic in Matthew," *JBL* 104 (1985) 611–35.

[79] See chap. 1, under "The Language of Sectarianism."

[80] See the discussion in E. Schweizer, "Observance of the Law and Charismatic Activity in Matthew," *NTS* 16 (1969–70) 213–30.

however, they both receive the epithet "lawless" because of their corruption of the law and will of God. "Lawless" then does not refer to a specific group within the Matthean community which is creating tension; it is the preferred Matthean term for anyone who does not accurately understand God's law and will or corrupts it. This is a term—more importantly, a sentiment—Matthew shares with other sectarian groups in the late first century. Matthew's use of this term tells us much more about him and his community than it does about the people or group that is causing dissension.[81]

Thus Matthew 5–7 functioned to order and instruct the community in its behavior and relationships. This section is not primarily oriented toward the world, but rather is concerned with the community itself, the guiding and shaping of the community's life. Relationships within the community, resolving disputes, and the values and attitudes the members are to embrace represent the primary concerns of the Sermon. Chapters 5–7 constitute an example of what Hans Mol has called "sacralization," the process by which a community over time orders itself and brings stability to its beliefs and values. By the term "sacralization" Mol refers to the holy or larger-than-life dimension which these values and beliefs take on. Indeed they must take on this larger-than-life dimension if they are to endure and be adopted by subsequent members. This process is really the institutionalization of the pivotal values of the community, vesting the necessary authority and stature in them so as to ensure adherence to them and their perpetuation.[82]

The Sermon on the Mount, as it has been constructed by Matthew, does exactly this. Through the authoritative teaching of Jesus, the values and attitudes of the members are spelled out. The actions and ethics expected of the community are reiterated in chaps. 5–7 in a way that establishes them as accepted and essential priorities for the ordering of the ongoing life of the community. Here the actions and attitudes that are to control the life and relationships within the community begin to be reified. These initially abstract and constructed values and attitudes begin to be accepted by the community as

---

[81] We will discuss our hypothesis concerning the conflict within the Matthean community in the concluding chapter. Here it is enough to recognize the significance of Matthew's use of this term, and not that it is a *terminus technicus* for the Matthean opponents.

[82] H. Mol, *Identity and the Sacred* (Oxford: Basil Blackwell, 1976) 14, 266. Mol makes clear that this order and the values it possesses play a large role in establishing the identity of the community.

absolute.[83] This results in firmly establishing the values and beliefs and provides a ready-made set of priorities for ensuing members to "inhabit."[84] These values and the ordered life of the community must be regularly reiterated for purposes of reinforcing the actions and beliefs of the community against opposing (anomic) forces and for purposes of education and guidance.

Viewing the Sermon in this way, the developed liturgical form of the Lord's Prayer as it appears in Matt. 6:5-15 takes on significance. Most scholars concur that Matthew's form of the prayer is liturgical and was most likely used by the community in its worship or gatherings.[85] Matthew provides a far more extensive set of instructions concerning prayer than Luke (Matt. 6:5-8//Luke 11:1) or, in any case, Mark (Mark 11:25-26). Matthew's version of the prayer is much longer (Matt. 6:7-15//Luke 11:2b-4). Within the prayer is the distinctive Matthean concern to see God's will in heaven enacted "on earth as it is in heaven" (Matt. 6:10//Luke 11:2b). The prayer includes also petitions about debts, freedom from concern about daily needs, and forgiving others.

The import of the Lord's Prayer in terms of ordering the life of the community can be found in the way the prayer, reiterated and often repeated by the community, would reinforce the shared values and actions of the community. The prayer contains the values and priorities expressed elsewhere throughout the Gospel, particularly in chaps. 5–7. To include these values and priorities in the worship and petitions of the community is, to borrow Peter Berger's phrase, to invest the values and beliefs of the community with "cosmic significance."[86] In their prayers to God the members continually remind each other of the actions and attitudes which the members are to embrace and enact. The prayer reinforces the community concerning its life and relationships.

One could perhaps develop and discuss a variety of functions and aims for the Sermon on the Mount. The Sermon may have fulfilled several functions within the Matthean community itself. It is clear, however, that one function was the ordering and directing of the life of the community. In chaps. 5–7 Matthew has provided instruction about relationships, worship, and the priorities and values which are

---

[83] Concerning "reification," see Berger, *Sacred Canopy*, 37.

[84] Ibid., 30–31.

[85] First proposed by Kilpatrick, *Origins*, 72–100; see also the discussion by Luz, who refers to this as a "Gemeindeliturgie" (*Matthäus*, 334ff.).

[86] Berger, *Sacred Canopy*, 37.

to control the members. These values are portrayed with unusual authority (7:29). Understood to have its origin in Jesus, and having found a place in the community's worship, the content of chaps. 5–7 quickly took on a significance that was larger than life and doubtless played a powerful role in ordering the life of the Matthean community.

Community Discipline in Matthew 18

The order that is developing and being imposed on the life of the Matthean community is clearly reflected in chap. 18. The process and purpose of discipline in chap. 18 have to do with errant or stumbling members and with the community's response to this problem.[87] As W. Pesch has recognized, Matthew has altered the Lukan material in the parable in Matt. 18:10-14//Luke 3–7 so as to speak about members who have strayed (*Verirrte;* see Matt. 18:12), not lost sheep (*Verlorene*), as Luke portrays it (see Luke 15:4). Luke's arrangement of chap. 15 represents the proclamation of the Gospel to the lost. This parable in Luke serves the purpose of describing the ministry of Jesus and his followers to the "lost sheep" and has a decidedly missionary thrust. Matthew has allegorized this parable from Q to instruct the community about members who have strayed and are deviating from the community's norms.[88] Indeed, scholars concur that Matthew has shaped and constructed this traditional material in such a way as to provide instruction for his community about dealing with dissension and erring members.[89] "Matthew arranged and composed this section of the Gospel to help members confront the problem of internal dissension."[90] The whole of chap. 18 constitutes a redactional unity and aims at dealing with the problem of division within the community through stressing service to one's "brother," emphasizing forgiveness and, if all else fails, the institution of discipline and expulsion.[91]

---

[87] Trilling, *Das Wahre*, 113.

[88] W. Pesch, *Matthäus als Seelsorger* (Stuttgart: Katholisches Bibelwerk, 1966) 71ff.

[89] See most recently M. C. De Boer, "Ten Thousand Talents? Matthew's Interpretation and Redaction of the Parable of the Unforgiving Servant," *CBQ* 50 (1988) 214–32.

[90] W. G. Thompson, *Matthew's Advice to a Divided Community: Mt. 17.22−18.35,* AnBib 44 (Rome: Biblical Institute, 1970) 264ff.

[91] G. Forkman, *The Limits of Religious Community: Expulsion from the Religious Community within the Qumran Sect, within Rabbinic Judaism, and within Primitive Christianity* (Lund: Gleerup, 1972) 123.

Matthew's hand is evidenced throughout this chapter as seen
through the use of distinctive Matthean locutions like "my Father
who is in heaven" (18:10, 14), the "little ones" (*mikroi*) (18:6, 10, 14),
and "brother" (*adelphos*) (18:15, 21, 35).[92] Matthew begins this chapter
by adapting a tradition found also in Mark 9:33-37 and Luke 9:46-48,
concerning the question of who is the greatest. Matthew makes no
mention of the quarrel between disciples, which we find in Mark and
Luke. G. Forkman has pointed out that this no longer constitutes a
dramatic episode between two key players but rather emerges as a
fundamental question about life and relationships within the Matthean community.[93] Matthew equates true greatness with the humility of a child. Here, as in other places, Matthew aims at equality as
an ideal between members and attempts to discourage any sort of
hierarchy within the community.[94] In the life of the Matthean community the relationships between members are to be based on service
and deference toward one another. They are to apply the values and
traits equated with the kingdom of heaven in their own lives and
relationships.[95]

Matthew's treatment of Mark 9:43-47 in Matt. 18:8-9 is important in
terms of his attempt to order the life of the community. Both the
Markan and Matthean passages refer to the cutting of the hand or the
foot or plucking out the eye in order to avoid stumbling. Mark's treatment of this passage represents an admonition concerning the
general life of the disciple. Should anything encumber the disciple in
his or her attempt to follow Jesus, it should be cut out and done away
with so that the follower will remain "in life," and "enter life" (Mark
9:43). True disciples in Mark are to avoid influences that might
hinder them in following Jesus.

Matthew has used this passage to address the issue of the health
of the community. The part of the body which must be excised is the
one that corrupts the other members of the brotherhood. If there is
something in their midst that is causing the *mikroi* to stumble or be
led astray, it must be cut off for the sake of the community and its
sanctity. Matthew has transformed a passage that initially appears to
have been a word about the disciples loosing themselves from worldly

---

[92] See J. P. Meier, *The Vision of Matthew: Christ, Church, and Morality in the First
Gospel* (New York: Paulist, 1979) 134.

[93] Forkman, *Limits*, 119–20.

[94] Cf. 23:8-12. However, as we will see, the egalitarian spirit within the community is not being applied as thoroughly as Matthew would like.

[95] See Trilling, *Das Wahre*, 107.

encumbrances into a word of caution and protection for the community against corrupting influences and people.

Perhaps most significant for our purposes in chap. 18 is the process of discipline and expulsion that appears in 18:15-18. Matthew begins his instruction about the member who sins by first encouraging the other members to reprove this errant brother in private. At this point there is no need for other members of the community to be involved. Should this fail, Matthew cites the tradition of two witnesses (see Deut. 19:15; Lev. 19:7). This procedure can be seen also in varying forms in both the Qumran documents and in Josephus.[96] However, there is no such parallel in either Mark or Luke. Failing this, the church (*ekklēsia*) must be notified. If this person refuses to listen to the church, then "let him be to you as a Gentile and a tax gatherer" (18:17). These two terms, as in 5:46ff.; 6:7; or 9:10ff., clearly have a pejorative tone. Those who refuse to rectify their behavior and follow the advice of the witnesses or the community become outsiders.[97] The application of discipline is done in a communal setting. The entire *ekklēsia* enacts the punishment upon the sinning member.

An important point in understanding the development of the processes and modes of discipline in the Matthean community is the context in which Matthew has placed this important passage. Both W. G. Thompson and W. Pesch have noted the emphasis on forgiveness and reconciliation in chap. 18.[98] This is a pronounced and important part of this chapter and of Matthew's thinking about community order and discipline. The parable of the one lost sheep (18:12-13) and Peter's question about the number of times one should forgive one's brother (*adelphos*) frame the discussion about discipline and expulsion in chap. 18. The parable of the king, which concludes the chapter, reiterates this principle of forgiveness between members of the community (18:35).

Forgiveness is stressed in chap. 18. W. Trilling may be right that the disciplinary aspect of chap. 18 does not stand in the foreground.[99] Matthew may have included this disciplinary process reluctantly; but it is clearly there, and it constitutes an important element in the social

---

[96] See CD 9, in Vermes, *The Dead Sea Scrolls in English* (New York: Penguin, 1975) 111. See also 1QS 6; Josephus, *Life* 49 and *Ant.* 4.8.15 §219.

[97] Forkman, *Limits*, 124–25; 129–32.

[98] Thompson (*Matthew's Advice*) and Pesch (*Seelsorge*) both emphasize the focus on forgiveness in chap. 18.

[99] Trilling, *Das Wahre*, 123.

development of the Matthean community and in the ordering of its life.[100]

The process of excluding a member from the Matthean community concludes with these words: "Truly I say to you, whatever you bind on earth shall be bound in heaven, and whatever you loose on earth shall be loosed in heaven" (Matt. 18:18). In context of the expulsion of the erring member this seems to imply that the member is not only excluded from the community now but also finally excluded from salvation.[101] The actions and decisions of the community carry the force and authority of heaven. This notion is seen in a number of places in the Gospel (see 5:48; 6:10; 12:32; 16:19). The Matthean community understands itself as embodying and living out the order, structure, and values of the kingdom which is in heaven. In their power to bind and to loose, the Matthean community represents "a mimetic reiteration" of the power and authority of the kingdom of heaven. Their actions and decisions here below are binding in heaven. In sociological terms the social nomos and the universal cosmos appear as coextensive.[102] Here it is asserted that the Matthean community acts with, and indeed represents, the authority of heaven.

Here we wish to inquire about the meaning of the terms "bind" and "loose." Some maintain that these terms refer to the authority to forgive sins or the authority to teach.[103] These pregnant terms most likely imply both of these activities and more. It is noteworthy, however, that Matthew clearly refers to the authority to forgive sins in other places in his Gospel, and with other words (see 6:9; 9:8; 18:35). Similarly, the authority to teach is expressed more directly by Matthew (5:19; 28:20). It seems reasonable to assume that these terms imply more than the authority to teach or forgive sins, which Matthew has emphasized in others ways and in other places in his Gospel.

H. Strack and P. Billerbeck observed that the authority to bind and loose in Matthew has numerous parallels in rabbinic Judaism.[104] The

---

[100] This issue reflects a concrete situation of some urgency in the community. "Something had to be done"; see Thompson, *Matthew's Advice*, 264–66.

[101] G. Bornkamm, "The Authority to Bind and Loose in the Church in Matthew's Gospel," in *Jesus and Man's Hope* (Pittsburgh: Perspectives, 1970). We will discuss the parallel passage in 16:19 under the portrait of the disciples.

[102] See Berger, *Sacred Canopy*, 34–39.

[103] Bornkamm, "Bind and Loose," 90; see also Schweizer, *Matthäus*, 155.

[104] H. L. Strack and P. Billerbeck, *Kommentar zum Neuen Testament aus Talmud und Midrash* (6 vols.; Munich: Beck, 1922–61) 1:732–38.

that Matthew would choose a function—and even the precise terms for a function—within his community which at the same time represents a position and role within emerging rabbinic Judaism supports the view that Matthew's development was provoked by, and was a response to, formative Judaism. However, because the rabbinic texts which Strack and Billerbeck cited are later than the first century, their use in the reconstruction of the social developments and tensions within the Matthean setting is problematic. One need not rely on these later texts for insight into the meaning and freight which these terms carried within first-century Palestine.

In describing the transition of power from Alexander Jannaeus to his wife, Alexandra, Josephus mentions the power and influence of the Pharisees and the need for Alexandra to court their favor if she is going to rule successfully. Josephus writes that "they [the Pharisees] became at length the real administrators of the estate, at liberty to banish and recall, to loose and to bind whomever they would. In short, the enjoyments of royal authority were theirs" (*J.W.* 1.5.1-3 §111-16). We have alluded to this passage above in the context of the political role of the Pharisees as "retainers" within Palestinian society.[105]

This story from Josephus most likely involves both some accurate historical reflection and a projection of the Pharisees' present status backward onto the story of Alexandra's ascension to power, some 150 years prior to the writing of Matthew's Gospel.[106] It is striking that Josephus, writing around the time of the composition of Matthew's Gospel, here employs the same terms as Matthew in 16:19 and 18:19. The words "to bind" (*deō*) and "to loose" (*lyō*) are used by both Josephus and Matthew. Josephus uses these terms to describe the authority of the Pharisees, while Matthew uses these terms to describe the authority of the community (18:19) as well as Peter and the disciples (16:19).

The parallel passage to *J.W.* 1.5.1-3 §111ff. appears in *Ant.* 13.16.2 §407-11. This may help to explicate the authority Josephus has in mind concerning the Pharisees. In this passage Josephus writes, "The Pharisees had the power. For example, they recalled exiles, and freed prisoners, and, in a word, in no way differed from absolute

---

[105] See the discussion of the Pharisees in chap. 1 under "Fragmentation and Factionalism."

[106] S. Cohen has discussed extensively the tendentious nature of the Josephus corpus in *Josephus in Galilee and Rome: His Vita and Development as a Historian* (Leiden: E. J. Brill, 1979).

rulers." Here the power to banish and to recall, to bind and to loose, described in *War* 1, is described as a legal authority which the Pharisees, due to their position, possessed.

According to Josephus, the Pharisees had the power to make a crime and its punishment stick, or they could waive it. They could imprison or free people. They could grant amnesty to those who had been banished or exiled. The political and legal force of these terms distinctly emerges from the Josephus passages. We have here a clear example from Palestine at the close of the first century of the content of these two terms. Binding and loosing refer to the political and juridical power to punish or excuse, to imprison or set free. It is this power, analogous to that of the Pharisees, that Matthew bestows both on his community and on Peter and the disciples. Authority depicted in this way within the Matthean community would appear as a challenge to those existing structures and authorities outside of the community, and would create inevitable conflict.

The development of modes of communal discipline and the claiming of the power to bind and to loose are significant developments in Matthew's community. The community has drawn back from the existing civil structures and replaced them with its own. "In 18.15-17 the church appears as an organized society with prescribed modes of discipline."[107] The development of modes of community discipline is important for two reasons. First, such means stabilize the community and control deviance. Second, they constitute both a challenge and a substitute for those processes already established in the civil realm outside of the community. It is to this issue, Matthew's view of the civil realm, that we must now turn our attention.

Matthew and the Civil Realm

The authority to bind and to loose which Matthew ascribes to his community indicates a withdrawal from or rejection of the established avenues of civil and judicial authority by Matthew in favor of the procedures which the community has developed. The Matthean community has developed procedures and institutions which fulfill the tasks formerly belonging to the civil and legal authorities in the Matthean setting. However, the community has come to reject or regard with considerable suspicion the authorities and institutions outside of their community. They have sought to replace these

---

[107] D. Otto Via, "The Church as the Body of Christ in the Gospel of Matthew," *SJT* 11 (1958) 271–86.

institutions with their own—even, on occasion, to the point of imitating those procedures and institutions within the setting of the community. This appears to have been the case with the authority to bind and loose, which Matthew has claimed for his community and the disciples. However, this is by no means the only indication of this response to the civil realm on Matthew's part.

It is characteristic of sectarian groups to withdraw from the secular realm. Such groups seek to establish structures and procedures that will limit contact with the world or with those with whom the group contends.[108] Matthew's community is emerging in our study as a sectarian community, as is evidenced by its hostility toward the parent group in its setting, by its developing internal structure, and by its suspicious view of the civil realm and those outside the group.[109] It is not surprising, then, that Matthew and his community would seek to avoid contact with the courts and the civil or legal realm generally. The governing bodies, those who possessed the power and executed penalties, would represent the "world" over against which the Matthean community is defining itself. They are the dominant body from whom the Matthean community is trying to distance itself.

In chap. 5 Matthew has included instructions about the courts and legal disputes which demonstrate this concern. In 5:25 Matthew has inserted the Q saying about making friends with your opponent on the way to court. In Luke 12:58-59 this logion appears not as part of the Sermon on the Plain but as an independent saying placed at the end of an explanation about the strife and division that following Jesus will bring. Matthew has worked this saying into a group of passages relating to the theme of the law and the courts. In the context in which Matthew has placed it, 5:25 appears as an even stronger admonition to avoid the courts and to try to do all one can to avoid coming before the judge. The court, the judge, and the jailer will squeeze every last cent out of you, should you go before them (5:26).

Matthew 5:40 is another clear statement about avoiding the courts and legal proceedings. If someone should want to sue you for your coat, give it to him. Matthew has added the details about suing in

---

[108] B. Wilson, *Magic and the Millennium: A Sociological Study of Religious Movements of Protest among Tribal and Third World Peoples* (London: Heinemann, 1973) 16–20; see also P. L. Berger, "The Sociological Study of Sectarianism," *Social Research* 21 (1954) 470. The term "secular," a modern construction and distinction, is not entirely appropriate for Matthew.

[109] We will discuss Matthew's view of the outsider below.

v. 40. Luke's version serves as another example of the selfless life of
the disciple (Luke 6:29-30). Luke says nothing about the legal process
of suing or about the courts. The fact that Matthew has added the
overt reference to the courts (*krithēnai*) in 5:40 lends credence to
R. Guelich's reading of 5:39b as being yet another statement by Matthew about avoiding the courts and the civil, judicial realm. Guelich
sees the key to 5:39b to be the Matthean addition of "the right cheek."
Being slapped on the right cheek emphasizes the degrading nature
of this act and not only its violence, as in Luke 6:29-30. The addition
of the right cheek implies that one has been slapped by the back of
the hand, a particularly offensive act. Here one could take legal
action to gain recompense and vindication.[110] With these modifications Matthew has encouraged the offended to forgo the usual
legal action.

The Matthean version of the Lord's Prayer contains the word
"debts" (*opheilēmata*) in Matt. 6:12, and not sins (*hamartias*) as in Luke
11:4. Matthew, it can be observed, has an interest in the word
hamartias. He has inserted it into older traditions at several points. In
1:21 Matthew interprets the significance of Jesus' name as being, "he
will save his people from their sins (*hamartias*)." Matthew has also
inserted this word into his version of the last supper in 26:28 when
he writes, "This is my blood of the covenant, which is poured out for
many for the forgiveness of sins (*hamartias*)." Also, the disciples'
ministry and the forgiveness of sins are closely related. In 6:15; 9:8;
16:19; and 18:15, 18, disciples are granted the authority to forgive
sins, or at least charged with the ministry of forgiveness of sins.
Matthew 6:15; 9:8; and 18:15 all specifically use the term *hamartias*.
Given this interest in *hamartias*, it is striking that Matthew has
deleted it from the older version of the Lord's Prayer and inserted
instead this other term, "debts." Again we might infer from this
modification by Matthew an attempt to discourage legal actions and
proceedings against one another and to enjoin avoidance of the
courts and civil authorities in his setting. In his version of the Lord's
Prayer Matthew intends to draw attention to the problem of debts
between members, and he encourages them to "forgive" the debt,
not pursuing legal recourse.

One interesting judicial procedure that seems to have developed
within the Matthean community and is betrayed in 5:22 is the punishment incurred for insulting or speaking ill of a community member.

---

[110] See R. Guelich, *The Sermon on the Mount: A Foundation for Understanding*
(Waco: Word, 1982) 221-22.

Matthew 5:22 reads: "But I say to you, that everyone who is angry with his brother (*adelphos*) shall be guilty before the courts (*tē krisei*); and whoever shall say to his brother "Raca" (literally, "empty head" or "air-head") shall be guilty before the council (*synedrion*); and whoever shall say "You fool" shall be guilty enough to go into the fire of Gehenna."[111] By speaking about insult or injury to a "brother" and about the subsequent penalty for his behavior, Matthew betrays the presence of additional guidelines for behavior and penalties for deviant behavior. The penalties described indicate the presence of some sort of judicial body (*synedrion*) within the Matthean community.

The courts and penalties of 5:22 do not refer to the civil authorities and courts. Members of the Matthean community have been encouraged to avoid these people and institutions (5:25, 26, 40). Matthew 5:22, along with 18:15-18 (discussed above), provides evidence within the Matthean community for the construction of a judicial body and legal process which parallels and replaces the civil structures and authorities within the Matthean setting. Here we see the Matthean community drawing away from the existing civil authorities, developing instead its own procedures for discipline and guidance.

We see here that the Matthean community viewed the courts and the civil, legal realm as a hostile environment. It was to be avoided at all costs. These civil structures pose a threat to the community. The community has responded to this threat by withdrawing and avoiding contact and developing instead their judicial and legal procedures to guide their internal life and affairs. In this regard the Matthean community resembles a sectarian community, which develops its own procedures and structures to replace those of the civil realm and the parent group or authoritative body in their setting. Some of these developments are clearly in evidence within Matthew's Gospel. Another example of Matthew's suspicion of the world around him, an indication of the sectarian nature of his community, is his response to those outside the community, a subject to which we now turn.

Matthew and the Outsider

Matthew reflects a suspicion of "the world" in other ways than by his rejection of the civil and legal institutions and authorities in his setting. Along with this rejection of the civil realm, Matthew reveals

---

[111] The sectarian community at Qumran had similar legislation for slandering a member; see 1QS 7; CD 9:1ff.

an apprehension toward those outside the community. The form and definition of the Matthean community were not vague or amorphous. Matthew had a clear understanding of who was in and who was out of the community. Matthew knew what constituted membership. Matthew's community required allegiance in a manner that is not seen among the other Synoptic evangelists. This is seen in striking fashion by Matthew's deletion of the so-called strange exorcist found in Mark 9:38 and Luke 9:49 and in his alteration of the notion of allegiance.

The saying about allegiance, "He who is not against us is for us," appears in Mark 9:40 and Luke 9:50.[112] This is the concluding verse to the story of the strange exorcist. The verse regards allegiance to a particular group or community and not simply or generally to Jesus and his work. The disciples' tendency is to expect or demand that those laboring in the name of Jesus join their community or group. Placed in this context, the story of the strange exorcist and the concluding verse about allegiance are specifically aimed at the expectation that all those who share the common cause or belong to the movement should also belong to the specific community in question. John, on behalf of the disciples, asks Jesus about a man they saw casting out demons in Jesus' name, but would not join them in following Jesus. Jesus tells the disciples to leave the exorcist alone, "for he who is not against us is for us." Mark and Luke have constructed this passage in such a way as to address—and renounce—the expectation of particularism or exclusivity on the part of some members of the community.

Quite differently, Matthew has deleted the story of the strange exorcist altogether, which we can be certain he had access to. In 12:30 Matthew has retained only the Q version of this saying, which originally pertained to the impending apocalyptic judgment: "He who is not with me is against me, and he who does not gather with me scatters." Noting Matthew's deletion of the story of the strange exorcist and his striking of the Markan saying about allegiance, one can say that Matthew has reversed the principle of allegiance as it is presented in the other Synoptic Gospels. Membership in the Matthean community is critical. In Matthew's view, one is required to make a conscious decision to become a disciple and join the community. E. Schweizer's comment may be slightly overstated, but he

---

[112] Luke does contain a certain contradictory version of this logion in 11:23; however, the apocalyptic context of this Q passage is sufficiently different that it need not concern us here.

certainly captures the essence of Matthew's redactional activity in this regard: "The existence of a genuine Christian exorcist, who 'does not follow us,' that is, he is not a member of the Matthean community, is unthinkable for Matthew."[113]

A slight but similar modification by Matthew can be seen in 12:49, when it is compared with the parallels in Mark 3:33 and Luke 8:21. Here Jesus' family comes to see him and speak with him. Jesus asks rhetorically, "Who are my mother and my brothers?" Matthew notes that Jesus gestures toward his disciples, saying, "Behold my mother and my brothers" (12:49). Mark and Luke make no such explicit reference to the disciples as those who constitute Jesus' true family. As we will see below, "disciple" is not a generalized term for Matthew, but rather refers to fellow community members.[114] The members of the community are his family. This is further emphasized in Matthew's metaphorical use of the term "brother" to denote a member of the community.

A subtle but significant shift is betrayed here. Loyalty to Jesus and the Jesus movement is connected with loyalty to a specific community or church. This is seen neither in Luke nor in Mark, and we take this as an indication of a greater emphasis on communal loyalty and commitment in the Matthean community. This implies at the same time also the necessity in Matthew of a clearer understanding and definition of who the members are and what constitutes membership. This is a significant and substantial social development.

There are other indications of Matthew's concern about and apprehension toward the world outside the community. It can be seen in the unique addition to be "shrewd" while doing your work in the world (10:16b). Similarly, Matthew has inserted in the instructions in the sending in chap. 10 to "beware of men" (10:17), for which the closest Synoptic parallel is found in the Markan apocalypse (see Mark 13:6, 21). Matthew's suspicion of the world is seen also in his concern about dangerous people from outside the community who sneak in and destroy the community and its members (Matt. 7:15ff.). These people seem harmless, but will actually devour the members (7:15b). The community must test these people, observe their actions, and be on their guard so they will not be done in by the destructive forces from the outside. The community must protect itself from *the world*.[115]

---

[113] Schweizer, *Matthäus*, 115.

[114] See the discussion below under "The Disciples in Matthew."

[115] Matthew allows for a *corpus mixtum*, the good with the evil. The parable of

The community's view of and response to the world will have a significant impact on the structure of the group. The community's view of the world dramatically affects the degree of openness which it exhibits toward its environment.[116] More elaborate and sophisticated defenses develop within the community when the world appears not as the locus of the community's activity and the focus of its attention but rather as a force to be feared and avoided. Naturally, with this apprehension toward those outside the community, the Matthean community would find it necessary to be able to define just who is a member and who constitutes an outsider. The latter are viewed with suspicion by this community. Such a view of the world and of outsiders would be reckoned by B. Wilson to be a sectarian response to the world on the part of the Matthean community.[117] Mark's Gospel exhibits very little concern about the world. The world is the locus for the disciples' activity and the dawning of the kingdom.[118] The Markan community is "world open," while the Matthean community appears as "world concerned" and suspicious of those outside the community.

In a word, the Matthean community had developed clear means for ordering and guiding its life. The concept of *righteousness* in the Matthean community summarizes the proper behavior and disposition of the community members. This term in Matthew, one that is commonplace among the sectarian communities of this period, denotes the response and the behavior expected of the true follower of Jesus. Righteousness stands for an all-embracing value or ethic which the community has developed, and which serves to distinguish the members of the Matthean community from those outside the community.

The content of this all-embracing value is explicated in chaps. 5–7, the Sermon on the Mount. Within this section of the Gospel, Matthew has provided instruction for the community members about relationships and attitudes about a variety of issues and has made explicit the community's view of the law. One can observe in this section fragments of the liturgy of the community and the important role it plays in establishing and reiterating their values and beliefs.

---

the wheat and the tares suggests that the bad should remain together with the good, until the harvest, or judgment, when God will separate them.

[116] Berger, "Sectarianism," 479.

[117] Wilson, *Magic and the Millennium*, 16ff.

[118] For example, see Mark 3:9ff.; 6:7ff. See also D. Senior and C. Stuhlmueller, *The Biblical Foundations for Mission* (Maryknoll: Orbis, 1983) 211ff.; E. Best, *Following Jesus*, JSNTMS (Sheffield: JSOT Press, 1979) 15ff.

The order which the community has adopted has made its way into its worship and helps to legitimate the beliefs and interpretations of the community. The themes of love, forgiveness, and deference toward the other members are emphasized in the Sermon. Matthew, through his redactional activity, has constructed a Sermon which serves as a kind of constitution for the community concerning their relationships and their internal life.

A process for disciplining those members who fail to live according to the norms of the community has been established. Matthew somewhat reluctantly includes a means by which the community can rid itself of those who will not adopt the behavior and norms of the group. This sanction in chap. 18 is set within the context of several passages which stress forgiveness. It is clear, however, that the community has established a distinct means by which order can be maintained within the community. Those who refuse to heed the direction of the church become outcasts.

The procedure of expulsion is not the only legal procedure adopted by the community. The Matthean community's suspicious view of the civil realm has led it to withdraw from the courts and the judicial institutions in its setting and to establish instead its own procedures for discipline, evidenced in chaps. 18 and 5. Likewise, the community is apprehensive concerning those outside the group. Loyalty to the community is something that Matthew seems to expect. The order within the life of the Matthean community is a significant social development. The community has pulled back from the world around the community and constructed instead its own set of beliefs, values, and procedures. On more than one occasion the procedures which the community adopted and developed approximates those in the world around them—even, ironically, the group with which Matthew is so clearly in contention, namely, the Jewish leadership. This phenomenon can be seen also in the roles which the Matthean community developed. Let us look now at these roles.

Institutionalization: Roles within the Community

Matthew's Gospel reflects obvious and significant developments which are aimed at ordering the life of the community. Matthew instructs the members concerning the values and behavior embraced by the community and explains or legitimates the beliefs of the community to the members. These explanations and extended teachings offer a defense against whatever charges may be leveled against the community and its beliefs and actions. The Matthean community has ordered its own life and it has also sought to protect itself from those outside the community who appear hostile toward them. Significantly, though Matthew stresses love, forgiveness, and mutuality, the community has developed a means by which members can be expelled from the *ekklēsia*.

Just as significant in terms of the social development of the Matthean community is the emergence of what we are calling institutional roles. While the ordering of the life of the community led to an emphasis on the ethics, values, and attitudes which should control the community and its members, the institutional roles represent explicit offices or functions operative within the community. The term "institutionalization," then, refers to what appear to be these established offices or functions within the community.

At certain points the Matthean community seems to have established roles within the community which resemble and indeed seem to parallel the roles and functions developing within formative Judaism. This is clearly the case with the role of the scribe within the community; it is also the case, albeit in a negative way, with other titles used in the community. That is to say, Matthew is aware of the titles and functions which are developing within formative Judaism, and there is indeed clear evidence that some within the Matthean community are adopting those very titles. Matthew encourages the community to reject some of those titles (23:8). However, he does not reject their function and importance for his community. The titles are beginning to be associated with particular roles within formative Judaism, and the community should reject them. Matthew claims that the members are all equal (23:11-12), though, as we shall see, there are in fact leadership roles and positions of authority in the community. Matthew's description in chap. 23 of an egalitarian community is somewhat idealized, though it is something the members are to strive toward. The emergence of explicit roles and offices within the Matthean community is a significant social development. There is virtually no evidence of such offices or roles within the Markan community.[119] The Matthean community, however, has developed roles and offices which represent certain functions within its life. Certain people perform certain functions. Some roles emerge as more important than others, while some roles are beginning to be viewed with suspicion.

---

[119] H. C. Kee, *The Community of the New Age: Studies in Mark's Gospel* (London: SCM, 1977) 152.

The Scribe

In Matthew the Pharisees stand in the foreground. The opposition toward Jesus and the Jesus movement is concentrated within the Pharisaic party, according to Matthew.[120] In numerous places Matthew has deleted "scribe" from the Markan material and inserted or retained only "the Pharisees" (9:11; 12:24; 17:14; 21:23; 22:35, 41; 26:3, 47; 27:1). The scribes, however, are not completely removed from all the conflict scenes in Matthew (9:3; 12:38; 15:1).[121] The scribes are also named together with the Pharisees in chap. 23 in what appears to be a rather fixed formula. In chap. 23 the scribes are denounced along with the Pharisees. R. Hummel may be right in saying that for Matthew "scribe" is, in and of itself, a neutral term.[122]

One reason that Matthew seems to present a more neutral and balanced portrait of the notion and role of the scribe is that for Matthew scribe is still a valid title and function. Matthew will speak about "their (*autōn*) scribes" (7:28). The pronoun is a Matthean insertion into the Markan material (see Mark 1:22). Similar to the phrase "their gathering places" (Matt. 12:9; 13:54), these scribes are part of the developing institution and structure of formative Judaism. To say that "their gathering place" exists implies that the Matthean community has its own gathering place. Indeed they do, and Matthew calls it an *ekklēsia* (see 16:18; 18:17). Similarly, to speak of "their scribes" implies the existence of "our" or "your" scribes. The Matthean community has started to build up its own scribal role, which parallels that of formative Judaism.[123] It is clear that the scribes and Pharisees represent the dominant leadership in the Matthean setting. The scribes who are associated with the Pharisees ("their scribes") are blind guides and false leaders (15:14; 23:16). These scribes do not truly understand and are lawless, failing to produce fruit. These scribes can be contrasted with the scribes of the Matthean community.

According to Matthew the corrupt leaders in the Matthean setting have been sent scribes, and these *true* scribes have only been rejected, persecuted, and scourged in "their (*autōn*) gathering places" (23:34). These scribes, who have been sent by Jesus, in Matthew's view, are operative in the Matthean community. But they have been rejected and persecuted. The teaching of the Matthean scribes has

[120] R. Hummel, *Die Auseinandersetzung*, 17.
[121] Ibid.
[122] Ibid., 18.
[123] J. Koenig, *Jews and Christians in Dialogue* (Philadelphia: Westminster, 1979) 87.

met with serious opposition from the scribes of the Pharisees and in the gathering places of the Jewish opponents. One might well assume, along with Stendahl, Strecker, and others, that the Gospel of Matthew itself reflects considerable "scribal-like" activity.[124] This can be seen in the creative and learned application of Old Testament citations in the so-called introductory formulas, discussed above.[125] Also, the manner in which Matthew engages in legal disputes with the Pharisees, in contrast to Mark, reflects the presence of extended teaching and study of the Law and the Prophets in the Matthean community.[126]

The most striking and well-known indication that the Matthean community possesses its own scribes and honors that role and function is in Matt. 13:52. This verse follows Jesus' teaching on parables. When he had finished, Jesus asked the disciples, "'Have you understood all these things?' And they said, 'Yes.' And Jesus said to them, 'Therefore every scribe who has become a disciple of the kingdom of heaven is like a head of a household, who brings forth out of his treasure things new and old'" (13:51-52).

This verse may in fact be a reference to certain scribes who have decided to join the Matthean community. The community was clearly involved in missionary activity (see 28:20). However, there is no evidence in the Gospel that this activity met with any success within the Jewish leadership. The note of rejection and denunciation in Matthew of the Jewish leadership in his setting is too strong and definitive to suggest that Matthew either experienced or held out hope for their acceptance of the Matthean community and their message.

This verse, however, does reflect the presence of Jews within the Matthean community who possess the same training and skills as those of the opposition. But these skills are now being employed for the kingdom of heaven. The scribe is trained or discipled (*mathēteutheis*) into the kingdom of heaven. He is like a leader (*oikodespotēs*) who takes from his treasure things old and new. Things old and new refers to the teachings of the Matthean community. The new element is the Jesus tradition, and it has been applied to and serves as the interpretive framework by which the community will understand the old things, namely, the Law and the Prophets. We will see below that the portrait of the disciples in Matthew corresponds in significant ways to the activity and function of the scribe. The disciples are

---

[124] See n. 10 above.
[125] See above under "Scripture, Interpretation, and Tradition in Matthew."
[126] See the discussion of the conflict stories.

teachers who understand the teaching of Jesus and are even charged with unusual authority concerning the actions and behavior of community members.

The office and function of the scribe were developing in Matthew's setting. There were good scribes and bad. Scribes who were trained for the kingdom of heaven and who used their skills and tools for the kingdom were good scribes. The scribes of the Pharisees were using their authority and knowledge to lead people astray. They had obviously studied the law and knew it well. This becomes clear in the conflict stories and is virtually admitted by Matthew (23:3). What the scribes and Pharisees say, Matthew asserts, is to be obeyed. It is rather the actions of the scribes and Pharisees that should be avoided. They do not practice the Law and the Prophets. The scribe of the Matthean community will be a leader in the community and will provide treasure for its life. These scribes parallel and rival the scribes of formative Judaism. Scribes play a definite role within the Matthean community. Their instruction and knowledge of the law are now interpreted in light of the teachings and gospel of Jesus as the Matthean community understands it.

Prophets

The presence and nature of prophets within the Matthean community have received considerable attention.[127] The Matthean church doubtless included prophets (10:41; 23:34).[128] Clearly, however, this is not a pronounced role within the Matthean community. Matthew 10:41 is problematic, because it is difficult to determine what Matthew means by "prophet." The larger context of the saying in chap. 10 has to do with missionary activity. Matthew does not sufficiently expound on the term "prophet" for us to be completely sure what he means by it. His possible lack of interest in present prophetic activity may have resulted in a rather indiscriminate use of the term, which may have stood for a classical prophet (23:34), a miracle worker (7:15), or a missionary (10:41).[129]

---

[127] E. Schweizer, "Observance of the Law," 213–30; D. Hill, "False Prophets and Charismatics: Structure and Interpretation in Matthew 7.15-23," *Biblica* 57 (1976) 327–48; see also Luz, *Matthew 1–7*, 438ff.

[128] Schweizer, "Matthew's Church," 131.

[129] Matthew makes some thirty-five references to Old Testament prophets. The classical prophets of Israel's history are very important for him; however, in the present setting of the community *instruction* receives primary focus.

The most significant passage for the Matthean concept of "proph-et" is 7:15ff. Here Matthew explicitly asserts that there are people whom he considers prophets in the community. The focus here is on false prophets who have come in from the outside but are never-theless inside and, one would assume, members of the community. As Luz observes, the extensive Matthean redaction and the intensity of the struggle against these false prophets suggest a concrete situa-tion in the community.[130] A striking feature of this passage is the realization that Matthew believes there are members of the commu-nity who will not enter the kingdom of heaven (7:21). A similar senti-ment is expressed in the parable of the wheat and the tares (13:24ff.), where the tares remain among the wheat until the harvest.

Because 7:15ff. is Matthew's most extended discussion about the prophets within the community, we do not learn much about the *true* prophets, except through inference based on what the false prophets do or fail to do. The false prophets appear to be harmless and seem similar to other prophets (7:15). But they are a threat to the com-munity. The activity of the false prophets appears as decidedly charismatic in nature.[131] They prophesy, cast out demons, and perform many miracles in the Lord's name (7:22). These authorita-tive acts of power and the obvious charismatic activity seem to have no relation to the judgment decreed upon them. "Their activities are insufficient to insure entrance into the kingdom."[132]

Luz is correct to draw attention to the criteria which this passage contains for true prophets.[133] These false prophets have failed in their *praxis*. This is a recurring Matthean theme and in no way pertains only to prophets. The relation between hearing or teaching, on the one hand, and *doing*, on the other, is an absolutely fundamental notion for Matthew (see 5:19; 7:24; 23:3). These charismatic prophets are deemed lawless because they have failed to act out the demands of the kingdom as Matthew perceives them (7:23).

It is difficult to imagine that the miracles and exorcisms themselves constitute *anomia*. Matthew's own story of Jesus contains many such acts. Also, the abbreviated sending in chap. 10 charges the mission-aries to engage in this activity. It is certainly true that Matthew does not emphasize this sort of activity (see below).[134] But we should not

---

[130] Luz, *Matthew 1–7*, 446ff.

[131] See Schweizer, "Observance of the Law."

[132] D. Hill, "False Prophets and Charismatics," 348.

[133] Luz, *Matthew 1–7*, 446ff.

[134] See below under "Missionaries."

infer from this that Matthew rejects such activity altogether. These false prophets have failed to "bear fruit" (7:16), a favorite Matthean euphemism for failing to fulfill the will of God. This refers more to what they have not done than to what they have done. Always for Matthew failure to bear fruit means the failure to bring one's actions, attitudes, and behavior in line with what one says or what one has heard. As Luz says, Matthew "demands the proof by deed for Christian faith."[135] This connection between hearing and doing is made explicit in the concluding parable in 7:24.

There are prophets in the Matthean community. They may even be cast in a pejorative light because of the focus of 7:15ff. The authoritative and charismatic activity of prophets, true or false, does not replace the fundamental demand to act in accord with the Law and the Prophets. Matthew uses the presence of these prophets to emphasize that, despite one's marvelous acts, the fruit of service and love must be evident in one's actions and relationships. This is what bearing fruit means and is the demand placed upon all members of the community. Prophets within the community are not excluded from this demand. They too must bear fruit and fulfill all the Law and the Prophets (7:12).

Missionaries

Our primary focus in discussing the role of missionaries in Matthew's Gospel is chap. 10. This is Matthew's version of the sending of the Twelve. Many discussions about this chapter have been concerned with its theological significance, how it relates to the sending in chap. 28, and, above all, what this chapter represents in terms of Matthew's view of salvation history;[136] these are not our primary concern here. Chapter 10 and the sending recorded there are of interest to us primarily because of the information provided about the role of missionaries in the Matthean community and the status that position held.

The sending in chap. 10 finds its closest parallel in Mark 3. In Mark the disciples are called that they might be with Jesus and that he might send them out to preach (Mark 3:14). The Twelve in Mark 3 are also given authority over demons. There is no explicit evidence that on this occasion the disciples in Mark were in fact sent out; the work the Twelve are enjoined to do in Mark 3 seems to have reference to

[135] Luz, *Matthew 1–7*, 446.
[136] See Frankemölle, *Jahwebund*, 256ff.; and Senior, *Biblical Foundations*, 250.

the future. In Mark the reader naturally sees this fulfilled in chap. 6, in the sending reported there. In Mark 6:30 the "disciples" return to report on their missionary activity.

Matthew does not contain the second sending found in Mark chap. 6. In Matthew the "twelve disciples" (10:1) or "twelve apostles" (10:2) are given the same charismatic authority to heal and perform exorcisms but also to raise the dead (10:8). In the Matthean account there is no return or report about the mission of those supposedly sent out. Outside of the brief reference in 10:5a, there is no indication that these missionaries were actually sent out; this can only be inferred from the narrative. This passage may be simply a historical reflection or remembrance of an event in the ministry of Jesus. Matthew has so curtailed the sending and the healing and preaching mission of the disciples that one wonders if this ministry was in fact still operative in the Matthean community. Matthew has paid close attention to the disciples and their ministry, as we will see.[137] However, the ministry of the disciples has changed drastically compared to the Markan portrait. Healings, exorcisms, and preaching are essential features of the disciples' ministry in Mark.[138] This is not the case in Matthew. The truncated version of the mission in chap. 10 serves as a prime example of this.

However, Matthew's editorial hand and his arrangement of the material suggest that there is something more here than simply a historical reflection or recollection. The context in which the sending has been placed or framed is important. The plea from Jesus to the disciples for more people to go out serves as the introduction to chap. 10 (9:35-38). There is a shortage of workers who are willing to be missionaries (9:37); the disciples are asked to pray for more workers (9:38). The body of the mission chapter consists of material Matthew has drawn from Mark and Q, with special Matthean material concentrated in vv. 5-24. The bulk of chap. 10 consists of instructions to the Twelve about their mission to Israel, how they are to act, what they will do, and how they will overcome hardship and inevitable persecution. The thrust of chap. 10 is the instruction about and the description of the mission which awaits the ones who will be the workers, "sent out into the harvest" (9:38).

A small but significant change has been made at the conclusion of the mission chapter in 10:42. Matthew has made the striking change

---

[137] See "The Portrait of the Disciples" below.

[138] N. Perrin, *The Kingdom in Mark: A New Place and a New Time* (Philadelphia: Fortress Press, 1974) 67ff.

to the Markan material to the effect that whoever should give even one cup of water to one of the missionaries (here they are called *mikroi*) *in the name of a disciple* shall not lose his reward. Mark says the water — assistance to the missionaries — should be given in the *name of Christ* (Mark 9:41). Why Matthew would strike the name of Christ here and insert "disciple" in its place is curious, and we would not take this to be a slip of the pen or a casual alteration on Matthew's part.

Matthew 10:42, taken together with the introduction in 9:35ff., seems to suggest that the disciples or their successors in the Matthean community actually did send out people on missions. The rather small amount of attention which this kind of activity receives in Matthew, compared particularly with Mark, suggests that this was no longer a central activity and focus of the community. However, there were still people going out on missions of sorts, and there were apparently missions to be fulfilled. The harvest was still plentiful; however, few were becoming workers in the harvest. This is why the disciples are asked to pray for more people to be "sent out." There are still people in the community who go out on missions, though they appear to be few. Those that do go out are sent by disciples and go in their name. This is the source of the missionaries' authority, and it is the disciples who commission the *laborers* in their work. "The Evangelist does not conceive of this discourse merely as a moment in the past story of Jesus, but as an exhortation to the ongoing mission of his community."[139] While this kind of activity does not receive much attention in the Gospel and does not appear to be highly popular within the community, Matthew nevertheless seeks to encourage some people within the movement to be missionaries in a much more traditional sense. That is to say, the activity these missionaries are encouraged to pursue is far more reminiscent of the ministry and mission of Jesus and of the Markan disciples than it is of the Matthean disciples and their principal activity.

The sending at the close of the Gospel in 28:18-20 warrants some attention. Here the disciples, and through them the entire Matthean community, are charged to go to the gentile world, making disciples, teaching them, and baptizing them. This is a mission that the Matthean community understands itself to be involved in. The community is turning toward the wider world. Here the substance of the mission is of great importance. The community is charged to go into the world with Jesus' authority. They are to disciple or instruct the world, baptizing adherents with the liturgical formula and teaching

---

[139] Senior, *Biblical Foundations*, 250.

them to observe what Jesus has taught. This is the mission of the Matthean community. They are teachers and disciplers. This is the central focus for the Matthean disciples and the entire community. This, however, is substantially different from the mission activity described in chap. 10.

Chapter 10 describes the more charismatic activity of healing, exorcism, and resuscitation. Here these "workers" appear more like the Markan disciples. Within the Matthean community there now appear to be few such missionaries. The thrust of the mission and life of the Matthean community has changed toward education and teaching. The few missionaries who do go out—and it is not an activity Matthew has emphasized by any means—go in the name of a disciple, are sent by him, and most likely report back to him. This suggests somewhat of a hierarchy within the community. There are those who possess the authority to send out members, implying that this activity is now being left to a certain group of people, or specialists, as is the case in the *Didache* 11:1ff. Missionary activity fostered by the community, however, is waning in importance and popularity. Teaching and education seem to have taken priority.[140] The role of missionary, as it was originally portrayed in the early church and in the Gospel tradition, still exists in the Matthean community, but these missionaries do not possess great authority, and there are not many left.

"Don't Be Called Rabbi . . ."

One cannot discuss the presence and development of certain institutional roles and positions within the Matthean community without taking up the apparent rejection of such roles contained in Matt. 23:8-11. This is distinctive Matthean material inserted into the protracted denunciation of the Jewish leadership in chap. 23, represented in the Matthean formula "the scribes and the Pharisees." In this passage Jesus claims that the scribes and the Pharisees love the place of honor at feasts and the best seats in the synagogues, salutations in the marketplaces, and being called rabbi (23:6-7). Verse 8 continues, "But you are not to be called rabbi, for you have one teacher, and you are all brethren. And call no man your father on earth, for you have one Father, who is in heaven. Neither be called masters, for you have one Master, the Christ. He who is greatest

---

[140] See the discussion about teaching in "The Ministry of the Disciples," below.

among you shall be your servant; whoever exalts himself will be humbled, and whoever humbles himself will be exalted."[141]

The concern over the use of these titles, as both Trilling and Schweizer assert, presupposes that there were people in the community laying claim to them.[142] One can safely assume the presence of ministries within the community which approximate these titles and claims. There is unusual emphasis on teaching in Matthew and, as we have seen, extensive use of Scripture and *halakah*. All of this could have easily resulted in the use and application of the very same title, representing the very same function, within the Matthean community as that which was emerging within formative Judaism. Obviously this would make for competition and resentment, and it would raise the acute question, Who are the true teachers?

Matthew has tried to stress equality and service within the community. Greatness involves service and humility. The constant reference to the *brotherhood* emphasizes the Matthean ideal of mutuality and deference toward the other. Here, as in 18:1-4, the issue of greatness and of equality among the members emerges as a fundamental question about the structure, life, and relationships within the Matthean community.[143] That Matthew must add this admonition in 23:8ff., together with the stress on mutuality and deference toward other members throughout the Gospel, particularly the Sermon on the Mount, indicates that the egalitarian ethic which Matthew encourages is not completely taking hold within the community. The people who fulfill certain roles and positions are claiming a position of honor and prestige because of their role within the *brotherhood*. That v. 8 should directly follow v. 7 and the negative description of those who love to be called rabbi suggests that there are those in the Matthean community trying to keep up with the Jewish leadership in position and prestige. Matthew rejects this and reminds them of the importance of humility and service in the teaching of Jesus.

This passage alone virtually establishes the presence of certain institutional roles and a developing hierarchy within the Matthean community. In this passage, as elsewhere, Matthew is trying to counter a developing hierarchy that could destroy the brotherhood

---

[141] In this passage Matthew understands "rabbi" as an honorific title: "They love being called rabbi." Matthew makes clear that this is an honor given a teacher (23:8).

[142] Schweizer, "Matthew's Church," 139; and Trilling, *Das Wahre*, 36ff.

[143] See Forkman, *Limits*, 121.

and ethic of mutuality and service which ought to control relationships within the *ekklēsia*.[144] Trilling is right in seeing in this passage a rejection of the titles and the claim of honor and authority they appear to bring, but not the *functions* which the titles represent.[145] Neither the function of teaching nor the teachers are rejected by Matthew. What Matthew is responding to is the hierarchy that seems to be emerging in the community and the temptation to try to keep up with the Jewish teachers in both position and prestige. Leaders, teachers, and other positions are all part of the Matthean community. Ideally, Matthew would have the members fulfill their roles in a way that does not disrupt the egalitarian spirit which should pervade the life of the community. Ministry or function should not relate to status in the community.[146]

Clearly, institutional roles and functions developed within the Matthean community. At times this resulted in an emerging hierarchy among members which Matthew rejects. These developments were necessary if the community was to survive, and they are quite understandable in light of the community's struggle with formative Judaism. The struggle with formative Judaism affected also an important dimension of Matthew's Gospel, namely, the portrait and presentation of the disciples. It is to that important development which we now turn.

The Disciples in Matthew

Matthew has particular interest in the designation and the role of the disciples. Matthew employs the term disciple (*mathētēs*) some forty-five times without parallel in Mark or Luke.[147] Essentially two tendencies have been evident in Matthean scholarship concerning Matthew's presentation of the disciples. One tendency has been to see in the disciples a reflection of the Matthean community. The disciples are "transparent";[148] that is to say, in the portrait of the disciples one views the life and situation of the Matthean community

---

144 Schweizer, "Matthew's Church," 140.

145 W. Trilling, "Amt und Amtsverständnis bei Matthäus," in *Mélanges Bibliques*, Festschrift B. Rigaux, ed. A. Descamps (Gembloux: Duculot, 1969) 31.

146 Schweizer, "Matthew's Church," 140; and U. Luz, "The Disciples in the Gospel according to Matthew," in *The Interpretation of Matthew*, 110. However, Luz is incorrect to say that this passage, or a variety of others, does not indicate certain institutional problems within the Matthean community.

147 See Guelich, *Sermon on the Mount*, 52.

148 Hummel, *Die Auseinandersetzung*, 154.

and the plight of the community members.[149] "Disciple" is understood in this way as an ecclesiological term. It has become a designation for a follower of Jesus within the Matthean community.[150]

The other tendency in understanding the disciples in Matthew is associated with what has been called Matthew's "historicizing" of the story of Jesus. Thus, for G. Strecker, Jesus and the disciples are set in unrepeatable, holy past.[151] The disciples do not reflect the ongoing situation of the contemporary community, but rather are historical relics of the Jesus movement, serving to support and substantiate Matthew's view of salvation history. Some scholars have seen a combination of both of these elements in Matthew's portrait of the disciples.[152]

In light of the sociology of knowledge and the observations of E. D. Hirsch that the text always interacts and is influenced by the setting and horizon of the writer, Strecker's historicizing view of Jesus and the disciples in Matthew must be rejected. It is true that Matthew tells a story about Jesus and the Jesus movement. To suggest, however, that this story is not influenced by and indeed reflects the contemporary situation of the Matthean community is untenable. Matthew seeks to address his community and the issues and problems they face. At many points his Gospel directly addresses struggles within his community. We will see that Matthew's portrayal of the disciples is one crucial place where the setting and situation of the Matthean community have dramatically influenced the shape and the content of the Gospel.

In all of the Gospels the disciples emerge as central players and figures. While the understanding of the disciples in Mark has been pursued at some length within New Testament scholarship,[153] this is not the case with Matthew.[154] Matthew has made some significant

[149] So Frankemölle, *Jahwebund*, 150ff.

[150] Luz, "Disciples in the Gospel according to Matthew," 98; and Trilling, "Amtsverständnis," 41.

[151] Strecker, *Weg*, 194.

[152] So B. Rigaux, who speaks of the oscillation in Matthew between history and typology concerning the disciples (*Témoignage de l'évangile de Matthieu* [Brussels: Desclée de Brouwer, 1967] 205ff.).

[153] See N. Petersen, "Point of View in Mark's Narrative," *Semeia* 12 (1978) 97–121; J. Dewey, "Point of View and the Disciples in Mark," in *Society of Biblical Literature 1982 Seminar Papers*, ed. K. H. Richards (Chico, Calif.: Scholars Press, 1982) 97–106; R. Tannehill, "The Disciples in Mark: The Function of a Narrative Role," *JR* 57 (1977) 386–405; also E. Best, *Mark: The Gospel as Story* (Edinburgh: T. & T. Clark, 1983) 44–50, 83–92.

[154] With the notable exceptions of U. Luz's article, "The Disciples in the Gospel

changes in his characterization of the disciples. His view of discipleship and his portrayal of the disciples betray a great deal about the
issues facing the community and the setting of the Gospel, as well
as the priorities and values of his community and its developing
social structure.

The Ministry of the Disciples

There are some significant modifications in the ministry of the
disciples in Matthew that can be seen when Matthew is contrasted
with Mark or Luke. First, as was noted by Trilling, the ministry of
both Jesus and the disciples is greatly curtailed geographically.[155] The
so-called northern trip in Mark 7:24 is reported briefly and without
detail in Matt. 15:21ff. Unlike Luke, Matthew's Jesus never sets foot
in Samaria. The swing through the Decapolis, referred to in Mark
7:31, is altered by Matthew so that the crowds from the Decapolis,
beyond the Jordan, and Jerusalem and Judea, come to Jesus (4:25).
Jesus and his disciples do not venture into these areas. In Matthew
they remain essentially within Galilee. Even when Jesus and the
disciples do go north toward Tyre and Sidon, they merely cross over
the border, and Matthew records that the Canaanite woman there
"came out from the region to meet them" (15:22). Matthew gives the
impression that Jesus and the disciples barely set foot in this region.

There is an unusual concentration on Capernaum in Matthew, not
found even in Mark. For example, only Matthew records that Jesus
in fact "dwelt" in Capernaum (4:13). In 9:1 Capernaum is described
as Jesus' own city. There is repeated activity around the house in
Capernaum, so much so in fact that it has led some commentators to
suggest that the house may have been understood within the tradition as Jesus' own home.[156] Galilee tends to be the place of activity
for the ministry of Jesus and the disciples in Matthew. In Matthew
Jesus and the disciples are less itinerant and appear more settled and
fixed in their locale. J. D. Kingsbury is quite right in saying that in
view of this localizing and settling of the Jesus movement and the
ministry of Jesus and the disciples, "Matthew has blunted considerably the ostensible force of the statement that the Son of man has
nowhere to lay his head."[157]

---

according to Matthew." See also Barth in *Tradition and Interpretation in Matthew*,
106ff.

[155] Trilling, *Das Wahre*, 132.

[156] Kingsbury, "The Verb *Akolouthein*," 64–66.

[157] Ibid., 65.

In Mark, Jesus and the disciples are continually portrayed as being "on the way" (*en tē hodō*). E. Best and N. Perrin both have noted the strategic use of verbs of motion by Mark and the importance of the phrase "on the way."[158] Several occurrences of this phrase appear in the central section of Mark's Gospel (8:22–10:52), which bears the imprint of Mark's composition.[159] The mobile and itinerant nature of the ministry of Jesus and the disciples is a Markan redactional motif which Matthew deletes with telling regularity.[160] The Markan community reflects an awareness of and an appreciation for the itinerant mission initiated by Jesus. The Markan community and disciples are to continue in this mission.[161] We have already noted Matthew's curtailing of the sending and missionary activity of the disciples, when compared with Mark. The disciples in Matthew do not venture out on their own, as the Markan disciples do (Mark 6:1ff.). Rather, they remain "with Jesus" and are instructed about the kingdom and the proper understanding of the same.[162]

The mobile and itinerant, more charismatic ministry of preaching, healing, and exorcism of the Markan disciples is toned down or deleted by Matthew. The Markan "community on the way" (*Weg Gemeinschaft*) and the traditions from that community have been transformed and appropriated by a community with a deeper concern for teaching and instruction. Teaching and education have become the primary substance of the ministry of the disciples in Matthew.

The ministry of teaching for the disciples in Matthew is foreshadowed in the Matthean portrait of Jesus. Even the casual reader of Matthew's Gospel notices the shift in emphasis in Jesus' ministry regarding teaching. Jesus is portrayed as an authoritative and effective teacher in Matthew more than any other Gospel. This is evidenced in the Sermon on the Mount, in chap. 18, as well as in the debates over the law and its proper interpretation. In Mark, Jesus is described as possessing authoritative teaching (Mark 1:22), but the emphasis clearly falls on the powerful acts of healing, miracles, and exorcisms performed and presented in "breathless fashion."[163] Matthew develops extensively the portrait of Jesus as authoritative

---

[158] Best, *Following Jesus*, 15; Perrin, *Kingdom in Mark*, 67ff.

[159] See also E. Haenchen, "Die Komposition von Mk. 8.27-9.1," *NT* 6 (1963) 81–109; see also Perrin, *Kingdom in Mark*, 67.

[160] Perrin, *Kingdom in Mark*, 69.

[161] R. Pesch remarks that "the way of Jesus becomes the way of the community" (*Das Markusevangelium* [Freiburg: Herder, 1980] 1:60).

[162] This is a major emphasis in Frankemölle, *Jahwebund*, especially chap. 1.

[163] Senior, *Biblical Foundations*, 215.

teacher, and it is this feature of Jesus' ministry that the Matthean disciples inherit and perpetuate.

This shift in the substance and focus of the ministry of the disciples can be seen clearly in the final commission in chap. 28. Here the disciples are sent out not to heal, cast out demons, or raise the dead but rather to teach (*didaskontes*) people about Jesus' commands (28:20). They are to *disciple* the world (28:19). The function of the disciple here is to train people in the way of the community and the kingdom. Observance of and consonance with the established norms and order are essential for true discipleship. "Making disciples is the process of bringing people into the community, that is the Church."[164] Once these people have been instructed and observe the commands of Jesus as reflected in Matthew's Gospel, then membership is theirs through the rite of baptism and the litany reflected in the commission. The instruction to the disciples in 5:19 assumes that they are about the business of teaching and warns against false or misleading instruction. We may recall as well the explicit mention in 23:8-10 of teachers within the community. The scribes and teachers of the Matthean community take their lead from the portrait of the disciples in the Gospel. The scribe trained for the kingdom is a leader who offers accurate and true teaching for the community (Matt. 13:52).

Directly related to the Matthean emphasis on teaching in the Gospel—and especially in the ministry of the disciples—is the consistent removal by Matthew of the Markan motif of the failure of the disciples to understand. Matthew, for example, omits Mark 9:6, 10, and 32, all of which speak of the Markan disciples' failure to perceive. Conversely, Matt. 13:51; 15:16ff.; and 16:9-12 make explicit that the disciples do indeed understand or come to understanding.[165] In contrast to the dull or hardhearted people, the disciples understand (*synienai*) or perceive (13:16, 23; 17:13). Unlike the Markan disciples, who may also be hardhearted or unbelieving, the Matthean disciples are of "little faith" (6:30; 8:26; 14:31; 16:8; 17:20).[166] The Matthean disciples never fail to believe or understand.

Thus in Matthew both positive and negative aspects of the disciples are found. Though never hardhearted or unbelieving, the disciples are fearful and exhibit little faith (8:26; 14:27ff.). Jesus is an effective

---

[164] K. Tagawa, "People and Community in Matthew," *NTS* 16 (1969–70) 149.

[165] See P. Bonnard, "Matthieu, Éducateur du Peuple Chrétien," in *Mélanges Bibliques*, 3.

[166] H. Frankemölle, "Amtskritik im Matthäus-Evangelium?" *Biblica* 54 (1973) 255.

teacher who instructs the disciples about the kingdom of heaven and the life of discipleship.[167]

Perhaps the high point in the Matthean disciples' proper understanding of Jesus and the kingdom is the Petrine confession in 16:13ff. Here Peter and the disciples do understand who Jesus is. Peter is praised because he responds to Jesus' question about his identity by saying, "You are the Christ, the son of the living God" (16:16). Jesus then says that God has revealed this to Peter; it was not something he was told or perceived on his own (16:17). God revealed to Peter Jesus' true identity. This is in stark contrast to Mark's version of the Petrine confession, where Peter is rebuked for having addressed Jesus with a technical term reserved for demons and demonic powers.[168] In the Matthean version not only do the disciples understand, but their knowledge is portrayed as having been given to them by God.

Matthew consistently alters the Markan portrait of the disciples. The Matthean disciples know who Jesus is and are now able to instruct others about him and the way of life which the community is called to live. The disciples receive far more frequent instructions in Matthew than in Mark or Luke.[169] Full understanding is for Matthew a presupposition of discipleship and Christian existence. As Luz says, "In Matthew the disciples are men who have heard and understood all that Jesus taught in his lifetime; they are *earwitnesses.*"[170]

This modification on the part of Matthew is necessary if the disciples are to be teachers. How can these disciples teach if they never quite understood Jesus? How can Jesus be presented as a great teacher with unusual authority if he was never able adequately to instruct his coworkers? Matthew has responded to these questions by portraying the disciples as followers of Jesus who understood his message and now carry it on in the form of instruction within the community.

How does this teaching ministry of the disciples function within the Matthean community, and what does it reveal about the social development of the community? Sociologist Bryan Wilson has

[167] Frankemölle, *Jahwebund,* 153–55.

[168] The significant word in the Markan version is *epitiman,* which is deleted by Matthew; see H. C. Kee, "The Terminology of Mark's Exorcism Stories," *NTS* 14 (1967–68) 232–46.

[169] See Matt. 9:37; 11:1; 13:10-23, 36-52; 15:12ff.; 16:5ff., 33ff.; 18; 19:23–20:19; 21:21ff.; 24:1ff.

[170] Luz, "The Disciples in the Gospel according to Matthew," 105.

described how sects gradually become more concerned with training the second generation. The attempt to socialize younger and subsequent members leads to an increasing concern with education.[171] As Peter Berger has said, education legitimates—it helps members to "inhabit" the same social world, and it helps denounce threatening or anomic forces in the community's setting.[172]

Thus Matthew's emphasis on teaching and the transformation of the disciples' ministry into essentially a teaching post are developments that help maintain and protect the community and its world.[173] This focus on education helps to ensure the continuance of proper beliefs and values within the community. It explains and justifies the beliefs of the community and offers a defense against opposing views and beliefs.

The bare fact that someone is called to teach assumes a body of knowledge that has to be passed on and protected. This development within the community either anticipates or responds to the problem of authority and order in the community. That the primary role of the disciples in Matthew is that of teachers once again reveals the influence and threat posed by the Jewish leaders and their competing views about Scripture, tradition, and their response to the life and beliefs of the Matthean community. Matthew, through his presentation of the disciples, has responded by developing a teaching office which instructs the members concerning belief and behavior and responds to the accusations leveled against the community by the Jewish leadership in their setting.

The Authority of the Disciples

Matthew is unique among the Synoptic evangelists in the amount of authority he invests in the disciples. Perhaps the most striking aspect of this change is the authority the disciples are granted to forgive sins. Matthew 6:15; 9:8; 16:19; and 18:18 all ascribe to the disciples, in one form or another, the authority to forgive sins. This is something reserved exclusively for Jesus in Mark and Luke. The disciples are depicted as possessing unusual authority. Naturally this responds to questions of authority and order within the community and to challenges from authoritative figures outside the community; it

---

[171] Bryan Wilson, *Religion in Sociological Perspective* (Oxford: Oxford University Press, 1982) 96–97.

[172] Berger, *Sacred Canopy*, 30–31, 56.

[173] The term "world-maintaining" is Berger's (*Sacred Canopy*, 47).

supports the disciples' role as teachers and authorities within the community.

The Matthean community understands itself in certain respects as the reflection and embodiment of the kingdom which is in heaven. The Matthean social reality has in some way become closely identified with the ultimate reality of the kingdom of heaven.[174] There is a parallelism between the behavior and the will of the Matthean community and the will of God in the kingdom of heaven. In the words of Berger, the social structure and cosmic structure have developed along the lines of "microcosm" and "macrocosm." The roles and patterns of behavior of the society reflect and represent the heavenly society of which they are a *mimēsis*.[175] The community understands itself as living out the order, structures, and values of the sacred cosmos. It is for this reason that Matthew can claim such unusual authority for his community through his portrait of the disciples.

This claim on the part of Matthew for his community is summed up in the uniquely Matthean phrase, "on earth as it is in heaven." This is an obvious expression of the belief that everything here below has its heavenly analogue up above. In Matthew's version of the Lord's Prayer, the desire and conviction that the community should embody and reflect the kingdom which is in heaven here and now are clearly expressed in 6:10. God's will is to be done not only in heaven but here on earth. By contrast, in Luke's version one prays only for the eschatological arrival of the kingdom (Luke 11:2). This eschatological dimension in Luke's prayer, most certainly the older of the two forms, is toned down in Matthew and augmented by the new development that the community can in fact embody and reflect the kingdom here on earth.

This same understanding of the community and the unusual authority it possesses is seen also in the binding and loosing, granted to the community in 18:18 and to Peter in particular in 16:19. Here the decisions of the community and its leaders are depicted as possessing the authority and sanction of heaven. The decisions that are made in the community are at the same time also made in heaven. The community members behave as does God, who is in heaven (5:48), and their decisions are consonant with the will of God, and indeed are the very decisions of the kingdom in heaven. This is an unusual claim for the community and those who make decisions in their setting. Yet

---

[174] Berger, *Sacred Canopy*, 47.
[175] Ibid., 34, 38.

Matthew claims that the disciples and the members of the community through them possess the authority and power of the kingdom of heaven. Their will and behavior parallel God's will in heaven. They enact decisions within the community which in Mark and Luke belonged only to Jesus or his Father.

Matthew reveals this belief in the community's authority in two other subtle but significant passages. In 12:32 Matthew records his version of the logion dealing with the sin against the Holy Spirit (see Mark 3:29; Luke 12:10). Matthew has inserted that those who sin against the Holy Spirit will not be forgiven, "in this age" or in the age to come. Both Mark and Luke record the eschatological fate of the blasphemers against the Spirit: "they will not be forgiven." Matthew has emphasized the fact that these people will be condemned now, in this age, as well as the age to come. The community even now metes out punishment—forgiveness or judgment.

This development within the Matthean community and the authority they claim to possess are seen also in a subtle modification made by Matthew in 9:8. This is the story of the healing of the paralytic (see Mark 2:1ff.; Luke 5:18ff.). In the story Jesus forgives the sin of the paralytic (Matt. 9:2; Mark 2:2; Luke 5:20). In the conclusion to the story Mark and Luke record that the people were amazed, saying, "We never saw anything like this" (Mark 2:12) or, in Luke, "We have seen such strange things" (Luke 5:26). Matthew, however, records that the crowd (*ochloi*) glorified God because God "had given such authority to men (*anthrōpois*)."

In Matthew's version it is humans who possess the authority. It is not specifically Jesus, but humans. The change to the plural reflects that in fact the community, not just the historical person Jesus, possesses this authority. Only Matthew has made the issue in the conclusion of the story the authority to forgive sins. For Matthew this passage constitutes instruction about the unusual authority the community possesses. Matthew's version reiterates this authority, emphasizes that it was given "to humans" by Jesus and that they can now enact the very authority of heaven in their decisions and judgments.

Matthew portrays the disciples, and through them his community, as possessing unusual authority, paralleled only by Jesus in the other Gospels.[176] We have already seen how the Matthean community develops and enacts legal procedures formerly executed outside the

---

[176] What the disciples represent and why these modifications have been made are discussed below under "The Portrait of the Disciples."

community.[177] Along with this is the Matthean disciples' authority to bind and loose, expel from the community, and forgive sins. In short, the disciples reflect and enact the will and authority of the kingdom of heaven on earth, in the Matthean community.

The Portrait of the Disciples

What are we to make of this portait of the disciples by Matthew? What is the purpose of these significant developments in Matthew's presentation of the disciples? Matthew has consistently deleted the lack of understanding of the Markan disciples from his description of the disciples of Jesus. The substance of the ministry of the disciples in Matthew emerges essentially as that of education and instruction. In Matthew the disciples are primarily teachers. They received extended teaching from Jesus; they understood him and the mysteries of the kingdom; and they now are charged to instruct others about Jesus' commands and the life of the community. The more charismatic ministry of healings, exorcisms, and missionary preaching, more prominent in Mark, seems to play almost no role in Matthew's discussion about discipleship. Chapter 10 and the sending recorded there are all that is left of this sort of activity in Matthew's community. The sending is greatly curtailed: there is no report back, and it seems as if those who go are actually sent "in the name of a disciple" 10:42). Few people now go out on missions (9:37), and it may be a special or smaller group that now carries on this more traditional form of ministry.

Ministry for the disciples in Matthew involves understanding, instruction, and the exercising of unusual authority which the community believes was granted to them by Jesus. The actions and decisions of the disciples, and through them the community, embody in a binding way the decisions of God in the kingdom of heaven. These changes in the portrait of the disciples in Matthew reflect some significant social developments within the Matthean community. The community no longer looks to authorities outside of the community for guidance; indeed, the authorities outside the community are rejected. Any claim by another authority to possess the understanding of God's will and to enact the decisions and judgments of God would be rejected by the Matthean community. The Matthean community's portayal of the disciples and the authority and insight they possess is too exclusive to allow for other authorities, such as

---

[177] See "Matthew and the Civil Realm."

teachers, judges, or arbitrators of any kind. The Matthean community now has people who fulfill these roles. Their members possess
both the authority and the actual roles or positions parallel to those
authorities and roles outside the community (see 23:8ff.). Indeed, the
community claims that they possess the true judgments, the true
understanding, and true authority given them by God. Matthew's
portrait of the disciples is a key factor in communicating this to the
community and to those outside the community who would question
the authority and validity of the members and their judgments.

Instruction has developed as the central feature of discipleship
because of the false teachers in the Matthean setting (7:15ff.; 23:4,
13-16, 24, 29-31). The Matthean community must "beware" of these
false authorities and teachers. The disciples, in their role as teachers
and "true guides" (in contrast to the scribes and Pharisees), will
instruct the community and protect it from the corrupting instruction
of those outside the community.

Matthew also believes that the Law and the Prophets can be both
understood and fulfilled. The members of the community can properly and completely live out the righteousness which God expects of
them. The Sermon on the Mount emphasizes this.[178] The developed
and more defined ethics and values of the community, which the
members are to fulfill, call for teachers and education. The more
developed sense of community identity and order which we are
observing in the Matthean community would require both teachers
and a process of education, so that ensuing members would "come
to inhabit the same social world" which the community has now
constructed.[179]

The portrait of the disciples once again serves to legitimate the life
and order of the Matthean community. That is, the disciples and the
community members through them acting both as students (*mathētēs*)
and teachers explain and defend the life of the community. The
teachers will explain the interpretations, actions, and values of the
community to new members or to those who begin to doubt
the plausibility of the community's beliefs. Also these teachers, with
their authority and insight coming as if from God, defend the community's life and order from attacks from the authorities outside the
community who challenge their beliefs. The portrait of the Matthean
disciples constitutes a response to this threat and provides assurance
and guidance for the Matthean community.

---

[178] See above, "Ordering the Life of the Community."
[179] See Berger, *Sacred Canopy*, 30–31.

The disciples in Matthew's Gospel seem to represent the community members. "Disciple is the designation for a Christian in the Matthean community."[180] In many ways the disciples in Matthew have become ideal types; they are prototypes for the follower of Jesus. The disciples do not appear to struggle and at times fail in their attempt to follow Jesus, as the Markan disciples seem to do. The disciples in Matthew lack sharp contours, with little or no personal and biographical information provided about them.[181] The disciples are models (*Vorbild*) for the members of the community.

This can be seen in the fact that in the sections of the Gospel which are clearly intended as instruction for the community, especially chaps. 5–7 and 18, as well as 9:37ff. and 28:16ff., the disciples constitute the audience for the narrative. Even at the outset of the Sermon on the Mount, when Jesus sees the crowds around him, Matthew notes that Jesus called *his disciples to him*, and then began to teach them. The community, as represented by the disciples and not the *ochloi* or crowds, is the intended recipient and audience for the teaching.[182] This is further betrayed, as noted above, by the constant use of "brother" (*adelphos*), a favorite Matthean ecclesiological term, throughout the Sermon.[183] The same term emerges throughout chap. 18. Similarly, the disciples alone represent the audience in the extended teaching from 24:1 to 26:1. This includes the parable of the king and his judgment in 25:34ff. Here service and charity toward community members relate directly to one's fate at the judgment. The righteous (*dikaioi*) are the members who have employed the ethic of service and humility encouraged throughout the Gospel. The disciples, representing the community members, are to take to heart this message of service to other members. The entire community is called to be learners, to understand fully the teachings of Jesus and to fulfill them. The entire community is about the business of making disciples and teaching people what Jesus has commanded. These are all activities actually engaged in by the community, but in the Gospel they are enacted or represented by the disciples.

In his idealizing of the disciples and their emergence in the Gospel as followers of Jesus who truly learn, understand, and now *teach*

---

[180] Trilling, "Amtsverständnis," 41; Frankemölle, *Jahwebund*, 84–85, 150ff.

[181] Frankemölle, "Amtskritik," 256.

[182] P. Minear, "The Disciples and the Crowds in the Gospel of Matthew," in *Gospel Studies in Honor of S. E. Johnson*, ed. M. H. Shepherd and E. C. Hobbs; *ATR* Suppl. Ser. 3 (1974) 28–44.

[183] See above, "Ordering the Life of the Community."

others, Matthew has provided a model for the life and behavior of the community member. While Jesus is the hero and agent of God in Matthew's story, it is really the life and ministry of the disciples, centering as it does on learning, understanding, and instruction, which constitutes the primary focus of the member's own ministry in the present.[184] The community members are to identify and emulate the disciples of Jesus as they are portrayed in the Gospel. This is the case with the disciples as such, but not with the one disciple who receives unusual attention in Matthew's story, Peter. The figure of Peter in Matthew's Gospel deserves particular attention and discussion.

The Figure of Peter

Matthew does encourage equality and mutuality within the community. Service and humility are the marks of true greatness (18:1ff.). Members should eschew titles and places of honor (23:6ff.). Deference toward others and forgoing prerogatives and expressions of power or position which might be at one's disposal are to be practiced within the community and between members (5:22ff.). Though it is clear that these are priorities Matthew wishes to emphasize, it is also clear that Peter receives special attention within the Gospel. As Kingsbury has observed, Peter is *primus unter pares*, or first among equals.[185]

Peter is called "first" (*prōtos*) among the disciples in Matt. 10:2, and he is the first called to be a follower of Jesus in 4:18. There are occasions when it is clear that Peter is simply the spokesperson for the disciples or their representative. In 19:27; 26:35, 40 it is Peter who speaks, but all the disciples are addressed by Jesus, highlighting Peter's role as spokesperson or representative.[186] Matthew has even retained the plural response by Jesus, thereby addressing all the disciples, in his reworked Petrine confession (16:16ff.), which was already present in the Markan tradition (Mark 8:30ff.). Peter is not so important that he has become unreal in his characterization by Matthew. His denial of Jesus of course is retained (26:70), and he no longer receives special mention in the announcement of the resurrection in Matthew, as he does in Mark (Matt. 28:7//Mark 16:7).

---

[184] Bonnard, "Matthieu, Éducateur du Peuple Chrétien."

[185] J. D. Kingsbury, "The Figure of Peter in Matthew's Gospel as a Theological Problem," *JBL* 98 (1979) 71.

[186] Schweizer, "Matthew's Church," 135–36.

Peter, however, is not simply one of the disciples; he is not portrayed as an equal within the story. Peter emerges as a leader or, as Matthew says, "first" among the followers of Jesus. Peter receives special instruction about halakic matters in 15:15; 17:24-27; and 18:21. On all three occasions it appears that Matthew has inserted Peter's name into the pericope.[187] Peter has the foresight to inquire about the correct understanding and interpretation of the law and the ethical behavior which it mandates, and he receives this legal instruction from Jesus himself.

This special position of Peter in Matthew is most clearly seen in the so-called Petrine confession in 16:13-19. Matthew has inherited this encounter at Caesarea Philippi from Mark, but has made dramatic changes in the story. In particular, Peter's answer to Jesus' question about his identity and the blessing Jesus places upon Peter stand out as significant changes from the Markan tradition. Peter says to Jesus that he is "the Christ, the Son of the living God." In response to this Jesus tells Peter:

> Blessed are you, Simon Bar-Jonah! For flesh and blood has not revealed this to you, but my Father who is in heaven. And I tell you, you are Peter, and on this rock I will build my church, and the powers of death shall not prevail against it. I will give you the keys of the kingdom of heaven, and whatever you bind on earth shall be bound in heaven, and whatever you loose on earth shall be loosed in heaven. (16:17-19 RSV)

The two images employed by Matthew here of "rock" and "the keys" in v. 17 are of particular interest. The term "rock" is used by Matthew elsewhere to describe the person who hears and acts upon the teaching of Jesus in 7:24. Here the rock is the truth — namely, the teaching of Jesus — and relying on it results in one's safety and salvation. The one who does not rely on the rock is likened to a fool who will ultimately be destroyed.

This image of the rock was used by other communities within the wider setting of first- and second-century Palestine to communicate the same basic message. As O. Betz has pointed out, the rock was an important image at Qumran. In 1QS 11:4ff.; 1QH 6:25ff.; and 1QH 7:8ff., the rock represents the truth of God. In 1QS 8:5-10 the Qumran community is depicted as the "rock," the true Israel.[188] In a similar fashion, the *Odes of Solomon* 22:12 records that the "foundation

---

[187] Ibid.
[188] O. Betz, "Felsenmann und Felsengemeinde," *ZNW* 48 (1957) 49-77.

everything is your [God's] rock. And upon it you have built your kingdom, and it has become a dwelling place for your holy ones."

Here, as in Matthew, the term "rock" emerges as a rather exclusivistic term. Those who claim the rock claim to possess the truth. They possess God's favor and possess, or will possess, God's kingdom. It is a significant development to assign this term to a person, as Matthew does for Peter. This person Peter is now the rock or foundation of the kingdom. It is not the teachings of Jesus (Matt. 7:24) or the holy community (1QS 8:5-10) or God or the faithfulness of God (1QS 11:4ff.; 1QH 6:25ff.; *Odes Sol.* 22:12), but a person and the insight God has given to this person.

This metaphor for faithfulness and truth has been significantly transformed by Matthew essentially to legitimate and support the teaching of the community and its belief in Jesus. The confession of Peter and Peter himself constitute the foundation upon which the community rests (16:18a), and which provides a defense against the destructive forces that threaten the *ekklēsia* (16:18b). A significant aspect of this passage is the fact that it highlights the revelation Peter has received. No person told this to Peter; it was revealed to him by God (16:17). The understanding of the community and its belief about Jesus were revealed by God. Also, the authority which the present-day disciples carry out in the community was bestowed on them by Jesus.[189] Peter, in this passage, is portrayed as the guarantor of the correct understanding and teaching, and indeed of the community itself.[190]

Some of the same observations can be made about the term "keys," which Matthew inserts in this passage. Peter is granted the keys to the kingdom of heaven and, with them, the authority to bind and loose.[191] This passage appears to be based on Isa. 22:22. In 2 *Bar.* 10:18 and 4 *Bar.* 4:4 the keys to the temple are relinquished by the priests, who throw them up into heaven saying, "We give them to the Lord and say, 'Guard your house yourself, because behold, we have been found to be false stewards.'"[192] The priests relinquish the keys and are found unworthy to keep them. These documents, written around the time of Matthew, are attempting to deal with the

---

[189] See G. W. E. Nickelsburg, "Enoch, Levi, and Peter: Recipients of Revelation in Upper Galilee," *JBL* 100 (1981) 575–600.

[190] Trilling, "Amtsverständnis," 43.

[191] The authority to bind and loose was discussed above, "Community Discipline in Matthew 18."

[192] A strikingly similar passage occurs in ARNA 4. This document is much later, but chap. 4 could be based on an earlier *Vorlage*.

destruction of the temple, the obvious dissonance it would have caused, and the issue of the corrupt and unfaithful leadership in Israel.[193]

Quite in contrast to this picture, Matthew bestows on Peter the keys and all the authority they represent (Matt. 16:19). Peter is a faithful and true authority. We would not draw a direct connection between the keys of the temple in 2 and 4 *Baruch* and the keys of Matthew 16. Rather, we note that the image of the keys in this period was a symbol of authority and of the blessing and sanction of God. Those who possessed "the keys," whether to heaven, hell, or the temple, are claiming unusual authority. They claim also to be the representatives of God's authority on earth. Here again, however, Matthew bestows this symbol of significant authority on a person, Peter.[194]

The keys represent the authority and power of the kingdom of heaven on earth. Peter is empowered to exercise that authority through exclusion or inclusion from the community and generally in his role as the foundation or "rock" for the community. It is clear that Matthew understands this as the power to include or exclude, forgive or not forgive not only *in the community* but also in the future, in heaven. Peter, through his knowledge and confession, revealed to him by God, is granted the authority to be the gatekeeper both now, in the community, and eschatologically, in heaven.

What do the designation "rock" and the bestowal of the keys of the kingdom on Peter mean for Matthew's portrait of Peter and for the social development of the Matthean community generally? One significant factor has to do with the transfer of authority within the community. Max Weber observed that an important factor in the routinization of charisma is the problem of succession and the transferal of authority that must take place with the death of the charismatic leader. As the community develops and the memory of the leader wanes, the question inevitably arises, Who will be the leader? And upon what, or by whose authority, will they lead? The original charismatic power and authority must be transformed and legitimated by the successors of the leader into an acceptable right or force.[195] How can this transference of authority take place within the community?

---

[193] Discussed above in chap. 2.

[194] In Rev. 3:7 Christ possesses "the keys." In 3 *Bar.* 11:2 it is the angel Michael, and in 2 and 4 *Baruch* the "office" of priest, or all the priests, who have been found unfaithful, relinquish the keys. In Matthew 16 the apostle Peter is granted the keys.

[195] M. Weber, *Essays in Sociology*, ed. H. Gerth and C. Mills (Oxford: Oxford University Press, 1946) 262.

M. Weber noted that "designation" by the charismatic leader is one way in which communities deal with the issue of transference of authority. The leader clearly chooses the person who will carry the authority and sanction of the leader into the next generation and beyond. Revelation constitutes another way in which authority can be transferred and the problem of succession effectively resolved within the community. Through divine disclosure the successor of the charismatic leader within the community is selected and authority transmitted.[196] Both processes anticipate and respond to the question of authority within the community which, simply stated, asks, "Says who?"

Matthew has obviously combined both of the means of legitimation and transference of authority described by Weber. Matthew has described how Jesus set aside Peter to function as leader and protector within the community in this crucial passage. Matthew also made clear that Peter received this designation from Jesus on the basis of his correct answer to Jesus' question, an answer that was supplied to Peter by God. The Petrine confession in Matthew contains both elements of designation by Jesus of Peter as community leader and revelation, which supports the assertion that Peter is chosen and sanctioned by God for this role and the authority it carries.

Viewing the important terms "rock" and "keys" in their wider first- and early second-century context in Palestine, the claim made by Matthew for Peter being an authority and a leader emerges even more clearly. These two terms and images denote authority. Only Matthew assigns these pregnant terms to a person. This legitimates Peter as a community leader and also competes and conflicts with similar claims outside the Matthean community. Peter then emerges as a type or model within the Gospel for a community leader. The successors of Peter within the community enjoy the blessing and authority Matthew claims for Peter.[197] His role as spokesperson for the community and as protector of and authority within the community, whose judgments carry the authority of heaven, all point to the development of this significant office and position within the Matthean community.

---

[196] M. Weber, *Economy and Society*, ed. G. Roth and C. Wittich (Berkeley: University of California Press, 1978) 246ff.

[197] Peter as a type for a community leader is discussed in Frankemölle, "Amtskritik," 259.

Matthew and Judaism

The social developments and the forms of defense and legitimation evident within the Gospel of Matthew constitute responses to the pressure and authority of a developing Jewish body and institution within the setting of the community. The roles and structures which the community developed were a response to the threat they felt from formative Judaism. Indeed, we have seen on several occasions that the very developments within the Matthean community were appropriated from the Jewish leadership in the Matthean setting. The authority to bind and loose, we may infer from Josephus, is similar to the authority that was ascribed to the Pharisees.[198] The Matthean community constructed norms and values and essentially ordered its life in response to and over against their rivals, described by Matthew as *the scribes and the Pharisees* (5:20). Issues involving understanding and interpetation of Scripture—questions about who truly fulfills or lives out the law—have moved to the foreground in Matthew.

Throughout the Gospel the contention with and response to formative Judaism and the Jewish leadership are clear. The portrait of the disciples, Peter in particular, constitutes a response to the Jewish authorities in the Matthean setting. Learning and teaching are essential in Matthew. This is in order to train members in the *proper* understanding and to challenge the other leaders and teachers in the Matthean setting, the scribes and Pharisees.

Matthew and the Jewish Leadership

The Matthean rejection of and attack upon the Jewish leadership which runs throughout the Gospel culminate in chap. 23 and the woes (*ouai*) upon the scribes and Pharisees. Matthew has taken over the woes from Q, but has expanded them considerably.[199] The hostility and animosity between the Matthean community and the Jewish leadership come to fullest expression in this chapter. S. Van Tilborg and D. Garland, whose monographs discussed this chapter in depth, concur that Matthew 23 reflects extensive Matthean redaction.[200] Matthew has modified the tradition in order to address the

---

[198] See above, "Community Discipline in Matthew 18."

[199] Hummel, *Die Auseinandersetzung*, 87.

[200] S. Van Tilborg, *The Jewish Leaders in Matthew* (Leiden: E. J. Brill, 1972); and D. Garland, *The Intention of Matthew 23* (Leiden: E. J. Brill, 1979).

nature of the Jewish leadership in his setting and to instruct his community about the danger they represent. As Garland has correctly observed, chap. 23 has essentially a pedagogical function for the Matthean community. This chapter teaches about true and false leadership.[201]

As noted above, the different Jewish groups are dealt with rather indiscriminately by Matthew.[202] For the reader, the Jewish leadership emerges as one homogeneous group. In the Matthean setting, the distinctions within the Jewish leadership are no longer maintained, or they are not that pronounced. The Jewish leadership has converged into one single, dominant group. The Gospel, and Matthew 23 in particular, reflects this. The failure on Matthew's part to accurately reflect the distinctions between the different Jewish groups that functioned historically within Palestine may have been what led some to conclude that the struggle with the Jewish leadership is no longer a lively issue for Matthew. The struggle between the Jewish leaders and the Matthean community has been distanced over time, and there no longer exists serious competition between the two groups.[203] This is a mistaken conclusion. The Jewish leadership is summed up and converges in the fixed Matthean formula, "the scribes and the Pharisees." This formula represents the single, dominant group in his setting. This phrase is understood in this manner by his audience when it is heard or repeated.

All groups within the Jewish leadership share the same traits and faults. This is another aspect of the indiscriminate use of Jewish titles and proof that in the view of Matthew and his community they are essentially the same. The denunciations and epithets pronounced upon the Jewish leaders by Matthew are done with emotion and in the harshest terms. This does not sound like a distant struggle that lives on only as a relic in the memory of the community. These leaders are described as murderers (23:29-39), hypocrites (23:13, 14, 15, 23, 25, 27, 29), and blind guides and fools (23:16,24) who inwardly are corrupt and lawless (23:28).

It is perhaps here, more than anywhere else in his Gospel, that Matthew exposes the sectarian nature and stance of his community over against the dominant *parent group* in his setting, the Jewish leadership referred to as the scribes and the Pharisees. Like many

---

[201] Garland, *Intention*, 38; see also Minear, "The Disciples and the Crowds," 32.
[202] Hummel, *Die Auseinandersetzung*, 31; Van Tilborg, *Jewish Leaders*, 1–6; Garland, *Intention*, 44.
[203] Garland, *Intention*, 45.

other sectarian communities in this post-70 period, Matthew views the Jewish leadership as the source of many problems, as corrupt and faithless leaders who misguide and corrupt the people. The hostility toward the leadership and the harsh terms of denunciation and rejection employed by these groups help to locate these sectarian communities in the post-70 period. They have clearly rejected the dominant leadership in their setting. This much is an understatement. They constitute the minority and feel powerless in their present situation. These sectarian groups are not making the rules and have become outsiders in relation to those who are in control. God, however, will soon judge these so-called hypocrites and corrupt leaders. The sectarian community and its beliefs and practices will be vindicated.[204] Matthew has employed some of the very same terms which, as we noted above, emerge as part of the common stock of sectarian vocabulary in this period. The leaders are corrupt, lawless, and hypocrites, while the sectarian community is righteous, faithful, and the true people of God.[205]

Matthew, like other sectarian communities, tries to condemn the leadership through association with evil generations in Israel's past.[206] Matthew seeks to legitimate the position of his community by associating and implicating the current leadership with the widely accepted sins and errors of past leaders. Matthew, along with other sectarian documents from this period, tries to associate the present leadership with some of the villains of Israel's history. The persecution of the apostles and the Matthean community at the hands of the Jewish leadership parallels the persecution and rejection of the prophets by the false leaders of Israel's history.

The parable of the wedding feast in 22:1ff. is a thinly veiled story about the rejection of "the king's" son by Israel, who has mistreated and killed him, and the subsequent destruction of Jerusalem and the selection of others who were "found" to take the place of those who had rejected the son. Matthew 23:34 claims that the contemporary Jewish leaders, like those of old, have been sent prophets and wise men, but they were killed, crucified, and scourged in their synagogues. Indeed these contemporary leaders are implicated in the murder of all righteous blood in the history of Israel (23:35).

---

[204] See the discussion in chap. 1, "Fragmentation and Factionalism: The Sectarian Nature of Judaism."

[205] Similar passages are in the *Lives of the Prophets* 3:15; 15:6; 16:3; *2 Baruch* 25–30; *T. Levi* 10:3; 14:4-6; 16:2-4; 4 Ezra 7:22-24.

[206] See chap. 1, "Hostility toward the Jewish Leadership." Examples are *T. Levi* 16 and 5 Ezra 1:32ff.

The evil (*ponēroi*; see 9:4; 12:34; 16:1; 22:18) leaders are to be avoided, because they corrupt others and "tie up heavy loads upon men," and "make their converts twice the sons of Gehenna as themselves." They lie and are not to be believed (28:15). Following them leads to destruction (15:12-14), and their teaching (*didachē*) is to be avoided (16:12).[207] It is here that the pedagogical aspect of Matthew's portrayal of the Jewish leadership emerges most clearly. Matthew's depiction of the Jewish leadership, culminating as it does in chap. 23, serves as a warning to leaders and members of the Matthean community.[208]

The audience of chap. 23, like that of the Sermon on the Mount, begins with both disciples and *ochloi* present. However, also as with the Sermon, the primary audience shifts quickly to the community members. Verse 8 ("but you") reflects the focus of the chapter as being instruction for the community. Not only are the Jewish leaders rejected and denounced, but they constitute, through their exaggerated and stereotyped caricature, examples and agents of instruction, albeit in a negative way, of the essence of leadership and guidance. The leaders of Israel are the antithesis of the disciples.[209] They represent all that the disciples should not be or do. The actions of the Jewish leadership should not be followed or imitated. The same is true for their attitudes and motives. The members of the community will emulate the Jewish leaders at great peril. They should not be found as false stewards. The potentially negative fate of the false disciple is essentially the same as the corrupt Jewish leader in the Matthean setting, understood by his community as *the scribes and the Pharisees* (7:12ff.). Through Matthew's excessive and harsh denunciation of the Jewish leadership, something Matthew shares in common with many sectarian communities in his provenance and period, we learn much about what Matthew believes are the qualities of a leader and what he thinks is the nature of true leadership. The members are instructed through this overwhelmingly negative depiction of false leadership and the fate of false leaders to live according to the values of the community and the life to which Matthew feels they have been called.

For all the criticism and rejection of the Jewish leadership in chap. 23, Matthew curiously begins the chapter by ascribing a position of authority and power to the scribes and Pharisees by saying that they

---

[207] Van Tilborg, *Jewish Leaders*, 169.
[208] Garland, *Intention*, 117.
[209] Ibid., 123.

"sit upon the seat of Moses." It is quite unlikely that this refers to a specific object in the gathering place. We have no archaeological evidence to support the development of an actual "seat of Moses" in the gathering places at this early stage.[210] I. Renov is certainly closer to Matthew's meaning when he states that this represents a symbol of authority.[211] The scribes and Pharisees hold this position of authority and respect, and this is acknowledged even by their most ardent detractors.

But Matt. 23:2 should be read in the larger context of chap. 23 itself. It therefore cannot be construed as an endorsement by Matthew, even in a limited way, of the scribes and the Pharisees. No reader of Matthew's Gospel could possibly gather that impression.[212] This verse, however, does reflect the position the scribes and Pharisees enjoy in the Matthean setting as authorities concerning the law and their judgments.[213] This is the only viable explanation for the inclusion of this curious passage. The scribes and Pharisees really do possess authority and clout in Matthew's setting, and the community members should do what they tell them to do. It is the actions of the scribes and Pharisees, however, that must be avoided (23:3).

There are other elements in chap. 23 which reveal that the Jewish leadership in Matthew's Gospel does in actuality possess authority and position in the world of Matthew's community. These leaders have the authority to bind heavy loads upon people (23:4). Though Matthew finds this distasteful, the scribes and the Pharisees are granted the places of honor at banquets and in the gathering places (23:6). They are called "rabbi" by the public. Along with being teachers and leaders (23:16, 19), they are also engaged in missionizing activity, bringing people into the movement or group.[214] All of this, together with the emotional and vehement attack on these leaders by Matthew, which runs throughout the Gospel, reveals that the *scribes and Pharisees* truly are the leaders and authorities in Matthew's setting. It is against this consolidating and dominant group of Jewish authorities that the Matthean community struggles.

---

[210] *Contra* E. Sukenik, *Ancient Synagogues in Palestine and Greece*, The Schweich Lectures (Oxford: Oxford University Press, 1934) 90ff.

[211] I. Renov, "The Seat of Moses," *IEJ* 5 (1955) 262–67.

[212] Bornkamm laid too much stress on v. 2 alone and neglected the larger context which surely controls how one should understand this passage; see *Tradition and Interpretation in Matthew*, 21.

[213] Garland, *Intention*, 45ff.

[214] For Matt. 23:15, see J. A. Overman, "The God-Fearers: Some Neglected Features," *JSNT* 32 (1988) 20.

The Jewish leadership has emerged as the controlling body in Matthew's setting, and it is this group of leaders which casts such a long shadow over the Gospel of Matthew.

The claim of some scholars that Matthew lived in a world in which Judaism was no longer serious competition for the Matthean community has not taken into account the position and authority of the Jewish leadership depicted in concrete terms in the Gospel, and in chap. 23 in particular.[215] The threat and competition from this single, dominant group of leaders are described in the most real and threatening terms by Matthew. There is no note of distance or historical perspective in this lively struggle between the Matthean community and the Jewish leaders in their setting. This is an issue that has controlled and shaped Matthew's Gospel. From the fulfillment citations to the debates about the law to Jesus' teaching to the Matthean community, which sets its life and values over against the values and behavior of the Jewish leadership, to the denunciations of chap. 23 and elsewhere, the struggle with formative Judaism has dominated the horizon of the Matthean community. Moreover, to deny that this struggle with formative Judaism was a real issue and conflict for the Matthean community fails to take into account what recent studies in social conflict have shown.

Louis Kriesberg, in *The Sociology of Social Conflict*, notes that an awareness on the part of two groups that they constitute separate, collective entities in opposition to one another must be present for conflict such as that between the Matthean community and the Jewish leadership to exist.[216] The animosity with which the Matthean community views the Jewish leadership confirms the actual competition and conflict between these two groups. Further, these two groups, as is often the case with social conflict, "unwittingly help to define each other."[217] This is obviously true with the Matthean community. The community defines its interpretation of the law in relation to the Jewish leadership with which it contends (5:20; 15:12ff.). The ethics and values of the Matthean community are contrasted with this group (6.1ff.), and true leadership is portrayed by means of contrast with the false leaders and guides, the scribes and the Pharisees (chap. 23).

Competing ideologies and beliefs must be present for conflict to erupt in the manner and with the emotion that it has in the Matthean

---

[215] Van Tilborg, *Jewish Leaders*, 171.

[216] L. Kriesberg, *The Sociology of Social Conflict* (Englewood Cliffs, N.J.: Prentice-Hall, 1973) 61.

[217] Ibid., 87; Coser, *Functions of Social Conflict*, 95.

community.[218] These communities live close to one another, share similar beliefs and practices, and have now gone separate ways. As J. Gager observes, the conflict between the Matthean community and formative Judaism should be seen above all as a struggle between kindred communities.[219] The strong emotions and the sweeping manner with which the Jewish leadership is attacked and rejected by Matthew suggest a current and hotly contested struggle which the Matthean community seems to be losing. Matthew's accusatory language and name-calling indicate the position of power the Jewish leadership holds as well as the status of the Matthean community as the minority or underdog in this struggle. This harsh language has been called "safety-valve behavior," because it provides an opportunity to vent frustrations and anger which the group feels toward those in power.[220]

There is a single, dominant group of leaders in this setting which the Matthean community rejects and struggles against. Matthew has not created this struggle. It is a conflict that Matthew and his community must face daily, one that has played a controlling role in the shape of Matthew's Gospel. The struggle and break between Matthew's community and formative Judaism have forced a crisis upon the community. We must ask finally, in light of this, how Matthew understood the relationship between his community and Judaism in the post-70 period.

Jesus and Judaism in Matthew

The conflict that is evident throughout Matthew between his community and the dominant form of Judaism which has developed in his setting reveals an important aspect about the community and its relation with Judaism. It is clear that Matthew has sought to vindicate his community in the face of formative Judaism. That is to say, Matthew made no attempt to harmonize the life of his community with the developing leadership and authorities. Quite to the contrary, Matthew's portrait of Jesus and his followers takes up and disputes the very issues and concerns around which formative Judaism was

---

[218] Coser, *Functions of Social Conflict*, 82.

[219] Gager, *Kingdom and Community*, 88.

[220] Kriesberg, *Sociology*, 92, and Coser, *Functions of Social Conflict*, 41. As noted above, numerous other sectarian communities in the post-70 period exhibit this behavior and attitude toward the consolidating Jewish leadership; see chap. 1, "The Language of Sectarianism."

developing. Matthew does not do away with Sabbath laws or rules of ritual purity, as Mark seems to do (Mark 2:27; 7:19). Rather, he offers a reasoned defense of his community's understanding and application of the law. Matthew claims that his accusers do not understand the law but pervert it (12:7; 15:3).

Contrary to their opponents, Jesus and his followers do not act in a manner that violates the law and the tradition; rather their actions are the very fulfillment of the same.[221] Jesus, like Moses of old, is the leader of God's true chosen people. This emerges as an exclusive claim. The Matthean community claims the same tradition and history as their opponents from the consolidating formative Judaism. This has placed these two movements in direct confrontation with one another. Both the Matthean community and the Jewish leadership claim to possess the true interpretation of the law. According to Matthew, Jesus himself, in his own biographical history (the birth narrative) and in his actions as Messiah in word and deed, is the fulfillment of the predictions of the prophets and the very will and plan of God. The community has developed its own leadership, which parallels and challenges the leadership within formative Judaism and now instructs the community members about the false and dangerous nature of the Jewish leaders and their teaching. The community has adopted its own definite set of ethics and priorities so that the members will not embrace the teaching and interpretation of the false leaders and guides of formative Judaism.

Matthew and his community in its social development, provoked in large measure by the conflict with formative Judaism, have not gone their separate way. They have not forged their own set of beliefs and behavior sufficiently distinct from formative Judaism, which would have enabled the two groups to live more or less in peaceful coexistence. On the contrary, Matthew and his community claim to have the true understanding of the law, to have the true leaders, and truly to have fulfilled the "will of their Father in heaven." In short, Matthew and his community claim to be the true Israel, and the leaders of formative Judaism are false leaders who will be rejected at the judgment, while the Matthean community will be vindicated.[222]

Matthew sees God's rejection of these leaders as already operative. God is turning to a people "who bear fruit" (21:43). God has *found* (*heuron*) in the Matthean community a people who will both hear

---

[221] This was discussed above, under "Scripture, Interpretation, and Tradition in Matthew."

[222] Thus the title and theme of Trilling's monograph, *Das Wahre Israel*.

God's call and do God's will (22:10). The claims of the Matthean community are exclusive and are expressed in a manner that would make resolution of the conflict between these two movements difficult. This position leaves little room for bargaining. The social construction of the Matthean community, developing as it did in response to and over against formative Judaism, left these two groups in direct contention with one another. Matthew has placed his community in a struggle characteristic of sectarian communities in the post-70 period. The Matthean community, like several other communities in this period, claims to be the true Israel, the only faithful body, and the fulfillers of the divine plan and law.

Several developments within the Matthean community—the authority of the disciples and their function primarily as teachers, the extensive legal instruction, the rejection of the scribes and the Pharisees, the emergence of Matthew's own leaders—take aim specifically at formative Judaism. Matthew has set the beliefs and life of his community over against those of formative Judaism in such a way that the people of his community and city would have had to make a choice between the two. One could not support or be loyal to both. Lines of separation have been drawn, in a manner that appears to offer no way back. The paths of the Matthean community and formative Judaism do not flow together from this point forward, but appear rather to diverge.

The Nature and World of the Matthean Community

W E ARE NOW IN A POSITION to summarize the results of this study, which has had as its focus the social development of the Matthean community. In the introduction, our point of departure was M. Weber's insight concerning the routinization of charisma. The introduction proceeded to claim that this study would assume a perspective informed by the sociology of knowledge, an approach that suggests that the social constructions and developments evident within a community are shaped and provoked by developments and events within their *life-world* or, in the words of E. D. Hirsch, within the *horizon* of the community.

Chapter 1 sought to highlight certain salient features of the horizon of the Matthean community and formative Judaism. This chapter developed a number of issues which loomed large on the horizon of most communities in Palestine during this period. Many of these same issues—hostility toward the Jewish leadership, the law as common ground and battleground, the sectarian nature of some of these communities, and the question of the future of God's covenant people—all emerge as important issues within the life of the Matthean community. Matthew has been greatly influenced by his setting and the issues and attitudes which prevail there. Matthew's world has profoundly shaped the nature of his Gospel.

For example, it is clear that Matthew would have had many partners in debate over the law and its proper interpretation. It is also clear that many of Matthew's contemporaries would have claimed the same exclusive and (so it appears to the modern reader) rather dogmatic position concerning the law and its correct application to life. One suspects that the debates between Jesus and the scribes and Pharisees portrayed in Matthew were duplicated throughout Palestine by many competing groups and communities. Within these other communities the debates appear to have possessed the same vigor and emotion as are evident in the Matthean conflict stories.[1]

The same can be said for the response to the Jewish leadership or *parent group* in this period. Many communities rejected the Jewish leadership and viewed them as faithless and as a corrupting influence in their setting. God will soon judge these false leaders and vindicate the sectarian community. These attacks are carried out in the harshest terms, and the judgment of the leaders is depicted with some relish by the sectarian minority. There can be no doubt that this was a turbulent and unstable period. Matthew shares this perspective and the same harsh toned concerning the Jewish leadership. Many of the accusations—and, indeed, the very same terms that were commonplace within the sectarian milieu of this period and provenance—are employed by Matthew in his conflict with the Jewish leadership.[2] Certain disturbing and offensive passages within Matthew, such as 21:43; 27:25; or chap. 23 must first of all be read and interpreted in terms of this wider setting and horizon of the sectarian nature of Judaism. This is an important part of the world and setting of Matthew's community. Matthew's thinking, the emotion with which his convictions are expressed, and indeed some of the very notions he tries to communicate, especially concerning the Jewish leadership, are best understood and read in light of this wider setting within Judaism.[3]

The rejection of the Jewish leadership and the conviction that they are faithless and have corrupted the will and law of God lead naturally to the question about the future of God's people, specifically, Who will lead God's people? The exclusive nature of these communities and the claims they made led inevitably to the conclusion that the community constituted God's new or, more accurately, God's *true* people. The current leadership and order will be judged, and the sectarian community will be vindicated by God. God is turning to this

---

[1] This was developed in chap. 1, especially under "The Centrality of the Law."

[2] See chap. 1, under "The Language of Sectarianism."

[3] Concerning 27:25 particularly, this is a typical accusation by sectarian communities. A common means of discrediting the leadership is accusing them of shedding "innocent" or "righteous" blood (see chap. 1, under "Hostility toward the Jewish Leadership). Matthew, like other sectarians, also tries to implicate these leaders in the death of other righteous persons in Israel's history (see 23:34ff.). Note also concerning 27:25 the striking parallels in 1 Sam. 26:9 and 2 Sam. 1:16. Both of these are the words of David, who declares that the guilt (1 Sam. 26:9) or the blood (2 Sam. 1:16) is upon the head of the one who "kills the Lord's Christ." To my knowledge the connection here has not been explored. These explanations and the wider context in which this disturbing passage must be placed in no way excuse or explain the unfortunate abuses and history associated with this verse.

community and its people to carry God's will and message forward. This perspective is something Matthew shares with his contemporaries as well. God is turning toward a people who "bear fruit" (Matt. 21:43) and looks now to this people for the working out of God's will and kingdom here and now. This too, naturally, is an exclusive claim which would provoke conflict and competition among other groups making the same claim, but particularly between the sectarian community and those who are presently in power. This conflict is all too evident within Matthew's Gospel.

Chapter 2 of this study highlighted the development of formative Judaism and its emergence as the dominant form of Judaism in the setting of Matthew's Gospel. The institutional forms (the role of the rabbi, the means of expulsion and community definition and defense, and the gathering place) and the means of legitimation employed by formative Judaism (the tradition and the law) reveal the process of consolidation within formative Judaism and how it emerged as the dominant group within this milieu. It is here that Matthew's primary competition and opposition emerge. This dominant group constituted the leadership and most powerful body in Matthew's world. Matthew and his community contended with and responded primarily to formative Judaism, its developments, and the accusations it leveled against the Matthean community. It is no surprise, therefore, that the social developments within the Matthean community at so many points parallel and are analogous to the social and institutional developments evident within formative Judaism.

The social developments within Matthew's community respond to the developments within formative Judaism at a number of significant and telling points. Matthew's community has developed its own gathering place, an *ekklēsia*, which constitutes the community's institutional response to the gathering place of formative Judaism, *autōn synagōgē*, their synagogue. The disciples in Matthew emerge as teachers who understand the law and the instruction of Jesus, and they possess unusual authority to expel others from the community, forgive sins or not, and are granted the civil authority analogous to that of the Pharisees, "to bind and to loose."[4] The portrait of the disciples resembles in significant ways the image of the Jewish leaders as embodied in the Matthean antagonists, "the scribes and the Pharisees." The disciples are authorities within the community;

---

[4] Discussed in chap. 1, under "Fragmentation and Factionalism: The Sectarian Nature of Judaism."

they are essentially teachers, and they are contrasted directly with the Jewish leadership in the Matthean setting.

The figure of Peter is significant in this regard. Peter is a divinely inspired and guided leader given authority and insight from God. Peter and his successors in the community are granted this position and the authority it entails by God. Naturally this responds to and rivals claims being made by the dominant leadership, but it also serves to legitimate the role of the leaders within the Matthean community. The portrait of Peter supports and legitimates the role of leaders in the face of those in the community who may doubt the accuracy or viability of the Matthean authorities. Other sectarian communities possess their divinely inspired agent of God who interprets the word and message of God for the community.[5] These figures have been given a revelation from God, and they give it in turn to the community. These agents confirm the truth of the community's beliefs and reassure the community that God is truly on their side. Peter represents just such a figure within the life of the Matthean community.

Significantly, Matthew does not offer a way out of the conflict with formative Judaism. His use of the tradition, his extensive halakah and legal debates, and his claim that his community truly fulfills the law and that they are the true leaders, not their opponents, set the stage for direct conflict with formative Judaism and its emerging authorities. There is no evidence that a position was staked out by Matthew that would have allowed for reconciliation and mutual understanding between the two groups. One would clearly have to decide between membership in the two movements. Matthew and his community claim the same tradition, the same authority—even, at points, the same roles—as formative Judaism. Even more, Matthew claims quite explicitly to be the heir of God's kingdom and God's true people over against formative Judaism. The Matthean community, not the Jewish leadership, fulfills the law and will of God who is in heaven. This would clearly constitute a direct confrontation between the Matthean community and formative Judaism. The hostility and antagonism between these two groups are all too obvious within the pages of the Gospel. Matthew's Gospel reflects the confrontation between one Jewish community at the close of

---

[5] See chap. 1, under "The Centrality of the Law." Baruch, Enoch, Ezra, and Jeremiah are other such figures within sectarian Judaism; see G. W. E. Nickelsburg, "Enoch, Levi, and Peter: Recipients of Revelation in Upper Galilee," *JBL* 100 (1981) 575–600.

the first century and the developing formative Judaism which was emerging from this sectarian and fragmented period within Palestine as the dominant group within Judaism. This movement is the historical antecedent to rabbinic Judaism, which flourished in Galilee after 135 and began finally, in a protracted process, to consolidate its position after 200.[6] Within the immediate setting of Matthew's community that group already possesses significant power and influence. It is this group with which the Matthean community contends. What do this portrait and study of the Gospel of Matthew tell us about the Matthean community and its world?

First, Matthew's community was clearly sectarian, as we have defined that term.[7] The Gospel provides many indications that Matthew's community constituted the minority in a struggle with a parent group, which was in this case formative Judaism. The harsh language and epithets directed at the Jewish leadership betray the social location of the Matthean community; they were underdogs. The cautious and, at points, hostile response to the world further indicates the sectarian nature of the Matthean community. Relatively speaking, the Matthean community was more concerned with world-maintenance than being open to the world. This is in rather stark contrast to either Mark or Luke, where the world is depicted as the locus of Jesus' activity as well as the disciples. Matthew is interested in community formation, and not primarily world transformation.[8]

Matthew distrusts the institutions associated with the wider world. His response to the world is cautious at best, and at points clearly hostile. Indeed, the courts and their related authorities share many of the same characteristics as the scribes and the Pharisees.[9] In Matthew 5, for example, the two seem to coalesce and appear to be similar, if not the same body. The Jewish leadership seems to play a significant role in the administration and execution of legal and civil matters in the town or city which produced Matthew's Gospel.

This raises an important question which goes beyond the bounds of this study: What was the relationship of this consolidating Jewish body with the ultimate power and force in the region, the Roman Empire, and its clients and lords in Palestine? The struggle between

[6] A. Segal discusses the origins and development of rabbinic Judaism (*Rebecca's Children: Judaism and Christianity in the Roman World* [Cambridge, Mass.: Harvard University Press, 1986] 171ff.).

[7] A definition of "sectarian" is offered in chap. 1, under "Fragmentation and Factionalism: The Sectarian Nature of Judaism."

[8] See chap. 3, n. 63.

[9] See chap. 3, under "Matthew and the Civil Realm."

formative Judaism and the Matthean community would have almost certainly been between two rather minor factions in this place and period. One wonders whether the Roman rulers and authorities would even have been aware of the conflict we read about in Matthew's Gospel. Formative Judaism and the Matthean community may have been roughly equal in size and shape. They represent each other's primary opposition and competition. For the people of this setting these two movements would have represented basically "twin alternatives."[10] They were in many ways "kindred communities."[11] The reader of Matthew's Gospel enters into the history of this struggle and competition between formative Judaism and the Matthean community at a point when the Matthean community senses that it is losing ground against these opponents and obviously feels threatened by their growth and advance. It is in this sense and within this rather limited sphere that formative Judaism becomes the dominant power and influence in Matthew's world and setting.

This is not to dismiss the question concerning the relationship between formative Judaism and the Roman authorities in the region. The Jewish leadership in Matthew's setting may have enjoyed some sort of sanction or *de jure* authority from the Romans; they may have enjoyed popularity with the people as well, which Matthew seems to fear. Matthew has deleted the Pharisees' coalition with the Herodians (Mark 3:6), which is suggestive of the very relationship with the Romans which may have existed between them and the Jewish leadership.[12] However, this may also represent Matthew's desire to concentrate culpability for Jesus' death on the Pharisees. The Pharisees do emerge as the single and most powerful group of Jesus' opponents in Matthew. Deletion of the Heriodians from Mark 3:6 may simply be consistent with Matthew's desire to portray the Pharisees as the dominant antagonists in his setting.

The scribes and chief priests and scribes of the people appear together with Herod in Matt. 2:4. However, the Pharisees are conspicuous by their absence in this scene. The Pharisees appear as a Galilean group in Matthew; their activity and their power, to the

---

[10] Segal, *Rebecca's Children*, 2.

[11] J. Gager, *Kingdom and Community: The Social World of Early Christianity* (Englewood Cliffs, N.J.: Prentice-Hall, 1973) 88.

[12] See A. Saldarini, "Political and Social Roles of the Scribes and Pharisees in Galilee," in *Society of Biblical Literature 1988 Seminar Papers*, ed. David J. Lull (Atlanta: Scholars Press, 1988) 200–209.

extent they possess it, are limited to Galilee.[13] Formative Judaism and its leaders, represented by the Pharisees in Matthew, may in fact enjoy what we might think of as a degree of political power in Galilee. However, they are at best minor players in the political drama. Matthew provides too little evidence about the relationship of the Jewish leadership, with whom he contends, to the Roman authorities. He does depict them as friendly with judges and allied with the courts; this could easily explain Matthew's apprehension of the civil realm. In his particular setting, these Jewish leaders may well have enjoyed some *de jure* legal authority. This, however, is speculative.

More significant in terms of Matthew's Gospel than the question about the relationship between formative Judaism and the Roman authorities are the popular support and interest the movement is attracting in Matthew's setting. Formative Judaism is making converts and, to Matthew's chagrin, some members of his community seek to emulate these Jewish leaders at a number of points. Matthew must explicitly warn against fashioning one's righteousness after that of the Pharisees: "Do not act like them and do not pray or fulfill your legal obligations in the manner in which they fulfill theirs." One gets the distinct impression from this that indeed certain members of the Matthean community are doing exactly that. Matthew believes this *mimēsis* of the Jewish leaders is done at great peril. True leadership is regularly contrasted with the blind leadership of the Pharisees, and the Matthean understanding and application of the law are always set over against the view of the Pharisees. There is no doubt that the leadership of formative Judaism constitutes the primary competition and focus within Matthew's Gospel. It is also clear from the Gospel that formative Judaism is achieving some measure of popularity in Matthew's setting and even making inroads into the membership of the Matthean community. It is for this reason that Matthew offers such a reasoned defense of the beliefs of his community and such a harsh attack on the growing and now popular formative Judaism.

The popularity of formative Judaism and the threat it poses to the Matthean community help to explain Matthew's concentration on "ordinary Jewish issues."[14] Of course, these issues were of the utmost importance to Matthew and his opponents. Matthew is

---

[13] The exception here is 27:62-66, which is distinctive Matthean material. I take this as a Matthean insertion to emphasize the role of the Pharisees in the death of Jesus, and the subsequent hoax about the resurrection.

[14] Segal, *Rebecca's Children*, 146–47.

defending against and responding to the threats and the accusations from formative Judaism. The Matthean community has responded to the pressure from the Jewish leadership by developing analogous roles and institutions which teach the Matthean community's understanding of the law and its application to life as it is lived out now for them in light of the history and story of Jesus of Nazareth. For Matthew, Jesus was the one who fulfilled the will and plan of God for the people of God. The Matthean opponents view Jesus and his followers in the Matthean community as lax concerning the law. Matthew's response is that only his community, by enacting the law as it was taught and acted out by Jesus, truly fulfills the Law and the Prophets, and therefore constitutes the true Israel.

What about the composition or makeup of the Matthean community? One sees very little evidence of Gentiles (non-Jews) in the Matthean community. The slur concerning Gentiles or other nations or people (*ethnikoi*) (Matt. 5:47; 6:7; 18:17), even though it is a fixed formula, would not have found a sympathetic reception in a community with many, or even any, Gentiles. Further, the preponderance of Jewish issues and the obvious, thoroughly Jewish character of the Gospel warn against assuming too quickly any sizable non-Jewish population in Matthew's church.[15] Further, as we noted above, Matthew takes his stand within contemporary Judaism. That is to say, Matthew does not allow formative Judaism to go one way and his community to go another. Mark would be an example of letting the Jewish leaders worry about "Jewish issues," while his community essentially ignores those issues, focusing instead on others (see Mark 2:27; 7:19). This is by no means Matthew's position. Matthew argues that his community possesses the true interpretation and application of the law. Jesus freely debates about the law with the Jewish leaders. Formative Judaism and Matthew's community have overtly competing claims and would certainly, to an outsider, resemble one another. It is for this reason that the hostility between the two has reached the pitch it has in their setting.

Some might argue that the view of the law in Matthew represents a middle way between Jewish observance of the law and Gentile freedom from the law. This position would posit people within the

---

[15] While it is an argument from silence, the absence of any discussion concerning circumcision is striking. If the other books of the New Testament are anything to go by, a *corpus mixtum* of Jews and Gentiles tends to provoke questions, understandably, about circumcision. The absence of such discussion would indicate a primarily Jewish population.

community who are lawless and ignore the law. Matthew responds to this problem by offering an argument for the validity of the law. There are problems with this position. First, *anomia* does not refer to failure to keep the law, as we noted above.[16] Charismatic and seemingly legalistic Pharisees can both be *anomia*. Lawlessness in Matthew refers to failure to fulfill the will of God. It may or may not, and usually does not, refer to the Jewish law as such. Also, the arguments about the law in Matthew almost always concern the Jewish leadership and are not portrayed as internal issues. Matthew 5:17 might appear to be an exception to this; however, 5:17 responds, we believe, to accusations from the outside that certain members are perhaps beginning to believe. The opponents claim that the Matthean community fails to keep the law. Matthew responds by saying that Jesus and his followers fulfill the law and that their righteousness goes beyond that of the scribes and the Pharisees. Matthew 5, then, explicates the manner in which the halakah of the Matthean community surpasses that of formative Judaism.

However, there are several key passages which signal the community's turning toward other nations or people (see 21:43; 28:19). The hostility and animosity which characterized the relationship between formative Judaism and the Matthean comnunity as well as the poor reception Matthew's message was eliciting caused the community to look elsewhere for mission and perhaps a home. We would characterize the Matthean community, then, as mostly, if not thoroughly, Jewish but in the process of turning to the wider Gentile world. In their current setting the community was beginning to lose out to formative Judaism, as its attraction even to some of the members of the Matthean community attests; thus they are looking to another people who will receive them and their message in a more productive or fruitful manner.

Concerning the provenance or place of origin of the Gospel, certainty is impossible. However, there are features of the Gospel that suggest some possibilities. If one takes the struggle with formative Judaism seriously, as indeed this study does, then a Palestinian provenance is virtually assured. Both formative Judaism and its successor, rabbinic Judaism, were Palestinian in origin and provenance. Within Palestine, Galilee is attractive because of the central role it played in early rabbinic Judaism. This alone, however, would not necessitate Galilee. There are other features to be considered.

---

[16] See chap. 1, under "The Language of Sectarianism."

We have noted Matthew's unusual concentration on Galilee. Matthew seems to know Galilee quite well and essentially limits the activity of the Jesus movement to Galilee, and Capernaum in particular. This phenomenon in Matthew is not adequately explained by appealing to a theological agenda about the land of Galilee to which Matthew ascribes.[17] This seems to be one more reflection of Matthew's setting and world which has inevitably made its way into his Gospel story. As we noted earlier, the Pharisees, whom Matthew imports regularly as Jesus' partners in debate, are essentially portrayed as limited to Galilee. These Jewish leaders in Matthew, portrayed as the Pharisees, are in truth the Matthean opponents and not simply a literary device. The Galilean Pharisees represent the actual competitors of Matthew's community.

Within Galilee, the language and some of the imagery of Matthew, as has been noted by others before, suggest a city.[18] It is our view that this Galilean city would have to contain a court, because of the polemic against it in the Gospel, as well as environs large enough to accommodate at least the two competing factions of formative Judaism and Matthew's community. Both Sepphoris, three miles northwest of Nazareth, and Tiberias on the western shore of the Sea of Galilee were at different times during the first century the seat of the Sanhedrin, according to Josephus. There was only the one Sanhedrin or court in Galilee, and both of these cities were large enough (around thirty to forty thousand) and sophisticated enough to produce a Gospel such as this.[19] We would posit then a Galilean city, either Tiberias or Sepphoris, as the most plausible location for the Matthean community.[20]

---

[17] Along with several others, this would be the position of W. Trilling, *Das Wahre Israel: Studien zur Theologie des Matthäus-Evangeliums* (Munich: Kösel, 1964) 131ff.

[18] The urban origin of Matthew's Gospel, along with some of the vocabulary and terms that would support this, is discussed by J. D. Kingsbury, "The Verb *Akolouthein* as an Index of Matthew's View of His Community," *JBL* 97 (1978) 56–73. C. F. D. Moule discusses the "educated Greek" of Matthew in *The Birth of the New Testament* (New York: Harper & Row, 1962) 219; see also G. D. Kilpatrick, *The Origins of the Gospel according to St. Matthew* (Oxford: Clarendon, 1946) 124–25.

[19] See J. A. Overman, "Who Were the First Urban Christians? Urbanization in Galilee in the First Century," in *Society of Biblical Literature 1988 Seminar Papers,* ed. David J. Lull (Atlanta: Scholars Press, 1988) 160–68. The population of urban centers in Galilee, their institutional apparatus, and cultural sophistication are discussed there.

[20] We would tend toward Sepphoris because of the important role it played in nascent rabbinic Judaism; see F. Manns, "Un centre judéo-chrétien important: Sépphoris," in *Essais sur le Judéo-Christianisme* (Jerusalem: Franciscan Printing Press, 1977) 165–90.

From the Gospel itself the future of the Matthean community is difficult to reconstruct. The sectarian behavior and attitude and the emotional attacks on the Jewish leadership indicate a smaller, struggling body, which is drawing in from the world around it. The Matthean community feels persecuted and constitutes the minority in their competition with formative Judaism. It would seem that initially Matthew's Gospel was rather well received. It is possible to speak of a Matthean circle of sorts at the close of the first century and early in the second.[21] However, as is widely recognized, the distinctive kind of *Jewish Christianity* with which Matthew comes to be associated seems for the most part to have disappeared.[22] Matthew's Gospel may in fact show some initial signs of this fate in the upper hand which formative Judaism appears to be gaining in Matthew's setting. As we noted above, Matthew's position concerning the Jewish leadership left little room for negotiation; one had to choose between these two movements. The close relationship and the similarities between these two competing movements left little room for divided loyalties. In the world of Matthew's Gospel formative Judaism emerged finally as the dominant and more popular of the two. One can sense this development already in the pages of Matthew's Gospel.

Nowhere is the shared matrix of Christianity and emergent rabbinic Judaism more evident than in Matthew's Gospel. These two movements are fraternal twins.[23] They developed and defined themselves in light of one another. It is not surprising then that the most intense competition and perhaps the greatest struggle over the divergent paths these twins eventually take are also found in Matthew. The struggle and eventual separation between formative and Matthean Judaism have all the emotion and conflict of a family falling apart. One cannot be sure if the social developments and the forms of legitimation adopted by the Matthean community in the end resulted in the survival and perpetuation of the community. It is

---

[21] A Matthean circle might include the *Didache,* 5 Ezra, perhaps the *Kerygmata Petrou,* and other writings associated with a Petrine tradition. See H. Koester, "Gnomai Diaphoroi," in *Trajectories through Early Christianity* (Philadelphia: Fortress Press, 1971) 124ff.; see also G. Stanton, "5 Ezra and Matthean Christianity in the Second Century," *JTS* 28 (1977) 67–83.

[22] The distinctive history of Jewish Christianity is discussed by G. Strecker in *Orthodoxy and Heresy in Earliest Christianity,* ed. R. Kraft and G. Krodel (Philadelphia: Fortress Press, 1971) 241ff.

[23] Segal, *Rebecca's Children,* 179.

obviously true, however, that at least for a time the Matthean community and formative Judaism developed and grew alongside of and over against one another. In their competition and contention with one another they were forced to develop and change. To this extent, formative Judaism and the Matthean community have a stake in one another and cannot be understood or engaged apart from each other.

Bibliography

Anderson, H. "The Old Testament in Mark's Gospel." In *The Use of the Old Testament in the New and Other Essays: Studies in Honor of W. Stinespring,* edited by J. Efird, 280–306. Durham, N.C.: Duke University Press, 1972.

Avigad, N. "The Excavations at Beth She'arim." *IEJ* 4 (1954) 98–104.

——. "The Excavations at Beth She'arim." *IEJ* 7 (1957) 249–54.

Banks, R. *Jesus and the Law in the Synoptic Tradition.* SNTSMS 28. Cambridge: Cambridge University Press, 1975.

Baumgarten, A. I. "The Name of the Pharisees." *JBL* 102 (1983) 411–28.

——. "The Pharisaic Paradosis." *HTR* 80 (1987) 63-78.

Berger, P. L. *The Sacred Canopy: Elements of a Sociological Theory of Religion.* Garden City, N.Y.: Doubleday, 1969.

——. "The Sociological Study of Sectarianism." *Social Research* 21 (1954) 467–85.

Blenkinsopp, J. "Interpretation and Sectarian Tendencies: An Aspect of Second Temple History." In *Jewish and Christian Self-Definition,* edited by E. P. Sanders, 2:1–26. Philadelphia: Fortress Press, 1981.

Bonnard, P. "Matthieu, Éducateur du Peuple Chrétien." In *Mélanges Bibliques,* edited by A. Descamps, 1–7. Gembloux: Duculot, 1969.

Bornkamm, G. "The Authority to Bind and Loose in the Church in Matthew's Gospel." In *Jesus and Man's Hope,* 30–50. Pittsburgh: Perspectives, 1970.

——, G. Barth, and M. J. Held. *Tradition and Interpretation in Matthew,* translated by P. Scott. Philadelphia: Westminster, 1963.

Brown, R. E. *The Birth of the Messiah.* Garden City, N.Y.: Doubleday, 1979.

——. *The Community of the Beloved Disciple.* New York: Paulist, 1979.

Carlston, C. "Betz on the Sermon on the Mount: A Critique." *CBQ* 50 (1988) 47–57.

Charlesworth, J., ed. *The Old Testament Pseudepigrapha.* 2 vols. Garden City, N.Y.: Doubleday, 1983, 1985.

Cohen, S. *Josephus in Galilee and Rome: His Vita and Development as a Historian.* Leiden: E. J. Brill, 1979.

——. "Patriarchs and Scholarchs." *PAAJR* 48 (1981) 57–85.

——. "The Significance of Yavneh: Pharisees, Rabbis, and the End of Jewish Sectarianism." *HUCA* 55 (1984) 27–53.

Collins, J. *The Apocalyptic Imagination.* New York: Crossroad, 1987.

Coser, L. *The Functions of Social Conflict.* New York: Free Press, 1956.

Davies, W. D. *The Setting of the Sermon on the Mount.* Cambridge: Cambridge University Press, 1964.

Desjardins, M. "Law in II Baruch and IV Ezra." *Studies in Religion* 14 (1985) 25–38.

Elbogen, I. *Der jüdische Gottesdienst in seiner geschichtlichen Entwicklung.* Hildesheim: G. Olms, 1962.

Finkel, A. "Yavneh's Liturgy and Early Christianity." *JES* 18 (1981) 231–50.

Fitzmyer, J. A. *Essays on the Semitic Background of the New Testament,* Sources for Biblical Study 5. Missoula, Mont.: Scholars Press, 1974.

Forkman, G. *The Limits of Religious Community: Expulsion from the Religious Community within the Qumran Sect, within Rabbinic Judaism, and within Primitive Christianity.* Lund: Gleerup, 1972.

Frankemölle, H. "Amtskritik im Matthäus-Evangelium?" *Biblica* 54 (1973) 247–62.

——. *Jahwebund und Kirche Christi.* Münster: Aschendorff, 1974.

Freyne, S. *Galilee from Alexander the Great to Hadian.* Wilmington, Del.: Michael Glazier, 1980.

Gager, J. *Kingdom and Community: The Social World of Early Christianity.* Englewood Cliffs, N.J.: Prentice-Hall, 1973.

Garland, D. *The Intention of Matthew 23.* Leiden: E. J. Brill, 1979.

Gehlen, A. *Urmensch und Spätkultur.* Bonn: Athenäum, 1956.

Gnilka, J. *Das Evangelium nach Markus.* EKKNT. Zurich: Benziger, 1978.

——. "Matthäusgemeinde und Qumran." *BZ* 7 (1963) 43–63.

Goodman, M. *State and Society in Roman Galilee A.D. 132–212.* Oxford Centre for Postgraduate Hebrew Studies. Totowa, N.J.: Rowman & Allanhead, 1983.

Guelich, R. *The Sermon on the Mount: A Foundation for Understanding.* Waco: Word, 1982.

Gundry, R. *Matthew: A Commentary on His Literary and Theological Art.* Grand Rapids: Eerdmans, 1982.

——. *The Use of the Old Testament in St. Matthew's Gospel.* Leiden: E. J. Brill, 1967.

Halivni, D. W. "The Reception Accorded to Rabbi Judah's Mishnah." In *Jewish and Christian Self-Definition,* edited by E. P. Sanders, 2:204–12. Philadelphia: Fortress Press, 1981.

Hare, D. *The Theme of Jewish Persecution of Christians in the Gospel According to St. Matthew.* Cambridge: Cambridge University Press, 1967.

Harrington, D. "Make Disciples of All Nations (Matt 28:19)." *CBQ* 37 (1985) 359–69.

———. "Matthean Studies Since Joachim Rohde." *Heythrop Journal* 16 (1975) 375–88.

Hill, D. "False Prophets and Charismatics: Structure and Interpretation in Matthew 7.15-23." *Biblica* 57 (1976) 327–48.

Hirsch, E. D., Jr. *Validity in Interpretation.* New Haven: Yale University Press, 1967.

Hoenig, S. B. "The Ancient City Square: The Forerunner of the Synagogue." In *ANRW* II.19.1, 448–76.

Holmberg, B. *Paul and Power: The Structure of Authority in the Primitive Church as Reflected in the Pauline Epistles.* Philadelphia: Fortress Press, 1978.

Hultgren, A. *Jesus and His Adversaries: The Form and Function of the Conflict Stories in the Synoptic Tradition.* Minneapolis: Augsburg, 1979.

Hummel, R. *Die Auseinandersetzung zwischen Kirche und Judentum im Matthäusevangelium.* Munich: Kaiser, 1963.

Hunzinger, C. H. "Spuren pharisäischer Institutionen in der frühen rabbinischen Überlieferung." In *Tradition und Glauben: Das frühe Christentum in seiner Umwelt,* edited by W. Stegemann, 147–56. Festschrift K. G. Kuhn. Göttingen: Vandenhoeck & Ruprecht, 1971.

Josephus, Flavius. *Complete Works,* edited by R. Marcus. Loeb Classical Library. Cambridge, Mass.: Harvard University Press.

Kee, H. C. *Christian Origins in Sociological Perspective.* Philadelphia: Westminster, 1980.

———. *The Community of the New Age: Studies in Mark's Gospel.* London: SCM, 1977.

———. "The Transformation of the Synagogue after 70 C.E.: Its Import for Early Christianity." *NTS* 36 (1990) 1–24.

Kilpatrick, G. D. *The Origins of the Gospel according to St. Matthew.* Oxford: Oxford University Press, 1946.

Kimelman, R. "*Birkat Ha-Minim* and the Lack of Evidence for an Anti-Christian Jewish Prayer in Antiquity." In *Jewish and Christian Self-Definition,* edited by E. P. Sanders, 2:226–44. Philadelphia: Fortress Press, 1981.

Kingsbury, J. D. "The Figure of Peter in Matthew's Gospel as a Theological Problem." *JBL* 98 (1979) 67–87.

———. *Matthew: Structure, Christology, Kingdom.* Philadelphia: Fortress Press, 1975.

———. *Matthew as Story.* Philadelphia: Fortress Press, 1986.

———. "The Verb *Akolouthein* as an Index of Matthew's View of His Community." *JBL* 97 (1978) 56–73.

Koenig, J. *Jews and Christians in Dialogue.* Philadelphia: Westminster, 1979.

Kohler, K. "The Origin and Composition of the Eighteen Benedictions," in *Contributions to the Scientific Study of the Jewish Liturgy*, edited by J. Petuchowski, 52–90. New York: KTAV, 1970.

Kriesberg, L. *The Sociology of Social Conflict.* Englewood Cliffs, N.J.: Prentice-Hall, 1973.

Kuhn, H. "The Phenomenological Concept of Horizon." In *Philosophical Essays in Memory of Edmund Husserl*, edited by M. Farber, 164–86. Cambridge, Mass.: Harvard University Press, 1940.

Lagrange, P. J. *Évangile selon Saint Matthieu.* Paris: Gabalda, 1948.

Legasse, S. "L'antijudaisme dans l'Evangile selon Matthieu." In *L'Evangile selon Matthieu*, edited by M. Didier, 417–28. Gembloux: Duculot, 1970.

Levine, L. *Ancient Synagogues Revealed.* Detroit: Israel Exploration Society/Wayne State University Press, 1982.

———. "The Jewish Patriarch (Nasi) in Third Century Palestine." In *ANRW* II.19.2, 649–88.

Lewis, J. P. "What Do We Mean by Jabneh?" *JBR* 32 (1964) 125–32.

Luckmann, T., and P. L. Berger. *The Social Construction of Reality.* Garden City, N.Y.: Doubleday, 1967.

Luz, U. *Matthew 1–7: A Commentary.* Minneapolis: Augsburg, 1989.

———. "Die Erfüllung des Gesetzes bei Matthäus (5.17-20)." *ZTK* 75–76 (1978–79) 398–435.

———. "Die Jünger im Matthäusevangelium." *ZNW* 62 (1971) 141–71.

Manns, F. "Un centre judéo-chrétian important: Sépphoris." In *Essais sur le Judéo-Christianisme*, 165–90. Jerusalem: Franciscan Printing Press, 1977.

Martyn, J. L. *History and Theology in the Fourth Gospel.* Nashville: Abingdon, 1979.

Meeks, W. "Breaking Away: Three New Testament Pictures of Christianity's Separation from the Jewish Communities." In *"To See Ourselves as Others See Us": Christians, Jews and "Others" in Late Antiquity*, edited by J. Neusner and E. Frerichs, 93–106. Atlanta: Scholars Press, 1985.

Meier, J. P. *Law and History in Matthew's Gospel.* Rome: Biblical
    Institute, 1976.
——. *The Vision of Matthew: Christ, Church, and Morality in the First
    Gospel.* New York: Paulist, 1979.
Meyers, E. M. "The Cultural Setting of Galilee: The Case of Regional-
    ism in Early Judaism." In *ANRW* II.19.1, 686–702.
Meyers, E. M., and A. T. Kraabel. "Archaeology, Iconography, and
    Nonliterary Written Remains." In *Early Judaism and Its Modern
    Interpreters,* edited by R. A. Kraft and G. W. E. Nickelsburg,
    175–210. Philadelphia: Fortress Press, 1986.
Meyers, E. M., and J. Strange. *Archaeology, the Rabbis, and Early Chris-
    tianity: The Social and Historical Setting of Palestinian Judaism and
    Christianity.* Nashville: Abingdon, 1981.
Minear, P. "The Disciples and the Crowds in the Gospel of Mat-
    thew." In *Gospel Studies in Honor of S. E. Johnson,* edited by M. H.
    Shepherd and E. C. Hobbs, 28–44. ATR Suppl. Ser. 3 (1974).
Murphy, F. J. "Sapiential Elements in the Syriac Apocalypse of
    Baruch." *JQR* 86 (1986) 311–27.
——. *The Structure and Meaning of Second Baruch.* SBLDS 78. Atlanta:
    Scholars Press, 1985.
——. "The Temple in the Syriac Apocalypse of Baruch." *JBL* 106
    (1987) 671–83.
Neusner, J. *Development of a Legend: Studies in the Traditions Concerning
    Yohanan ben Zakkai.* Leiden: E. J. Brill, 1970.
——. "The Fellowship in the Second Jewish Commonwealth." *HTR*
    59 (1960) 125–42.
——. "First Cleanse the Inside." *NTS* 22 (1975–76) 486–95.
——. "The Formation of Rabbinic Judaism: Yavneh from A.D.
    70–100." In *ANRW* II.19.2, 3–42.
——. *From Politics to Piety: The Emergence of Pharisaic Judaism.* Engle-
    wood Cliffs, N.J.: Prentice-Hall, 1973.
——. "The Idea of Purity in Ancient Judaism." *JAAR* 43 (1975) 15–26.
——. *Method and Meaning in Ancient Judaism.* Vol. 2. Chico, Calif.:
    Scholars Press, 1981.
——. *Rabbinic Traditions about the Pharisees before 70.* 3 vols. Leiden:
    E. J. Brill, 1973.
——. "Religious Authority in Judaism: Modern and Classical
    Modes." *Interpretation* 39 (1985) 373–87.
——. "Two Pictures of the Pharisees: Philosophical Circle and Eating
    Club." *ATR* 64 (1982) 525–38.
Nickelsburg, G. W. E. "Enoch, Levi, and Peter: Recipients of Revela-
    tion in Upper Galilee." *JBL* 100 (1981) 575–600.

———. *Jewish Literature Between the Bible and the Mishna.* Philadelphia: Fortress, 1981.

———. *Resurrection, Immortality, and Eternal Life in Intertestamental Judaism.* Cambridge, Mass.: Harvard University Press, 1972.

Overman, J. A. "The God-Fearers: Some Neglected Features." *JSNT* 32 (1988) 17–26.

———. "Who Were the First Urban Christians? Urbanization in Galilee in the First Century." In *Society of Biblical Literature 1988 Seminar Papers,* edited by D. Lull, 160–68. Atlanta: Scholars Press, 1988.

Petersen, H. "Point of View in Mark's Narrative." *Semeia* 12 (1978) 97–121.

Pesch, W. *Matthäus als Seelsorger.* Stuttgart: Katholisches Bibelwerk, 1966.

Przybylski, B. *Righteousness in Matthew and His World of Thought.* Cambridge: Cambridge University Press, 1980.

Reumann, J. *Righteousness in the New Testament.* Philadelphia: Fortress Press, 1982.

Rothfuchs, W. *Die Erfüllungszitate des Matthäus-Evangeliums.* Stuttgart: Kohlhammer, 1969.

Saldarini, A. J. "The Adoption of a Dissident: Akabya ben Mahalaleel in Rabbinic Tradition." *JJS* 33 (1982) 547–56.

———. "Johanan ben Zakkai's Escape from Jerusalem: Origin and Development of a Rabbinic Story." *JSJ* 6 (1975) 189–204.

———. *Pharisees, Scribes and Sadducees in Palestinian Society: A Sociological Approach.* Wilmington, Del.: Michael Glazier, 1988.

———. "Reconstructions of Rabbinic Judaism." In *Early Judaism and Its Modern Interpreters,* edited by R. A. Kraft and G. W. E. Nickelsburg, 437–77. Philadelphia: Fortress Press, 1986.

———. "Political and Social Roles of the Scribes and Pharisees in Galilee Society." In *Society of Biblical Literature 1988 Seminar Papers,* edited by D. Lull, 200–209. Atlanta: Scholars Press, 1988.

Sanders, E. P. "The Covenant as a Soteriological Category and the Nature of Salvation in Palestinian and Hellenistic Judaism." In *Jews, Greeks and Christians and Other Religious Cultures in Antiquity: Essays in Honor of W. D. Davies,* edited by R. Hamerton-Kelly and R. Scroggs, 11–44. Leiden: E. J. Brill, 1975.

Sayler, G. "II Baruch: A Story of Grief and Consolation." In *Society of Biblical Literature 1982 Seminar Papers,* edited by K. H. Richards, 485–500. Chico, Calif.: Scholars Press, 1982.

Schäfer, P. "Die Flucht Johanan b. Zakkais aus Jerusalem und die Gründung des 'Lehrhauses' in Jabne." In *ANRW* II.19.2, 43–101.

Schiffman, L. *The Halakah at Qumran*. Leiden: E. J. Brill, 1975.

Schutz, A., and T. Luckmann. *The Structures of the Life-World*, translated by R. Zaner and H. Engelhardt, Jr. Evanston: Northwestern University Press, 1973.

Schütz, J. H. "Apostolic Authority and the Control of the Tradition: I Cor. 15." *NTS* 15 (1968–69) 439–57.

Schweizer, E. *Matthäus und seine Gemeinde*. SBS 71. Stuttgart: Katholisches Bibelwerk, 1974.

――――. "Observance of the Law and Charismatic Activity in Matthew." *NTS* 16 (1970) 213–30.

Senior, D., and C. Stuhlmueller. *The Biblical Foundations for Mission*. Maryknoll: Orbis, 1983.

Shanks, H. "The Origins of the Title 'Rabbi,'" *JQR* 59 (1968) 152–57.

Stanton, G. "5 Ezra and Matthean Christianity in the Second Century." *JTS* 28 (1977) 67–83.

――――. "The Origin and Purpose of Matthew's Gospel: Matthean Scholarship from 1945-1980." In *ANRW* II.25.3, 1889–1951.

――――, ed. *The Interpretation of Matthew*. Philadelphia: Fortress Press, 1983.

Stendahl, K. "Quis et Unde? An Analysis of Matthew 1–2." In *The Interpretation of Matthew*, edited by G. Stanton, 56–66. Philadelphia: Fortress Press, 1983.

――――. *The School of St. Matthew and Its Use of the Old Testament*. Philadelphia: Fortress Press, 1968.

Strange, J. "Archeology and the Religion of Judaism in Palestine." In *ANRW* II.19.1, 646–85.

――――. "Review Article: The Capernaum and Herodium Publications." *BASOR* 226 (1977) 65–73.

Strecker, G. *Der Weg der Gerechtigkeit: Untersuchung zur Theologie des Matthäus*. Göttingen: Vandenhoeck & Ruprecht, 1966.

Suggs, M. J. *Wisdom, Christology, and Law in Matthew's Gospel*. Cambridge, Mass.: Harvard University Press, 1970.

Tagawa, K. "People and Community in Matthew." *NTS* 16 (1969–70) 144–61.

Tannehill, R. "The Disciples in Mark: The Function of a Narrative Role." *JR* 57 (1977) 386–405.

Thompson, W. G. *Matthew's Advice to a Divided Community: Mt. 17.22–18.35*, AnBib 44. Rome: Biblical Institute, 1970.

Trilling, W. "Amt und Amtsverständnis bei Matthäus." In *Mélanges Bibliques*, edited by A. Descamps, 29–44. Gembloux: Duculot, 1969.

Bibliography 169

———. *Das Wahre Israel: Studien zur Theologie des Matthäus-Evangeliums.*
Munich: Kösel, 1964.
VanderKam, J. *Textual and Historical Studies in the Book of Jubilees.*
HSM 14. Missoula, Mont.: Scholars Press, 1977.
Van Segbroeck, F. "Le Scandale de L'Incroyance: La Signification de
Mt. 13.35." *ETL* 41 (1965) 344–72.
Van Tilborg, S. *The Jewish Leaders in Matthew.* Leiden: E. J. Brill, 1972.
Vermes, G. *The Dead Sea Scrolls in English.* New York: Penguin, 1975.
Weber, M. *Economy and Society,* edited by G. Roth and C. Wittich.
Berkeley: University of California Press, 1978.
———. *Essays in Sociology,* edited by H. Gerth and C. Mills. Oxford:
Oxford University Press, 1946.
White, L. M. "The Delos Synagogue Revisited: Recent Fieldwork in
the Graeco-Roman Diaspora." *HTR* 80 (1987) 133–60.
Wilson, B. *Magic and the Millennium: A Sociological Study of Religious
Movements of Protest among Tribal and Third World Peoples.*
London: Heinemann, 1973.

Author Index

Subject Index